Divided Parties, Strong Leaders

CHICAGO STUDIES IN AMERICAN POLITICS

A series edited by Susan Herbst, Lawrence R. Jacobs, Adam J. Berinsky, and Frances Lee; Benjamin I. Page, editor emeritus

Also in the series:

LEGAL PLUNDER: THE PREDATORY DIMENSIONS OF CRIMINAL JUSTICE by *Joshua Page and Joe Soss*

THE MONEY SIGNAL: HOW FUNDRAISING MATTERS IN AMERICAN POLITICS by *Danielle M. Thomsen*

THE POLITICS OF SKIN TONE: AFRICAN AMERICAN EXPERIENCES, IDENTITY, AND ATTITUDES by *Nicole D. Yadon*

HOW POLITICIANS POLARIZE: POLITICAL REPRESENTATION IN AN AGE OF NEGATIVE PARTISANSHIP by *Mia Costa*

FALSE FRONT: THE FAILED PROMISE OF PRESIDENTIAL POWER IN A POLARIZED AGE by *Kenneth Lowande*

MORAL ISSUES: HOW PUBLIC OPINION ON ABORTION AND GAY RIGHTS AFFECTS AMERICAN RELIGION AND POLITICS by *Paul Goren and Christopher Chapp*

THE ROOTS OF POLARIZATION: FROM THE RACIAL REALIGNMENT TO THE CULTURE WARS by *Neil A. O'Brian*

SOME WHITE FOLKS: THE INTERRACIAL POLITICS OF SYMPATHY, SUFFERING, AND SOLIDARITY by *Jennifer Chudy*

THROUGH THE GRAPEVINE: SOCIALLY TRANSMITTED INFORMATION AND DISTORTED DEMOCRACY by *Taylor N. Carlson*

AMERICA'S NEW RACIAL BATTLE LINES: PROTECT VERSUS REPAIR by *Rogers M. Smith and Desmond King*

PARTISAN HOSTILITY AND AMERICAN DEMOCRACY by *James N. Druckman, Samara Klar, Yanna Krupnikov, Matthew Levendusky, and John Barry Ryan*

RESPECT AND LOATHING IN AMERICAN DEMOCRACY: POLARIZATION, MORALIZATION, AND THE UNDERMINING OF EQUALITY by *Jeff Spinner-Halev and Elizabeth Theiss-Morse*

COUNTERMOBILIZATION: POLICY FEEDBACK AND BACKLASH IN A POLARIZED AGE by *Eric M. Patashnik*

RACE, RIGHTS, AND RIFLES: THE ORIGINS OF THE NRA AND CONTEMPORARY GUN CULTURE by *Alexandra Filindra*

ACCOUNTABILITY IN STATE LEGISLATURES by *Steven Rogers*

OUR COMMON BONDS: USING WHAT AMERICANS SHARE TO HELP BRIDGE THE PARTISAN DIVIDE by *Matthew Levendusky*

DYNAMIC DEMOCRACY: PUBLIC OPINION, ELECTIONS, AND POLICYMAKING IN THE AMERICAN STATES by *Devin Caughey and Christopher Warshaw*

PERSUASION IN PARALLEL: HOW INFORMATION CHANGES MINDS ABOUT POLITICS by *Alexander Coppock*

RADICAL AMERICAN PARTISANSHIP: MAPPING VIOLENT HOSTILITY, ITS CAUSES, AND THE CONSEQUENCES FOR DEMOCRACY by *Nathan P. Kalmoe and Lilliana Mason*

Additional series titles follow index

Divided Parties, Strong Leaders

RUTH BLOCH RUBIN

THE UNIVERSITY OF CHICAGO PRESS   CHICAGO AND LONDON

The University of Chicago Press, Chicago 60637
The University of Chicago Press, Ltd., London
© 2025 by The University of Chicago
All rights reserved. No part of this book may be used or reproduced in any manner whatsoever without written permission, except in the case of brief quotations in critical articles and reviews. For more information, contact the University of Chicago Press, 1427 E. 60th St., Chicago, IL 60637.
Published 2025
Printed in the United States of America

34 33 32 31 30 29 28 27 26 25   1 2 3 4 5

ISBN-13: 978-0-226-84182-3 (cloth)
ISBN-13: 978-0-226-84184-7 (paper)
ISBN-13: 978-0-226-84183-0 (e-book)
DOI: https://doi.org/10.7208/chicago/9780226841830.001.0001

Library of Congress Cataloging-in-Publication Data

Names: Bloch Rubin, Ruth, author.
Title: Divided parties, strong leaders / Ruth Bloch Rubin.
Description: Chicago : The University of Chicago Press, 2025. | Series: Chicago studies in American politics | Includes bibliographical references and index.
Identifiers: LCCN 2024048569 | ISBN 9780226841823 (cloth) | ISBN 9780226841847 (paperback) | ISBN 9780226841830 (e-book)
Subjects: LCSH: United States. Congress. House—Speakers—History—20th century. | United States. Congress. House—Speakers—History—21st century. | Political leadership—United States. | Intra-party disagreements (Political parties)—United States. | United States—Politics and government—1945–1989. | United States—Politics and government—1989–
Classification: LCC JK1411.B56 2025 | DDC 324.27309/04—dc23/eng/20250106
LC record available at https://lccn.loc.gov/2024048569

♾ This paper meets the requirements of ANSI/NISO Z39.48-1992 (Permanence of Paper).

Contents

CHAPTER 1. Leading Divided Parties 1

CHAPTER 2. Analyzing Divided Parties 32

CHAPTER 3. How Nancy Pelosi Built Back Better 43

CHAPTER 4. How John Boehner Lost His Party and Then His Job 66

CHAPTER 5. How Tip O'Neill Lost the Budget Battle but Won the Public Relations War 94

CHAPTER 6. How Sam Rayburn Tamed the House Rules Committee 115

CHAPTER 7. How William Knowland Saved McCarthyism from McCarthy 134

CHAPTER 8. Learning from Divided Parties 156

Acknowledgments 173

Appendix A. Archival Collections Consulted 175

Appendix B. Interview Procedures 177

Notes 179

Select Bibliography 237

Index 249

CHAPTER ONE

Leading Divided Parties

> A leader who knows how to use his resources to the maximum is not so much the agent of others as others are his agents. —Robert Dahl[1]

Standing in the Capitol's Statuary Hall at the unveiling of Nancy Pelosi's official House portrait in the winter of 2022, John Boehner paid tribute to his former rival. Amid memorials to legislative giants past, Boehner declared, "No other speaker in the modern era, Republican or Democrat, wielded the gavel with such authority or such consistent results."[2] Boehner's assessment reflected a remarkable cross-party consensus. Even the combative Newt Gingrich avowed that Pelosi was "the strongest speaker in history," a leader who had demonstrated an exceptional "capacity to organize and muscle."[3] Such praise was surely warranted. Pelosi had managed her fractious party's affairs for nearly two decades—longer than all but the legendary Sam Rayburn. And as Speaker of the House of Representatives, she had helped pass landmark legislation to reform healthcare, address climate change, and limit the economic fallout of the COVID-19 pandemic, exercising "power more forcefully and effectively than *any* speaker since Joe Cannon."[4]

Pelosi's record is all the more remarkable when we look across the aisle. In the time she headed the House Democratic Caucus, House Republicans cycled through four leaders, each of whom floundered more desperately than his predecessor. Following a period of relative stability under Dennis Hastert—still the longest-serving Republican Speaker in American history—both Boehner and Paul Ryan struggled to keep their party in line. Tired of taking punches, both men chose to resign rather than face a recall.[5] Their immediate successor, Kevin McCarthy, fared worse. After fighting through more than a dozen ballots, he lasted only nine months on the job—becoming the first Speaker to be formally ousted from the post. Mike Johnson, who succeeded McCarthy, found governing no easier. In his first hundred days in office, the new Speaker suffered a slew of setbacks that prompted members to dismiss him as "Speaker in Name Only."[6] Within months, conservative hard-liners were vowing to oust him as they had McCarthy, leaving more moderate and mainstream Republicans to despair that, even if he kept his post, Johnson would struggle as his predecessors had.[7]

What explains this disparity in leadership performance? Why have House Republicans today experienced near-continuous leadership churn, while House Democrats have not? Legislative scholars are accustomed to thinking about questions like these in ideological terms. The consensus is that leader power is contingent on the extent to which a party is divided. The more a party's rank and file agree with one another, the stronger their leaders will be. The less members agree with one another, the weaker their leaders will be. As applied to contemporary politics, this approach has much to recommend it. Since 2010, the most conservative members of the House Republican Conference have consistently battled their more moderate colleagues on a wide range of issues, including government spending, immigration, and legislative procedure. Particularly as congressional majorities have narrowed, these divisions have made it more difficult for Republican Speakers to build winning coalitions and complicated their efforts to control the agenda.

Yet, over the same period, House Democrats have had pronounced disagreements of their own. Indeed, Pelosi's long tenure was marked by recurring fights between her party's moderate and progressive members, prompting no less an authority than Barack Obama to describe the caucus as a "diverse and contentious group of folks."[8] Pelosi, however, did more than simply survive in the face of such divisions—she thrived.

It is possible that Pelosi is an exception to an otherwise good rule. After all, she is renowned for her extraordinary "political instincts," "boundless energy," and capacity to "grind and grit."[9] But this book is motivated by the conviction that her record, and that of her Republican counterparts, provides an opportunity to think differently about the relationship between party divisions and leader power. Contrary to the conventional wisdom, I will argue that divisions are *not* inherently limiting. Rather, leaders are sometimes able to overcome, and even draw strength from, their divided ranks. In the chapters that follow, my aim is to explain why, and under what conditions, this is so.

Dating back to the work of E. E. Schattschneider in the mid-twentieth century, scholars have recognized that explaining political outcomes requires more than just identifying and aggregating the preferences of officeholders and citizens. It also matters whether and how those preferences are mobilized and institutionalized. As Schattschneider observed, the preferences "organized into politics" invariably shape outcomes to a greater degree than those "organized out."[10]

Congressional parties are no exception. Party divisions surely reflect important differences in what members believe and purport to want. But they also reflect differences in how like-minded members choose to work together, whether through ad hoc and sporadic interactions, informal but routinized cooperative arrangements, or more formally institutionalized intraparty blocs.[11] To capture this distinction, I use the term *faction* to refer to party members whose wants or beliefs across some related and politically salient issues overlap with each other, however imperfectly, but conflict with those of their co-partisans. On this definition, members of a faction may, but need not, regularly interact, coordinate their activities, or share a sense of camaraderie. Divided parties, so described, are those that encompass at least two competing factions.

This book's thesis is that variation in how rival factions collaborate helps explain why legislative leaders can sometimes exercise power even in the face of party divisions. As we will see, leaders' capacity to exercise power is at its apex when the collaborative efforts of their party's competing factions are evenly matched—that is, when the party's factional configuration is *symmetric*. By contrast, leaders' capacity to exercise power is more limited when one faction outcollaborates the competition—that is, when the factional configuration is *asymmetric*.

In defense of this thesis, I assemble and analyze a great deal of data from archives and interviews.[12] I use these records to construct detailed narrative case studies of some of the most storied leaders of the post–World War II Congress, including Rayburn and Pelosi, along with others, such as mid-twentieth-century Senate majority leader William Knowland, who have received substantially less attention from legislative scholars. Revisiting major policy and procedural battles from the 1950s through the 2020s, the book's empirical chapters explore the factional configurations leaders encountered and their consequences for how forcefully they wielded power. As I elaborate in chapter 2, the choice to employ qualitative, largely historical evidence is a deliberate response to the inferential challenges inherent in studying leader power and, indeed, in conceptualizing what it means to be a powerful leader in the first place.

For now, though, we need only take note of the fact that the book's chronological sweep offers considerable variation in how factions collaborate. At different times and for different reasons, competing factions have collaborated in different ways, with some eschewing collective action altogether and others developing robust institutional arrangements that last for decades. This variation, I suggest, makes it possible to track how certain factional configurations have conditioned leaders' power across congressional era, party, and chamber. It also permits us to understand how a faction's propensity to collaborate interacts with other variables legislative scholars deem important to the balance of power in Congress, including a faction's size and its spatial position relative to rival factions.

If this all sounds too abstract, we can make it more concrete by revisiting the disparity in leadership performance that opened this chapter. Pelosi, we will see, was able to consolidate power in ways her Republican rivals were not because she helmed an increasingly symmetric party. Her early years in leadership were marked by sustained and intensive collaboration by the party's moderate faction. Emboldened by Bill Clinton's successful presidential bid and the growing prominence of "third way" politics, moderate Democrats in the late 1990s and into the first decade of the twenty-first century outorganized their more progressive peers, pooling electoral and staff resources and meeting regularly to share information and strategize about policy and procedure. But midway through her tenure as leader, the party's progressive faction began to countermobilize, investing in their own institutional mechanisms to facilitate collective action on the left.[13] By the time she was reelected Speaker after the 2018 midterms, progressives and moderates were collaborating with equal vigor. As chronicled in chapter 3, these shifting dynamics help explain why Pelosi was able to consolidate control over her party in spite of its increasingly bitter divisions.

House Republican leaders have been considerably less fortunate. Since 2010, the collaborative imbalance between the Republican Party's conservative firebrands and its remaining moderates has become especially acute. Members of the party's right wing have adopted an array of organizational practices to unite their ranks—including internal voting rules, disciplinary tools (including expulsion), and norms of confidentiality—while the party's beleaguered moderates have struggled to coordinate in kind.[14] The consequence of this factional asymmetry has been persistent leadership weakness. As chapter 4 details, from Boehner to Johnson, those at the top of the party hierarchy have lacked the ballast of a comparably organized factional rival to match their highly mobilized right wing. In the absence of a factional equal to contend with, conservatives have instead turned against party leaders, whose equivocal response (at least so far) has vacillated between strategies of confrontation and appeasement in an effort to keep the conference intact. Thus configured, "*no one* can herd this version of the Republican Party."[15]

Beyond its analytic insights, this book's account of leader power offers a blueprint for how we might get more out of the first branch. In recent decades, it has become commonplace to lament an apparent decline in pragmatic, bipartisan dealmaking in Congress and a corresponding increase in aggressive partisan warfare. Especially on the Republican side of the aisle, the moderate lawmakers who remain committed to consensus building and "getting to yes" have become highly endangered.[16] This is thought to have deleterious consequences for American politics, as the absence of members willing to compromise may undermine the responsiveness, and perhaps even the stability, of our system of constitutional government.[17] It is not surprising, then, that many popular reform proposals aim to increase the number of moderates in Congress, whether by changing how primary elections are conducted or how our campaign finance regime is structured.[18] Proponents argue that, with more moderates advocating for bipartisan action on Capitol Hill, congressional leaders will be more willing to rebuff the hard-liners in their party who stand in the way of getting things done.

But this book suggests a different, and more effective, approach. A defining feature of American politics today is that Republican moderates have consistently eschewed the kinds of collaborative mechanisms that have enabled their more conservative colleagues to dictate terms to the party's leadership. These differences in mobilization across factional lines suggest that simply increasing the number of Republican moderates is unlikely to alter the status quo. Absent efforts to foster greater collaboration among their ranks—and, in so doing, to correct the party's factional asymmetry—such proposals will accomplish little. Moderates will remain under threat, and the party's leaders will find it no easier to govern.

For these reasons, reformers might consider directing their resources as much toward helping moderates already in Congress deepen their collaboration as toward recruiting a new generation of candidates to run. This may well be easier said than done. Particularly in today's Republican Party, moderate lawmakers have good reason to keep a low profile, lest they be tagged as "Republicans in name only" for failing to pursue the hardest of lines. But whatever the challenges of promoting moderate collaboration, it does not require broadscale changes in today's hyperpartisan electoral environment, be that shifts in how conservative media outlets cover political events, changes to campaign finance laws, or the undoing of partisan gerrymanders. All it requires is that those moderates who have already persuaded voters of their merits commit themselves to collective action.

I return to, and elaborate on, these prescriptions in the book's concluding chapter. The remainder of this chapter lays out the study's central thesis in greater detail, beginning with a discussion of how legislative scholars have generally understood the constraining effect of party divisions on leadership in Congress and why we ought to be skeptical of that understanding.

Before moving forward, it is important to be clear about the book's limitations. This study is not an effort to identify *all* the factors that might plausibly make congressional party leaders effective. Nor does it attempt to offer a comprehensive theory to explain patterns in leadership turnover or legislative productivity, or, for that matter, why intraparty conflict waxes and wanes. It is also agnostic about the factors that underly the emergence and persistence of party divisions throughout congressional history, although it offers some clues. My aims are decidedly more modest, if no less important. They are to establish that divided parties have, at times, been governed by strong leaders, and, in light of that empirical reality, to theorize anew about the relationship between party divisions and leader power.

Finally, like many studies of legislative leadership, this one focuses squarely on majority party leaders. In contrast to minority party leaders who have relatively few tools to bend legislative outcomes to their will, majority party leaders are institutionally empowered to do just that. Notwithstanding the obstacles to governance that bicameralism and the separation of powers impose, majority party leaders can, at least in theory, shape laws and legislative procedure to reflect what they want or believe is necessary for their members, their party, or the nation as a whole. With substantive policymaking and procedural decisions regularly at stake, the question of whether majority party leaders can effectively exercise power over divided parties matters greatly.

Divided Parties, Diminished Leaders?

To hear leaders tell it, a divided party is never good. Success, they counsel, is possible only when members "work as a team. Unity is . . . power."[19] Legislative scholars tend to agree. Party divisions are said to constrain majority party leaders by diminishing their power and limiting their agency—oftentimes both.

David Rohde and John Aldrich's theory of conditional party government (CPG) is a prime example of this way of thinking. Drawing on a principal-agent model of delegated power, the authors predict that the more lawmakers' preferences diverge from those of their co-partisans, the more they will seek to reduce their leaders' authority. With fewer shared policy priorities, members will want to limit their leaders' prerogatives and instead accumulate as much power as they can to pursue their aims individually. Thus, CPG predicts, leaders of divided parties will be consigned to a "caretaker or housekeep[er]" role, for "a fractionalized membership . . . ke[eps] leaders from being as powerful as they might . . . want . . . to be."[20] The authors also posit that leaders of divided parties will be "disinclined to make strong use" of whatever powers they hold on to—in effect, voluntarily restricting their own agency. As Rohde explains, "leaders will be reluctant to use the tools at their disposal" when their "party is deeply divided," and they will consequently "appear . . . weak."[21]

In more recent years, CPG's original formulation has been updated to take partisan polarization into account. Now, in addition to considering the distribution of preferences within each party, the authors theorize that the degree of ideological difference between the two parties will inform both members' willingness to delegate power and leaders' willingness to exercise it. Holding intraparty dynamics constant, they argue that as the ideological gap between the parties widens, members will be more willing to cede authority to their leadership, and leaders will be more comfortable exercising that authority on behalf of their members.[22] The logic is straightforward. However much members disagree or agree with one another, polarization ensures that they will disagree *more* with lawmakers on the other side of the aisle. The argument works in reverse, too. The smaller the ideological distance between the two parties, the less willing members will be to endow their leaders with authority and the less willing leaders will be to use whatever prerogatives they retain.

Legislative scholars have found substantial empirical support for the claim that ideological agreement will yield increases in majority party leaders' formal prerogatives and institutional resources. For example, in his meticulous account of party whip organizations, C. Lawrence Evans observes that it is "when the party is relatively homogenous" that "members tend to expand the size and organizational strength of their whip networks." But when a party is divided, its leaders will face "binding time and resource constraints," and must pick and choose their battles carefully.²³ Leaders, in Evans's view, have little choice in the matter; independent of the strategies or tactics they may choose to adopt, divisions invariably limit their ability to muscle their rank and file into line. Studies also find that checks on party leaders decrease in frequency as member preferences become more homogenous, just as CPG would predict.²⁴

Other scholars focus more intently on the ways in which party divisions are likely to discourage leaders from exercising the powers their members permit them to possess. Barbara Sinclair, for instance, observes that leaders are empowered by members to advance a positive legislative agenda and "keep the peace." But when "passing legislation that is controversial within the party . . . strains party harmony," Sinclair argues that leaders will inevitably choose peacekeeping over productivity. Rather than risk exercising authority in ways "that might exacerbate intraparty conflicts," they will prefer to "foster cooperative patterns of behavior."²⁵

Gary Cox and Mathew McCubbins's party cartel theory generates a similar set of predictions. Emphasizing leaders' role as custodians of the party's reputation, they, too, argue that leaders will use their authority to keep the peace, particularly when it comes to agenda setting. As they assert, "*Thou shalt not aid bills that will split thy party*" is "the first commandment of party leadership."²⁶ This form of self-effacing leadership has understandable appeal. When there is little that members can agree on, a prudent "senior partner" will seek to defuse calls for action on issues they anticipate may generate conflict between members.²⁷ Moreover, to the extent that leaders of divided parties seek to minimize public displays of discord, Cox and McCubbins suggest that they will also be reticent to advance a positive legislative program.²⁸ Majority party leaders, on their account, will only "sometimes obey the second commandment [of party leadership]—*Thou shalt aid bills that most in thy party like*."²⁹ The bottom line is that while leaders of unified parties are free to engage in both positive and negative agenda control, cartel theory predicts that leaders of divided parties are likely to lack such agency and will instead devote themselves to blocking potentially divisive legislation before it reaches the floor.³⁰

The presence of party divisions may restrict leaders' agency in still another way. Drawing on the same reputational logic that animates cartel theory, Frances Lee contends that "leaders . . . maintain their power by avoiding or suppressing issues that have the potential to weaken or tear apart partisan consensus." But where cartel theory predicts that leaders will rely exclusively on negative agenda control to navigate party divisions,

Lee argues that leaders of divided parties will aggressively deploy their positive agenda powers to advance "messaging" votes that tar the opposition but do not yield substantive policy change. Divisions, in her telling, compel leaders to shift their focus away from making "serious attempts to pass laws" and toward coordinating increasingly vitriolic critiques of their partisan adversaries.[31]

In sum, legislative scholars have offered a sensible and straightforward account of the relationship between party divisions and leader power. We are told that when a party is divided—that is, when the distribution of preferences within the party is heterogenous—members will seek to decentralize procedural power, and leaders will hesitate to use what power they retain. As member preferences become more homogenous, however, leaders' procedural power is expected to grow, along with their willingness to use the full range of tools their office makes available. Parties whose members largely agree with one another will thus be governed by energetic leaders, while those whose members are at odds will suffer at the hands of anemic ones.

Institutional Resilience and the Stickiness of Leadership Authority

It surely seems right that most of the time, leaders will be attentive to changes in the wants of their membership. But the claim that a leader will see their authority expand or contract with shifts in the ideological composition of their party is at odds with how we understand processes of institutional change more generally. Institutions, we have learned, often resist reform, even when individual-level preferences militate in favor of change.[32] As Paul Pierson argues, "actors do not inherit a blank slate that they can remake at will when their preferences shift or unintended consequences become visible. Instead . . . the dead weight of previous institutional choices often seriously limits their room to maneuver."[33] Applying the insights of historical institutionalism to the hypothesized relationship between party divisions and leader power gives us reason to doubt that party members can finely calibrate and recalibrate the amount of power their leaders wield based on how much they agree or disagree with one another.

In a variety of institutional contexts, including Congress, scholars observe that past allocations of authority shape how it is subsequently distributed.³⁴ Eric Schickler identifies one possible mechanism, suggesting that "preexisting institutions often create constituencies dedicated to the preservation of established power bases."³⁵ If this holds true for legislative leaders, we can anticipate that regardless of changes in member preferences strong leaders will remain strong, as efforts to diminish their authority encounter resistance from those who benefit from the status quo. Likewise, it seems plausible that weak leaders will remain weak, as constituencies who stand to lose out under a reshuffling of legislative authority—committee chairs, for instance—push back against reform.

Attending to the vested interests of existing stakeholders has also led scholars to observe that political processes in Congress and elsewhere are often open-ended in early stages but increasingly closed off in later ones.³⁶ As applied to legislative leaders, we should expect it to be more difficult for a divided party to revoke an expansive grant of authority at some later time than it would be for that same party to refuse to confer such authority in the first place. So, too, a homogenous party should have a harder time augmenting a leader's authority in the present than it would granting that authority were Congress to be organized afresh.³⁷

Initial choices about how to allocate authority might take on outsize importance for yet another reason. Historical institutionalists have shown that the passage of time itself tilts the playing field in favor of the status quo because the "costs of exit[ing]" from an initial set of institutional arrangements—that is, of "switching to some previously plausible alternative"—increase.³⁸ Congress should be no exception to this rule. As in other walks of political life, we would expect lawmakers to adapt to, or at least accommodate, the institutional arrangements they first encounter. Therefore, to the extent that members grow used to navigating Congress against the backdrop of a particular distribution of leader power, they may be reluctant to challenge that distribution, even if they later come to resent it.

For our purposes, once a leader is empowered with certain procedural prerogatives, members are incentivized to exploit the opportunities and maintain the advantages that flow from this delegation, even as the party's distribution of preferences fluctuates. Political entrepreneurs in Congress must consequently labor to convince their colleagues that the benefits of change exceed its costs. And when members do seek to alter the distribution of power within the party, they may well prefer "layering ... new arrangements on top of old ones" rather than making a clean break with the past.³⁹ This means that even when members of a divided party do mount a successful attack on their leaders' prerogatives, party leaders may well retain substantial residual authority.

Effecting institutional change in Congress is made still more onerous by the many obstacles to sustaining collective action on Capitol Hill. Even lawmakers with shared aims often struggle to work together, and these difficulties are likely to be magnified when parties are divided.[40] Faced with the task of curtailing a leader's power, members must try to find mutually acceptable answers to a host of thorny questions.[41] Should the leader be replaced, and, if so, by whom? Should some of the leader's procedural powers instead be revoked? If yes, then which ones and by what expedient? Given these challenges, it seems reasonable to conclude that rank-and-file members' ability to diminish their leaders' authority may well decrease with disharmony, even as their desire for change grows.

Consistent with this idea, those infrequent occasions when lawmakers successfully altered allocations of leadership authority are marked by exceptional organizational efforts to enlist members in a common plan of action. Consider the 1910 Cannon Revolt. While insurgent Republicans had long chafed at "czar" rule, it took considerable collaborative effort, unmatched by their factional rivals, to wrest control of House procedure from Speaker Cannon's grip. Despite widespread frustration with his authoritarian style of leadership, Republican dissidents struggled to reach agreement on practical matters of political strategy, including which of the Speaker's prerogatives they would target. It was only by organizing over the course of many months that they were able to settle on a shared approach, ultimately backing a proposal to strip the Speaker of the power to make committee assignments.[42]

This point can be recast by relying on the principal-agent framework that structures much traditional thinking about congressional parties. As we have seen, legislative scholars often describe leaders as the agents of party members.[43] Treating a party's membership as though it were a single actor makes sense when party members have shared goals. But this simplification has important limitations. Take a party cleaved into several rival factions, or one where there are so many viewpoints that even grouping members into identifiable blocs is difficult. In either case, it is perhaps more accurate to say that there are multiple principals the leader must serve.[44] Framed this way, members are likely to struggle to curb their leaders' power even as their party's growing heterogeneity increases their desire to do so. As Terry Moe observes, "without any common understanding of how authority is legitimately divided among competing principals," a party's vying factions may struggle to collectively monitor the behavior of their common agent, let alone discipline or replace them.[45]

From the perspective of potential dissidents, even that scenario is perhaps unrealistic. As party divisions deepen and opposing factions compete more aggressively to control the party, the resulting rivalry may prompt members to attempt to strengthen the prerogatives and autonomy of their leadership in the hopes of insulating their putative agent from their opponents' "intrusions."[46] Alternatively, members may come to fear that party divisions will create so much gridlock that the party will earn a "do nothing" reputation.[47] As James Curry and Frances Lee have recently highlighted, lawmakers may seek to avoid this outcome by centralizing power, believing that strong leadership is necessary to break through the logjam and secure the kinds of tangible legislative accomplishments members need to run on.[48] At the very least, the party rank and file may hesitate to curtail the authority of leaders for fear of exacerbating legislative dysfunction or the perception that Congress has fallen victim to it.[49]

Congressional history lends support to this perspective, too. Nearly two decades after the Cannon Revolt, Nicholas Longworth—himself one of the chamber's most formidable, if irascible, Speakers—capitalized on Republican members' fear that their divided party was incapable of legislating to recoup some of the power that Cannon had been forced to cede to Progressive reformers in 1910.[50]

Entrepreneurial Leaders, Ready and Willing

Not only is leadership authority likely to be resilient to shifts in member preferences, but there is little reason to think that growing ideological heterogeneity within a party would motivate leaders to voluntarily limit their own agency. Congressional leadership elections have traditionally attracted lawmakers of surpassing ambition and drive for power. As Matthew Green and Douglas Harris observe, what distinguishes those who run for leadership posts is "an inherent desire for more power or a higher profile."[51] They find that those who run are often dissatisfied by the drudgery of constituent service and tedium of committee work, and instead yearn to shape the broader agenda.[52] Would-be contenders for leadership positions want to have a voice in deciding, as Boehner has said, "Where's the ground that we fight on? Where's the ground that we retreat on? Where are the smart fights? Where are the dumb fights?"[53]

That leaders might want to have a say in these matters seems only natural. Instrumentally, if leaders anticipate that voters or members will hold them responsible for the party's actions, they should have strong incentive to retain control. But there is likely more at stake than reselection. Having reached the pinnacle of legislative power, leaders are often interested in shaping how they are remembered. A play for legacy tends to require leaving a distinctive imprint on Congress as an institution—whether, like Everett Dirksen, as the prime mover of a piece of landmark legislation or, like Thomas Reed, a key driver of procedural change. Or, like Gingrich, it can mean changing the party's direction. This suggests that, regardless of a party's ideological composition (or changes to it), leaders are likely to chafe at restraint and search for ways to subvert it.[54] Put another way, if by dint of selection, leaders are more ambitious than the average legislator, what are the odds that they will scale back their aspirations even when burdened by a fractious caucus?

Of course, leaders might well "discover the limits of leadership" should their actions prompt members to put aside their differences and rally against a common enemy.[55] But leaders are not fools. Rather, they are entrepreneurs, "creative, resourceful, and opportunistic." In consequence, they can "frame issues, define problems, and influence agendas" to avoid provoking member backlash while nevertheless accomplishing their ends.[56] Indeed, congressional leaders often use their agenda-setting powers to "structure decisions in ways that maximize support for the alternatives [they] favor."[57] So, too, leaders can craft "common carrier" proposals that bring together divergent factions within a party (or legislative body) to secure a winning coalition. Either way, the art is in identifying an intervention that can temporarily appease potential dissenters by giving members a variety of reasons to support the proposed course of action.[58] Alternatively, leaders can use the considerable resources at their disposal to grease the skids, offering members targeted rewards to cooperate when they disagree or threatening them with punishment should they refuse.[59] As Christopher Deering and Steven Smith put it, "successful leaders . . . exploit their hunting license to persuade."[60]

The fact that "information [in Congress] is not evenly distributed" between leaders and members enables entrepreneurial activity of this kind. Well aware that their knowledge of pending legislation, member preferences, and parliamentary procedure exceeds that of their rank and file, leaders are free to deploy information strategically, releasing favorable intel and withholding damaging material to minimize potential resistance.[61]

Leaders can also take steps to conceal the extent of their influence over chamber outcomes so as to mute or limit potential dissatisfaction. Like machine-era party bosses, they can obscure their involvement in party decision making by lodging de jure authority in party institutions like steering committees and task forces while retaining de facto control for themselves.[62] In this way, leaders can effectively launder the true source of power within the party. They can also leverage relationships with prominent figures outside Congress to help cover their tracks. Congressional history is replete with examples of legislative leaders who discreetly called upon a friendly president or interest group to cajole, threaten, or persuade errant or uncertain members to back the course of action the leader thought best. Often, members were unaware the intervention was done at the behest of their leaders, and even when members suspected leadership involvement, plausible deniability was maintained.[63]

Divided Parties, Strong Leaders

What can all of this teach us about leaders of divided parties? Recognizing that institutions are resilient, collective action difficult, and leaders entrepreneurial, this book argues that party divisions and strong leaders are not inherently incompatible. In fact, the twentieth and twenty-first centuries have been marked by congressional leaders who successfully leveraged intraparty divisions to pursue their aims and, in so doing, durably reshaped national politics and legislative procedure. Crucial to understanding when and why they managed this feat is to recognize that party divisions reflect more than just an underlying distribution of preferences. Regardless of how such preferences are distributed, every legislator has a choice about whether to join forces with like-minded colleagues or go it alone.[64] Thus, party divisions have a *collaborative dimension*—one that is distinct from, but related to, the ideological dimension that grounds most legislative scholarship. Appreciating this collaborative dimension can help us think systematically about the opportunity structures that leaders of divided parties are likely to encounter and explain why some leaders have been able to exploit party divisions more successfully than others.[65] As we will see, a leader's ability to transcend their party's divisions depends in part on whether and how members of a faction choose to work together, as well as how those choices compare to those made by their rivals.

Admittedly, the probability that a leader will seize on the opportunities afforded by divided parties will depend, at least in part, on the leader's aims. As Randall Strahan observes, no two leaders "have the same goals or hold those goals with the same degree of intensity."[66] Leaders primarily motivated by reselection may hesitate to leverage party divisions for fear of prompting a leadership challenge. But leaders whose "goals reach beyond office-holding ambition inside Congress" may be more comfortable taking advantage of the opportunities their parties' divisions create, whether to secure what they believe to be good public policy, bolster Congress's capacity and prestige, or have a say in what their party stands for.[67]

Conceptualizing the Collaborative Dimension of Party Divisions

It is understandable why party divisions are often framed in terms of the "political beliefs, values, and policy positions" that lawmakers carry around in their heads.[68] After all, a divided party is one whose members disagree with one another. But whatever the source of members' divergent "ideological values or tastes"—what we might call their *primitive* preferences— "the preferences *revealed in legislative behavior* are . . . [not] exogenous to legislative politics and policymaking."[69] At the very least, the things members publicly say and do reflect *both* their primitive preferences and any collaboration they may choose to undertake.[70] This is not a novel claim. Scholars have long recognized, for instance, that working within a political party shapes legislative behavior in ways that are distinct from members' underlying ideology.[71] But the point can be generalized. Collaboration has an independent and consequential effect on lawmakers' revealed preferences, which in turn can alter the substance and tenor of party divisions.[72]

To begin, consider that collaboration can redirect how like-minded lawmakers allocate their time and resources. As scholars have long appreciated, engaging in collective action invariably requires individuals to accommodate the needs of others. In Congress, as elsewhere, successfully joining forces is usually possible only when some legislators agree to set aside their own preferred approaches for those of others.[73] Encouraging participants to make these kinds of sacrifices is not always easy. A sense of solidarity or commitment to colleagues can sometimes be sufficient to persuade a member to pursue objectives that would not otherwise be at the top of their to-do list. Often, however, self-reinforcing collaborative arrangements that condition membership on participation or reward it through selective incentives may be necessary to initiate and sustain a joint enterprise.[74] Regardless, by inducing members of a faction to reconcile their wants with those of colleagues, collaboration can make it appear that members are in greater ideological alignment, and thus more unified, than their primitive preferences alone would dictate.

Collaboration can reinforce the perception that members share the same wants, beliefs, or priorities in still another way. Having agreed on a common plan of action, a collaborating faction's members can optimize how they allocate the labor necessary to pursue their chosen agenda in ways that leverage individuals' comparative competencies. For example, members with superior communications skills can be tasked with devising a collective public relations strategy, while those with expansive political networks can disseminate the message and materials their colleagues create. This may lead observers to overstate the degree to which members share the same priorities and commitment to them.

Mapping the Collaborative Dimension

Despite how consequential collaboration can be for legislative politics, like-minded members will not necessarily choose to work together. They must weigh the odds of achieving their ends independently against the possibility that, notwithstanding its costs, collective action offers greater likelihood of success. Indeed, even for members with overlapping preferences, going it alone often has strong appeal. In a system where legislators represent a single, geographically defined constituency, independent action ensures that members retain maximum autonomy to serve their constituents as they see fit.[75] Likewise, lawmakers eager to burnish their own reputations may find themselves reluctant to share the spotlight with others.

But independent action in pursuit of a shared goal does not guarantee success. Most of Congress's core tasks are cooperative in nature, and it is rare that one lawmaker's actions will be decisive. These features of legislative politics create a troubling incentive. When members of a faction cannot be certain that their participation is necessary to achieve a common goal, they may prefer to use their time and resources to pursue goals that they—and they alone—can accomplish and credibly claim credit for. Thus, as Mancur Olson writes of group dynamics more generally, "unless the number of individuals is quite small, or unless there is coercion or some other special device to make individuals act in their common interest, rational, self-interested individuals will not act to achieve their common group interests."[76] Simply put, a faction's members may choose to free ride on their fellows' labor, notwithstanding their overlapping aims.[77]

Members of a faction can lower the risk that some within their ranks will free ride by opting to collaborate. At minimum, even sporadic efforts to work together can yield better information about participants' activities and help members monitor their colleagues' contributions to the cause. Collaboration can also foster solidarity. As members work together and forge personal bonds, they may become increasingly reluctant to abandon their colleagues. Structured forms of collaboration offer additional insurance against free riding. Members can agree to make certain perks—for instance, the promise of help gaining a desirable committee post or additional campaign resources—available only to those who do their fair share. These types of selective incentives give lawmakers an immediate and tangible reason to support the collective enterprise. But collaboration in any form comes at a cost. To facilitate collective action, participants may be asked to subordinate their priorities in favor of those of their peers. Worse still, these sacrifices of autonomy may be for naught, whether because others renege on the bargain or because the group's agreed-on course of action fails to bear fruit.

Because the costs and benefits associated with collective action are different for every lawmaker and faction, the form that collaboration takes will vary. Among other things, members must decide what information to share with one another, whether to meet and how frequently, whether to correspond and how frequently, and whether to adopt formal organizing mechanisms such as a leadership structure or internal voting rules. Choices regarding one need not imply a similar choice for another. Thus, members may decide to meet irregularly but correspond frequently. Alternatively, they may adopt a leadership structure but eschew a fixed meeting schedule and share only limited private intel. Other, secondary choices follow. Will members choose to pool resources such as campaign funds or staff? Will they regularize their interactions—for example, picking a recurring meeting time or location or agreeing to circulate a weekly or monthly update detailing their activities? Or will they rely on more informal coordinating mechanisms—for example, a phone call or memo suggesting a meeting to address a particular issue or topic?

Those factions whose members believe that the benefits of collective action only modestly exceed the costs tend to adopt a minimalist approach. This can mean an occasional meeting preceding a vote or the infrequent exchange of news and intel via letters, phone calls, or—increasingly—text chains. Or their collective action can take the form of a hub-and-spoke model, where members interact irregularly, instead relying on the entrepreneurial activity of one or several among their number to take the lead in coordinating communication and sharing information. Other factions may work to lower the costs of collective action by favoring participatory practices, such as "feeling out the room" or informal straw polls, to coordinate joint decision making.[78]

There are also factions whose members believe the benefits of collective action significantly exceed the costs and are thus willing to tolerate a maximalist approach, usually characterized by elaborate and clearly defined rules and procedures to structure their collaboration. These factions tend to establish formal intraparty organizations: internally bounded alliances of co-partisans, with specialized institutional arrangements to support and enforce members' commitment to work together. Such organizations typically demand that members identify publicly with the group, meet regularly, pool private information, and consent to be bound by group decision making.

In between these minimalist and maximalist modes of collaboration is a broad middle ground. Some factions opt for arrangements that aim to encourage members' participation without overly constraining their autonomy—for instance, having flexible attendance requirements that do not penalize individuals for missed meetings. Others require their members to commit to hold the faction's line by staging binding votes on some joint priorities but provide a "three strikes" policy allowing members to defect without consequence on at least a few occasions.[79]

As a faction's members decide whether and how to collaborate, they do so against the backdrop of various institutional and electoral considerations. For example, the prerogatives afforded to even junior senators help explain why factional collaboration is more uncommon in the upper chamber, as individual senators are well positioned to exercise meaningful influence on their own. In the House, by contrast, factional collaboration is quite common, as the larger size of the lower chamber and members' more limited procedural rights tend to encourage members to join forces to get things done.[80]

The choice of whether and how to collaborate may also be shaped by an array of variables beyond Capitol Hill. For instance, electoral incentives can alter how a faction's members weigh the benefits of collaboration against the costs.[81] Members aiming to keep a low profile may determine that collaboration risks unwanted exposure; members eager to make a name for themselves may see collaboration as a useful vehicle for their own ends. Other aspects of the broader political environment can also influence whether and how members choose to collaborate. A faction's members may decide to join forces if they sense their shared outlook is politically or culturally under threat. Members may also choose to strengthen their collaborative efforts if they come to believe that public opinion is suddenly with them, on the theory that their investment will yield more certain returns.

Members' working relationships and the practices that govern them are also subject to evolutionary pressures.[82] Indeed, it can take years for members of a faction to decide that collaboration is warranted. And, once established, collaborative arrangements are often revised and refined—sometimes in the direction of working together in a more structured way, while at other times not. Shifts in the degree to which members collaborate tend to reflect evolving goals or changes in the perceived costs of collective action.[83] Sometimes, ad hoc interactions remain sufficient to achieve a faction's aims; other times, more routine engagement proves necessary. Other factions' choices also come into the picture. One side's choice to collaborate more (or less) intensively, or to refrain from collective action altogether, can prompt rival factions to reconsider their commitment to organization, and sometimes to even mimic the arrangements adopted by opponents.

Collaborative Arcs and Factional Symmetry

Viewed in this way, collaboration is not a static state of the world. Variation in whether and how a faction's members choose to work together means that each faction will operate on its own time scale, governed by a discrete organizing logic and corresponding set of institutional arrangements. Many factions adopt and subsequently maintain minimalist arrangements, finding them suitable to achieving their ends. When existing practices prove insufficient, a smaller number will work together more extensively and adopt more elaborate arrangements. All collaborations ultimately end. Some dissolve when members prove unwilling to bear the costs of more structured collaboration, while others dissipate when a collective goal is achieved or member interest wanes.

We might say, then, that every faction has its own distinctive *collaborative arc*. Factions collaborating for years, or even decades, will have long arcs, while those that collaborate only briefly will have shorter ones. Some arcs will have a steep upward slope, as factions rapidly layer on additional collaborative arrangements. Others will quickly plateau, as their collaborative evolution stalls. Similar dynamics work in reverse. Some factions will decline slowly, their collaborative architecture eroding over a long period, while others disintegrate rapidly, returning members to a collaborative state of nature.

At the level of the party, the interplay of these distinct collaborative arcs results in factional configurations that are either *symmetric* or *asymmetric*. Symmetry occurs when the extent of one faction's collaborative efforts matches that of intraparty rivals. Symmetry of this kind may reflect minimal collaboration by all sides in a factional conflict. Like Senate Republicans in the mid-twentieth century, competing factions have sometimes chosen to prioritize independent action over collective efforts, meeting rarely (if at all), communicating sporadically, and eschewing institutional arrangements to govern group decision making. But symmetry may also reflect the choice by rival factions to each collaborate extensively. As with today's House Democrats, symmetric configurations can result from quite substantial investments in coordination by multiple factions, often characterized by the development of institutionalized intraparty blocs that facilitate frequent and substantive member interactions and maintain group discipline through written bylaws and a clear hierarchy. Symmetry may be the product of competing factions' strategic responsiveness, as members observe their opponents' efforts to work together and attempt to emulate them. But not necessarily. History suggests that competing factions will sometimes collaborate with similar levels of intensity for coincidental or serendipitous reasons, following their own internal clocks and organizing logics.

More often than not, however, one faction's collaborative efforts will exceed (or be exceeded by) those of opponents. Sometimes asymmetry describes situations where one faction opts to collaborate while its rivals do not. But asymmetry can also capture situations where one faction outcollaborates its competition—for instance, meeting and corresponding more frequently, sharing information more widely, and adopting more formal institutional mechanisms than the competition. The current House GOP offers a good example. While conservatives communicate extensively and openly with one another and have armed their intraparty organization, the House Freedom Caucus, with bylaws that commit members to vote the group's position and authorize leaders to negotiate on members' behalf, moderates in the Republican Governance Group (formerly known as the Tuesday Group) engage with one another less frequently, are more guarded in their conversations, and have so far refrained from adopting equally restrictive rules.

Factional Symmetry and Leader Power

With this conceptual architecture in place, we can now consider the book's core claim. Leaders, I argue, are best positioned to overcome, and even draw strength from, their divided ranks when their party's factional configuration is symmetric.[84] Asymmetric configurations, by contrast, provide more limited opportunities for leaders to pursue their ends.

To understand why factional symmetry might advantage party leaders, consider first a scenario where all factions have eschewed collaboration and members are instead pursuing their aims independently. These conditions are likely to minimize the degree of resistance a leader will encounter from dissenting factions should the leader pursue their own preferred course of action over that of any faction. Absent some degree of coordination, members of a faction opposed to the leader's intervention are likely to find it difficult to identify a mutually acceptable response or reach consensus on how to execute it. As Strahan argues, it is when members' preferences are "ill-defined, uncertain, or even in substantial conflict" that leaders will have an opportunity to "play an independent role."[85] Alternatively, members of a faction opposed to a leader's intervention may find themselves vulnerable to co-optation. As one former member of Congress observed, "it is very difficult for . . . factions to be internally cohesive. Individual members are easily picked off . . . [unless] you can form a group."[86] So long as resisting a leader is costly and members cannot be certain that their labor will be decisive, potential dissidents may prefer to stay out of the fight or, better yet, cut a favorable deal in return for their silence or support.[87]

Now imagine a scenario where rival factions are all collaborating extensively. Here, leaders may be able to leverage the resources of one faction to pursue their aims more efficiently and undercut the efforts of factions that might oppose them. These resources can include the selective incentives a faction provides its own members to discourage free riding (e.g., tangible materials like white papers, draft press releases, or brokered access to interest groups or donors) or the organizing mechanisms a faction has developed for its own use (e.g., a system of whips or internal voting rules). Access to such resources can make a leader's job easier by granting them a valuable "legislative subsidy."[88] For instance, by relying on a faction's internal whip counts, leaders can count more noses more frequently and accurately without allocating additional staff to the task. The particular virtue of party symmetry is that, for any course of action the leader wishes to undertake, they can be reasonably certain that the faction likely to be most amenable to that course of action will have the resources to equal the faction most likely to oppose it.[89]

Alternatively, by prolonging intraparty fights, or by making them appear intractable, factional symmetry can make members more accepting of a leader's attempts to intervene in the conflict. Often, the institutional arrangements factions adopt to battle one another sustain members' engagement and attention beyond what their primitive preferences would dictate. As rival factions dig in, each is likely to reassess their opponents' strength and tolerance for prolonged conflict. These calculations may make all sides more willing to support a leader-crafted settlement. At minimum, they will make more credible a leader's claim that resolution is unlikely absent their intervention. By the same token, the more capable a faction appears to its rivals, the more willing opponents may be to empower or insulate party leaders in the hopes of countering their adversaries.[90]

This is not to say that leaders will find it easy to pursue their preferred course of action. Factional symmetry does not suspend the ordinary laws of legislative politics. Leaders must still negotiate with important stakeholders, be they committee chairs, other senior members, interest groups, or donors. So, too, given the constitutional requirements of bicameralism and presentment, they must attend to the preferences of pivotal members of the other chamber, the president and key members of the executive branch, and the courts. Leaders must also work to shape public perceptions, whether through the media or by communicating directly with voters. For our purposes, however, the crucial point is that party symmetry will increase the odds that leaders will be able to transcend their party's divisions to achieve their aims.

Asymmetry, by contrast, offers fewer opportunities and more obstacles for leaders hoping to draw strength from their divided ranks. Consider a scenario where the faction that is outcollaborating its rivals is opposed to the leader's preferred intervention. The difficulties should be evident. At a minimum, the leader must face off against dissidents who have had the opportunity to work through their differences and agree on a plan of resistance. More extensive collaboration only compounds the challenge, as the cost to leaders of buying off individuals or singling out offenders for punishment is likely to increase.[91]

But what about a situation where the organizationally ascendant faction views the leader's preferred intervention favorably? We might expect these conditions to be propitious. Surely, a leader would be advantaged by the backing of a friendly faction that had resolved its coordination and collective action problems better than anyone else. But as we will see, members of an organizationally ascendant faction often have little incentive to work cooperatively with leaders when they can plausibly get what they want on their own. Indeed, a faction that outcollaborates its opponents may well insist that leadership compromise with it, rather than the other way around.

Even if a leader's priorities align with those of an ascendant faction in the short term, asymmetry is likely to present considerable obstacles in the longer term. Over time, the faction may begin to demand greater control over the leader, with members insisting that the leader serve more as their agent and less as a coprincipal. The seeds of discord are easily sown. Members of the ascendant faction may come to believe that they are contributing a disproportionate share of the labor in pursuit of their shared agenda. Or they may be increasingly uncertain that the bargains the party leader has struck reflect the leader's best efforts to get the faction the best deal possible. Alternatively, a new issue may emerge that jeopardizes the alliance and prompts the faction to try to limit the leader's autonomy going forward. Should the leader resist these efforts, an ascendant faction may seek a more pliable replacement.

Leaders may also suffer reputational costs from associating too closely with an organizationally ascendant faction. Consider that other actors, be it factional opponents, lawmakers in the other chamber, executive branch officials, or party stakeholders, can observe only that the leader is working with a powerful faction. They cannot easily discern the true nature of that relationship, including whether the leader is making key decisions or simply serving as a figurehead. Moreover, a leader's opponents may well attempt to undermine the leader's reputation further by promoting the perception that their ties to the ascendant faction make them an untrustworthy broker. The more doubt there is that a leader cannot (or will not) see beyond one faction's interests, the more difficult the leader will find it to obtain credible information from other power brokers or persuade them to negotiate in good faith.[92]

Regardless of whether the organizationally ascendant faction is favorably disposed to the leader's preferred intervention, asymmetry can create additional headaches. Factions are often eager to craft a brand that conveys meaningful information to voters and donors.[93] One way for a faction to do so is to distance itself from other power centers within the party. In cases of party symmetry, this may be a well-matched factional rival. But in cases of party asymmetry, members of an organizationally ascendant faction are likely to set their sights on leadership. For those factions keen to cultivate a reputation for pragmatic dealmaking, distinguishing themselves from the positions articulated by leaders can help signal that they are not mindless partisans. And for factions eager to cultivate a reputation for ideological fealty, distinguishing themselves from the positions articulated by leaders can signal that they are unwilling to sacrifice principles for expediency.

* * *

Thinking about party divisions in collaborative rather than exclusively ideological terms yields a counterintuitive conclusion. Although we have long been taught that the more divided a party, the weaker its leaders, a deep dive into the logic of collective action in Congress suggests that party divisions will not always debilitate the people who lead them. But understanding why leaders of divided parties only sometimes exercise power requires attending to the nature of the factional configuration they encounter. Leaders who helm symmetric parties will be better able to transcend their party's divisions and achieve their aims than those who govern asymmetric ones.

Factional Symmetry and Its Limits

This book's emphasis on factional symmetry is not meant to minimize the importance of other variables commonly thought to condition leader power—principally, the size of the leader's majority, the size of the party's respective factions, and each faction's spatial position. Rather, my contention is that a party's factional configuration will often mediate the effect of these other variables, making it difficult to draw generalized conclusions about how they might independently (or collectively) shape leader power.

Start with the size of the majority. The conventional wisdom is that a leader is best positioned to achieve their ends when they control a large majority. With more votes to spare, the leader will have greater flexibility to assemble a winning coalition in support of their preferred proposal and greater confidence that any defections will not threaten their control of the floor.[94] But the prospect of factional collaboration complicates the story.

Consider a large majority where members of a dissenting faction are collaborating extensively, while members of factions more sympathetic to leadership are collaborating minimally (or not at all). This kind of party asymmetry is likely to increase the costs of assembling a winning coalition. As Sinclair points out, "Ordinarily . . . leaders simply want to win, and as cheaply as possible."[95] Clearly, however, if a leader must rely on some of the dissenters to maintain a working majority, the leader may be compelled to expend more resources to secure their allegiance. As we have seen, collaboration makes it harder for leaders to buy off individual members with particularly favorable terms and instead may require them to strike a deal with the entire faction. But even if a leader does not need the dissenting faction's votes, their collective unwillingness to cooperate will make the leader more dependent on the votes of those outside the faction, which should drive up the price that even sympathetic members can demand in return for their support.

Now consider a narrow majority where no faction is collaborating. With members pursuing their aims independently, it may be possible for leaders to efficiently allocate the resources and bargaining chips at their disposal to secure just enough votes to carry the day. These dynamics suggest that absent attention to a party's factional configuration, it is hard to say with certainty how the size of a leader's majority will shape their time in office.

Without attending to collaboration, it is likewise difficult to know how a faction's size will condition its influence. It seems intuitive that the faction commanding the most votes within a party would have the most leverage. But bigger isn't necessarily better. As in settings outside Congress, the larger the faction, the greater the risk that members will free ride. And while large factions may seek to adopt stricter rules to monitor members' behavior or otherwise incentivize their cooperation, such restrictions are rarely popular and hard to execute. For leaders, this means that bigger factions may in fact be more vulnerable to co-optation than smaller ones.

It is no easier to generalize about how a faction's spatial position might shape intraparty power dynamics. We often assume that members situated at or near the chamber median will have outsize influence over legislative outcomes. Not only are their votes possibly pivotal to maintaining their party's control of the floor, but their proximity to the minority makes their threats to work across the aisle more credible.[96] By contrast, we tend to think that members farther away from the chamber median lack a credible threat of exit and must therefore accept what leaders give them. These intuitions scale up to the level of a faction. In expectation, factions at or near the median should have greater sway than those at the ideological extremes.

But collaboration muddies the waters. When members of a faction at or near the chamber median opt not to work together, they may all choose the path of least resistance and cooperate with leaders. By the same token, when members of a faction at the ideological extreme join forces, they may be able to control enough votes to deny the party its majority and credibly demand that leaders attend to their interests. Thus, collaboration may reduce the explanatory power of spatial theory, helping to explain why, as our current politics makes clear, leaders are sometimes forced to accommodate the wants of more extremist factions while simultaneously dismissing those of colleagues at the chamber median.

Factional Symmetry and American Political Development

Although this is first and foremost a book about Congress, it also endeavors to be sensitive to—and engage with—two of the central concerns that animate studies of American political development.[97] First, it offers a new way to think about time and congressional politics. By and large, legislative scholars demarcate time into discrete historical eras. This is sometimes done on the basis of prevailing institutional arrangements, where time is bounded by significant shifts in how the legislature is organized.[98] For example, it is common to speak of the era of "czar rule," the "textbook" Congress, or the "post-reform" Congress. At other times, coherent policy regimes serve as points of demarcation: for example, the Reconstruction Era Congress or the New Deal Congress. Still another possibility is to emphasize periods of long-term party control or its absence. Today's era of "insecure majorities" is often contrasted with earlier periods of unbroken one-party rule in one or both chambers.

These ways of keeping "secular" time link distinct historical periods to particular allocations of power both within Congress and among the other branches of the national government.[99] For our purposes, the implication is that leaders will have much in common with those who share their historical era (however defined) and less in common with their more distant predecessors or successors. But linear periodization schemes are not the only way to situate legislative leaders in time. Like presidents, legislative leaders encounter recurring background conditions that alternately empower or disempower them. By naming and categorizing these conditions, we can layer "political" time atop secular trends.[100]

Attending to factional configurations is one way to put this idea into action.[101] Leaders who govern under comparable factional configurations coexist in shared political time even if they inhabit radically different secular eras. Comparisons that keep political time constant but cut across secular time can yield surprising insights about the individual capacities of those who have held top leadership posts. Indeed, if the "test of leadership varies . . . from one incumbent to the next" on the basis of the factional configuration they encounter, then we can more fairly judge how individual leaders perform by taking that configuration into account. Some leaders will find factional politics "rigged in their favor" and so wield "an authority quite independent of the merits of their proposals" or their personal talents.[102] Others will confront less favorable factional configurations and struggle mightily through no fault of their own. So, too, leaders who coexist in the same wedge of secular time may find themselves in quite different political moments. This can help explain why, as in our current era, there is such variation in leadership performance across the two chambers and parties.

This book also underscores the continuing value of conceptualizing institutional development as the result of political actors resolving, however imperfectly, tensions between contemporaneous forces "with contradictory logics or purposes."[103] Often, those political forces originate outside Congress but nevertheless shape what happens in it. As Schickler describes, the Democratic Party in the 1930s incorporated new coalition partners—"CIO [Congress of Industrial Organizations] unionists, African Americans, Jews, and other urban liberals"—who were sympathetic to the party's economic policy. However, once embedded within the party, these new partners joined forces in a separate social movement to demand action on civil rights in defiance of Democratic leaders. It was the "convergence" of these "two initially distinct political trajectories" that spurred reluctant leaders to push for civil rights legislation, even as they worked to prevent a direct confrontation between the party's liberal northern and conservative southern wings. For this reason, Schickler contends, we cannot understand the timing of civil rights legislation or its partisan origins without attending to the intersection of the Democrats' party-building logic and the movement-building logic of civil rights activists.[104]

But this book suggests that tensions between vying forces can arise organically within Congress itself, with important implications for legislative development. As I have argued, every faction has its own collaborative logic that determines whether and how its members join forces—one that reflects their particular wants and needs and the specific contours of their institutional environment. Over time, a faction's organizational choices, whether to impose new collaborative arrangements or maintain or abandon existing ones, will plot a distinct collaborative arc, as members evaluate and reevaluate collaboration's costs and benefits. Congressional party politics can thus be viewed as a series of contingent intersections of vying factions' collaborative arcs, which leaders must navigate in pursuit of their ends. And one must follow each of these collaborative arcs to appreciate why the factional configuration any leader encounters at a particular moment in time is symmetric or asymmetric. It is to this task that we now turn.

Plan of the Book

With this theoretical framework in place, and before launching into the empirics, chapter 2 provides a detailed discussion of the book's methodological approach. It begins by explaining how we might define and measure our objects of interest: factions, symmetry and asymmetry, and leader power. The second half of the chapter outlines the book's case selection strategy and describes why archives and interviews are both vital and appropriate sources of data.

Organized in reverse chronological order, the book's empirical account begins in the modern era with Pelosi, who held the speakership twice in the first decades of the twenty-first century (2007–11 and 2019–23). In chapter 3, we will see that during her first stint as Speaker, moderate Democrats in the House outcollaborated their progressive rivals. This asymmetric configuration provided a consistent constraint on Pelosi as she worked to pass the Affordable Care Act (ACA). In confrontations with the Speaker, moderates prevailed in limiting the act's shape and scope, successfully weakening the public option and significantly curtailing women's reproductive rights. But by the time Pelosi was back in the Speaker's office, her party's factional configuration had evolved. Progressives were countermobilizing and investing in their own institutional mechanisms to facilitate collaboration. As the remainder of the chapter details, Pelosi used her newly symmetric party to pursue action on climate change, an issue she had longed hoped would be the "flagship of [her] speakership" but that moderates had resisted.[105]

Chapter 4 considers the peculiar predicament of Republican Speakers in the modern Congress. As the chapter describes, in the decades following Gingrich's Republican revolution, the ideological composition and organizational landscape of the House GOP shifted dramatically. The Republicans' moderate faction, once a vital force within the conference, struggled to counter the rising tide of antiestablishment conservatism and soon found its existing collaborative arrangements inadequate. By contrast, the party's conservatives, energized by the grassroots populism of the Tea Party movement and flush with new recruits, began to collaborate with greater intensity.[106] Though himself a committed conservative, Ohio's Boehner clashed repeatedly with the newly ascendant right wing during his time as Speaker (2011–15). With the party's pronounced asymmetry providing little room to maneuver, Boehner struggled—and failed—to persuade his right flank to set its sights on something other than defunding the ACA. Admitting defeat, the Speaker switched tactics. Publicly vowing to give conservatives the fight they wanted, Boehner agreed to greenlight a government shutdown, privately hoping the public fallout would turn his conference against "the crazies" in the party.[107] He turned out to be half right. Although the shutdown that followed proved deeply unpopular, the Speaker's strategy did not undermine the conservatives' influence or restore greater balance to his conference. Nor would his successors find it easier to govern. Burdened by an asymmetric conference, Speakers Ryan (2015–19), McCarthy (2023), and Johnson (2023–) struggled, much as Boehner had, to prioritize their wants over those of their mobilized right flank.

Moving backward in time several decades, chapter 5 profiles yet another Speaker who found his power constrained by an asymmetric factional configuration. As we will see, by the early 1980s, the collaborative arrangements liberal Democrats had used so successfully to influence the mid-twentieth-century House were fast degrading. Their more conservative colleagues, by contrast, had begun to re-organize their diminished ranks—buoyed by Ronald Reagan's election and public enthusiasm for the new president's economic agenda. Speaker Tip O'Neill, who for ten years (1977–87) presided over House Democrats' increasingly asymmetric caucus, tried and failed to prevent conservative Democrats from working with the Reagan White House. Unable to get what he wanted from his fractured party, the Speaker reluctantly pursued a public relations campaign he had little faith in. Much to his surprise, however, his second-best strategy proved remarkably fruitful. With the country's economy sputtering, O'Neill was able to discredit Reagan's fiscal policy and raise the profile of the speakership in the process.

Chapter 6 takes readers further back, into the mid-twentieth-century House, to consider a case of strong leadership under conditions of factional symmetry. As the chapter recounts, the Democratic Party that enacted the New Deal and steered the country through the Second World War roped together two opposing factions: one of northern and western urban liberals, the other of rural southern conservatives. In time, the liberal wing of the party grew to resent their southern colleagues' overt racial animus, and both factions began to develop formidable institutional mechanisms to structure their collaboration. As we will see, this emerging factional symmetry facilitated Speaker Rayburn's efforts to combat southern conservatives' influence within the Democratic Party. Chronicling the Speaker's audacious and ultimately successful bid to expand the House Rules Committee in January 1961, the chapter describes how Rayburn, who served as Speaker nearly uninterrupted for twenty years (1940–47, 1949–53, and 1955–61), leveraged the collaborative arrangements conceived by liberal Democrats to curb southern gatekeeping, secure key policy victories, and further consolidate authority in the speakership.

Chapter 7 completes readers' tour through congressional history, ending in the Senate of the late 1940s and early 1950s. This was an era when paranoia about the threat of domestic communism was at a fever pitch and Senator Joseph McCarthy at the apex of his power. As the chapter details, Senate Republicans were deeply divided over McCarthy's brand of populist conservatism. Moderate Republicans, backed by a sympathetic White House, decried the senator's incendiary tactics and sought to discredit his style of reactionary politics. Conservatives, in contrast, saw much to like in McCarthy's agenda. Despite the depth of their disagreement, however, neither faction opted to collaborate, and neither succeeded in gaining the upper hand. Leveraging this symmetric factional configuration, Senate Majority Leader Knowland—an ardent anticommunist and foreign policy hawk—intervened. Determined to guide Senate Republicans away from President Dwight D. Eisenhower's "middle way," Knowland maneuvered to sideline McCarthy while keeping the cause he championed at the top of the party's agenda. In so doing, he ensured that "despite Eisenhower's repeated attempts to govern in the middle of the road," conservatives maintained a "foothold in the GOP," from which vantage they would ultimately transform the party over the second half of the twentieth century.[108]

Chapter 8, the book's conclusion, revisits the study's central thesis and the evidence marshaled to support it. It then details the many ways that our understanding of Congress can be profitably enhanced by thinking about legislative politics along the collaborative dimension.

CHAPTER TWO

Analyzing Divided Parties

Chapter 1 laid out the book's core theoretical claim that a party's factional configuration conditions its leader's power. Here, I outline my approach to defending that thesis on empirical grounds. Because this study foregrounds power, it makes sense to start there. How might we define power and measure it as a dependent variable? The chapter next turns to the study's independent variable, specifying my strategy for identifying rival factions, categorizing the collaborative choices they make, and then determining whether their party is symmetric or asymmetric. With these pieces in place, the chapter closes with a discussion of case selection, detailing the considerations that motivated the inclusion of the leaders profiled in this book.

Conceptualizing Leader Power

As readers will no doubt be aware, power is among the most contested concepts in all of social science. Students of American politics are probably most familiar with Robert Dahl's definition. Power, on his account, means getting another actor to do what he or she would not otherwise do.[1] But in a legislative context, this definition offers more limited analytic traction. In a party caucus or chamber body, members possess a variety of policy preferences that they hold with varying levels of intensity. Thus, whenever a leader acts, they are likely to be pushing some lawmakers to deviate from their preferred course, while leaving the behavior of others unaltered. In other words, leaders under this definition are going to be simultaneously powerful and powerless. Applying Dahl's definition is also complicated by the reality that discerning what someone would not otherwise do is difficult in the setting of a congressional party. As James Curry notes, independent of leadership pressure, "rank-and-file lawmakers have numerous incentives to go along with their leaders, and most of them, most of the time, will not be interested in proving their leaders wrong."[2]

Accordingly, this book relies on a more forgiving definition of power. As I use it here, exercising power means getting more of what you want than others do. As to legislative leaders specifically, this outcome-focused view of power reasonably "encompasses influence over all of [Congress's] various doings."[3] In light of leaders' outsize ambition and demonstrated political acumen, we should expect that they will seek influence beyond the legislature's core constitutional tasks of statutory drafting and oversight. Among other things, leaders may wish to shape the content of chamber procedure; the identity of those appointed to important offices, including party leadership and committee posts; their party's electoral strategy; and the legislature's relationship with rival branches.

The challenge of defining power in this way is that even when we observe a particular outcome—the statute that was drafted, the procedure that was adopted, who was appointed to a contested position, or which strategy the party pursued to retain (or regain) its majority—it is difficult to know what relevant actors wanted before the fact, and thus to assess who got the most of what they wanted. A common path forward is to use a legislator's voting record to estimate their underlying preferences. Scholars can then assess how closely legislative outputs (typically, the results of floor or committee votes) correspond to this estimate of what each lawmaker wants. The most powerful lawmaker is the one for whom the calculated distance is smallest—that is, the member whose preferences are most directly reflected in the laws that Congress enacts. It is this logic that often leads us to conclude that the floor median in the House and the filibuster pivot in the Senate are powerful, as outcomes in both chambers often correspond most closely to those members' preferred policy or procedural interventions.[4]

While this account is appealing in its apparent objectivity, power dynamics in Congress are often more complicated. As myriad studies have shown, leaders work to shape members' votes before they are cast, whether by using their informational advantage to influence how rank-and-file lawmakers think about issues; setting the agenda in ways that foreclose otherwise-popular choices; or simply inducing members to vote the party line by promising reward or threatening punishment.[5] In short, what members vote on and how they vote are both subject to leader interference.

And because vote-based metrics make it difficult to disentangle those inputs that reflect members' preferences and those that result from leadership influence, it is hard to use them to make reliable inferences about exercising power.[6]

Aware of this inferential challenge, other studies have focused instead on the formal procedural tools leaders have at their disposal.[7] The intuition here is that the extent of a leader's capacity to intervene is a strong indication of their power, regardless of whether or how frequently that capacity is deployed. As is true of vote-based metrics, one important virtue of this approach is that scholars can rely on publicly accessible and easily replicable data—for instance, the operative chamber rules or those of the party caucus—rather than subjective evaluations by congressional insiders. This approach also enables comparison across chamber, party, and time. So, for example, we can say with some confidence that, all else being equal, a Speaker with the power to appoint members to the House Rules Committee has more power over legislative proceedings than one who lacks that authority.

But this approach, too, is less helpful if we are interested in assessing how much power leaders actually exercise. Knowing the panoply of paper powers leaders have at their disposal tells us little about how or why they will use (or not use) them in practice, let alone how the mere prospect of deploying those powers might aid or hinder their negotiations with others. If a leader fails to intervene, were they hamstrung by their membership or simply disinterested? If the leader does intervene, was their hand forced by their rank and file or did the leader freely choose to act as they saw fit? These questions become even more vexing when attempting to evaluate whether or how leaders might seek to leverage conflicts that divide their membership. Leaders, for their part, may be reluctant to admit—whether to colleagues or outsiders—that they have something to gain from the hostilities. So, too, members of vying factions may be unaware of a leader's interference or simply unwilling to acknowledge the leader's meddling, preferring to take full credit should the faction's goals be achieved. By the same token, we should not assume that when a leader acts with the apparent support of their party, they are not exercising power. The leader may well be shaping the particulars of the intervention to achieve the outcome *they* want most. Leaders, as Randall Strahan notes, often play "an independent role in determining the specific path that gets chosen," even when party members agree about the destination.[8]

This book assesses power from a different vantage. Consistent with much of the literature, it pairs systematic evaluation of what leaders and members say they want ex ante with an evaluation of who came closest to getting it ex post. But it departs from existing scholarship by relying primarily on interviews and archives—including the personal papers of congressional party leaders, executive branch records and those of party organizations, correspondence between members of congressional party factions, and detailed oral histories—to better ascertain what the relevant actors in a given political conflict wanted and thought they could get at a time before events or deliberate action on the part of leaders came to restrict the legislative agenda.[9] In this way, archival records and interviews enable the researcher to historicize legislative power rather than make ahistorical assumptions about what members might have thought possible. Armed with this information, we can look to how events unfolded and determine with greater certainty the extent to which a leader succeeded in getting their way.[10]

To be sure, archival materials and interviews are not fully insulated from the pressures of legislative politics, nor can we be certain that they will reveal what went on in a legislator's mind. Even in confidence, members of Congress may not be entirely candid or uncensored in articulating their wants. Yet, with "suitable witnessing and reporting," we can, as David Mayhew describes, "hope for fly-on-the-wall evidence."[11] Moreover, and crucially for our purposes, while reports of private conversations may acknowledge and perhaps be shaped by leader power, they are not themselves—unlike votes or public statements—its direct objects. Leaders may well be unaware of or uninterested in what members privately express, so long as they publicly comply with demands to toe the party line. And leaders themselves are most likely to be frank about their own wants and strategies in correspondence or conversations they know to be out of the public eye. For these reasons, relying on interviews and archives has the potential to help us estimate preferences with greater accuracy than prevailing approaches. Long before votes are cast, we can go behind the scenes to see how leaders and members perceived the lay of the land, understood their options, and aimed to promote their varied interests.

Yet another reason to rely on archives and interviews is that they bring many perspectives to the table. When examining a chain of events, we have more than just the records of leaders and members discussing possibilities in real time. We can, for instance, tap into contemporaneous assessments of nonparticipants, including members of interest groups and journalists, as well as reflections offered in retrospect by key figures themselves and their biographers. Taking advantage of this diversity of opinion allows us to profitably triangulate among competing perspectives. By adopting the techniques of a historical detective—sifting through the record, matching up accounts, and interrogating the biases of witnesses—we can better understand who exercises power in Congress and why.

Identifying Factions

So much for power. What about factions? Early American political thinkers used the term to encompass a wide variety of social groupings, including political parties and interests—both concentrated and diffuse. This broad definition held sway into the mid-twentieth century. As Harold Lasswell wrote in his 1931 entry in the *Encyclopedia of Social Sciences*, a faction is "any constituent group of a larger unit which works for the advancement of particular persons or policies."[12] In the years since then, many scholars have emphasized organization as the distinguishing characteristic of factions. Mayhew, for his part, defined a faction as "a traditional organization that regularly competes for a wide range of offices against one or more traditional organizations of the same party in the same city or county."[13] More recently, Daniel DiSalvo defines a faction as "a party subunit that has the ideological consistency, the organizational capacity, and the temporal durability to undertake significant actions to shift a party's agenda priorities and reputation."[14]

In this book, I take a different approach, defining factions with reference to their members' shared beliefs. On my account, a *faction* refers to lawmakers whose wants or beliefs across some related and politically salient issues overlap with each other—perhaps imperfectly—but conflict with those of their co-partisans. Crucially, members of a faction may, *but need not*, regularly interact or coordinate their activities. As I argued in chapter 1, the virtue of this approach is that we can acknowledge variation in the extent to which members engage in collaborative activities of this type. The difficulty, however, is that evidence of collaboration provides an accessible, and ostensibly objective, way to identify factions. If we remove collaboration from the equation, how can we systematically identify factions across time?

One possibility is to look to members' voting behavior. But for reasons that should now be familiar, I eschew this strategy. Vote-based metrics do not allow us to distinguish between members of Congress who vote together because they are in fact like-minded and those who find themselves on the same side of a cut point for other reasons, perhaps because of successful agenda setting or vote buying by party leaders. Instead, I turn again to more qualitative sources of data, drawing on a diverse array of secondary scholarship on the post–World War II Congress and synthesizing it with primary accounts that describe differences of opinion within a party firsthand. Admittedly, evaluations of this kind introduce bias, both mine and that of the source's author. In recognition of this possibility, I verify that the factions whose collaborative activity I trace in this book are also identified as factions by other legislative scholars.[15]

In tracking factional activity, I make two deliberate simplifications. First, the empirical chapters that follow reduce what are often nuanced, multi-faceted factional arrangements into contests between moderates (those partisans closest to the floor median on whatever policy dimension is salient) and progressive or conservative hard-liners (those partisans farthest away). Like many such simplifications, this one is based on political reality. Think here of the moderate members of the Republican Governance Group facing off against the conservative members of the House Freedom Caucus. This simplification is also intended to facilitate comparison across historical era. For instance, we might suggest that prosilver Republicans of the late nineteenth century are in some important ways analogous to contemporary GOP moderates, as both adopted issue positions that were consonant with those of their Democratic opponents.

Second, I treat factional configurations as exogenous to leaders' interventions. This is surely only partially true. As we will see, leaders have sometimes helped incubate factional collaboration with the intention of augmenting their own power. And those efforts have occasionally borne fruit, as in the case of liberal Democrats in the mid-twentieth century, who benefited from Speaker Sam Rayburn's protection and tutelage. Given the advantages of factional symmetry for leaders, it would be surprising if the world were otherwise. Nevertheless, to demonstrate the book's core thesis, and to keep the analysis within manageable confines, the empirical chapters largely proceed on the assumption that leaders simply encounter a particular configuration and then work within it. When factions develop new collaborative arrangements or abandon old ones, the main actors driving change are the rank-and-file members of that faction, with their party's leader along for the ride. In the book's conclusion, I reflect on the consequences of softening this assumption.

Assessing Factional Collaboration

It is necessary but not sufficient to identify a party's constituent factions. We must also make determinations about how extensively members of each faction are collaborating at any given point in time. Collaboration, on my account, requires that members interact and coordinate their activities in pursuit of a mutually agreed upon end. As we will see, there is considerable variation in how members collaborate. For example, members of some factions collaborate only sporadically, while others do so more regularly.

So defined, efforts to collaborate nearly always leave an evidentiary footprint. Legislative offices file away written correspondence and log calls. Intraparty organizations maintain their own records, preserving bylaws, membership lists, and meeting minutes. And to the extent that these materials fail to document informal or confidential interactions, members and staff can be called on to describe, whether in oral histories or interviews, their own collaborative activities and those of others.

In analyzing these records, I rely on the intuition that more extensive collaboration is likely to involve frequent interaction over a long duration and the regular exchange of closely held information, while more limited collaboration is likely to reflect infrequent interaction over a shorter duration, with the content of the exchange remaining superficial or reflecting professional formality. Thus, when characterizing a faction's collaborative efforts, I make note of the frequency of members' interactions. How often are they communicating with one another, whether in person or by letter, memorandum, phone, email, or text? I evaluate their regularity. Are members interacting at fixed intervals or are they doing so only intermittently? I also attend to the duration of members' collaboration. Are they working together over a period of weeks, months, or years? Finally, I consider the content of their communications. Are members conveying already public information or are they sharing private intelligence? Are their communications intended to elicit meaningful feedback from colleagues, or are they designed merely to notify recipients of a predetermined course of action or preferred outcome?

I also assess the degree to which a faction's collaborative activities are institutionalized. The logic here is that undertaking and sustaining collective action often requires the scaffolding of formal procedures and organizational arrangements. Although smaller factions may seek to institutionalize if their aim is to routinize members' interactions or further reduce coordination costs, we are especially likely to observe a greater array of formal procedures and organizational arrangements when factions are large and endeavoring to collaborate extensively. To track patterns of institutionalization, I consider whether a faction has taken steps to establish a formal organization, such as adopting membership rules, settling on a leadership structure, or imposing procedures to govern or enforce group decision making. I also look to whether members have worked to cultivate a recognizable brand or public image, as evidenced by their communications strategy and marketing materials. Table 1 summarizes the indicators of factional collaboration.

In doing this work, I am attentive to the problem of missing data. Not all interactions are documented. Even for those that are, legislative offices vary in what materials they save. No office preserves everything. Member and staff recollections are invariably imperfect. Fortunately, given that we are interested in comparisons, we need worry about missing data only if one faction in a dyad is disproportionately affected. To guard against the consequent possibility that we might mistakenly characterize a factional configuration as symmetric when it is, in reality, asymmetric (or vice versa), I examine a wide variety of sources. For any faction, I analyze the records of its members as well as those of lawmakers unaffiliated with the faction, party leaders, and intraparty and party organizations (if relevant). If there were unintentional biases in the creation or preservation of records that

TABLE 1 **Indicators of factional collaboration**

Frequency of interactions	Are exchanges between members regular or sporadic?
	Are exchanges between members lasting days, weeks, months, or years?
Quality of interactions	Do members convey private or public information?
	Do members insist on confidentiality or encourage sharing correspondence or information outside the group?
	Do members seek feedback from one another, or are they simply notifying recipients of a predetermined course of action?
Extent of institutionalization	Have members adopted membership rules? Are those rules stringent or lax?
	Have members established a leadership structure? Is it hierarchical or diffuse?
	Have members imposed procedures to govern decision making? Do they tend to insist on unanimity or allow for majority rule?
	Have members created mechanisms to enforce group decisions?
	Have members cultivated, or attempted to cultivate, a shared brand?

disproportionately affected one faction—or perhaps more concerning, if members of a faction were intentionally concealing evidence of their own collaboration or overstating its magnitude—then we would expect to see a disjuncture between how that faction's activities were described in their own records and others' characterization of those same activities.

Other materials can act as a further check against the possibility that deficiencies in the archival and interview record systematically favor one faction over its rival. Journalistic accounts often make reference to factional collaboration, as do congressional biographies and autobiographies. Secondary sources provide additional insight, as political scientists and political historians often describe factional activities during specific congressional eras, as the voluminous historiographies on the mid-twentieth-century Southern Caucus and Democratic Study Group make clear. By combining all of these materials, we can be reasonably confident that the available evidentiary footprint reliably indexes the extent of factional collaboration and thus that our classification of a party's factional configuration as symmetric or asymmetric is accurate.

Case Selection

This book's case selection strategy begins with the core theoretical distinction between symmetric and asymmetric factional configurations. As described in table 2, the empirical chapters profile leaders who presided over symmetric parties as well as those who presided over asymmetric ones. Several of these chapters chronicle a single episode in a leader's career. Others sweep more broadly, tracking multiple episodes in an effort to trace changes in a leader's fortunes as their party's factional configuration evolved. In this sense, the book leverages both *across*-case and *within*-case comparisons in defense of its thesis. As with any classification scheme, one is likely to encounter borderline cases. For instance, is a configuration symmetric or asymmetric if one faction is outcollaborating its rival by only a small margin? In the interest of clearly delineating the book's theoretical categories, I have deliberately excluded such cases here. Instead, I have chosen cases where there is little ambiguity as to whether one faction is collaborating more extensively than its rival or whether both factions are collaborating on equal terms.

Defending the book's thesis also requires selecting cases with an eye toward structural factors, separate from factional configuration, that

TABLE 2 **Case selection and chapter structure**

Symmetry	Asymmetry
Chapter 3: Nancy Pelosi (2019–23)	Chapter 3: Nancy Pelosi (2007–11)
Chapter 6: Sam Rayburn	Chapter 4: John Boehner
Chapter 7: William Knowland	Chapter 5: Tip O'Neill

might plausibly shape leaders' power. I start with party. To help ensure that the book's conclusions do not apply exclusively to Democratic or Republican leaders, the cases selected feature leaders of both parties. Next: chamber. To help rule out the possibility that the argument applies only to House leaders and not to Senate leaders (or vice versa), the book profiles leaders of both chambers. But, in recognition of the fact that extensive collaboration is more uncommon in the Senate, the cases are weighted more heavily toward House leaders. For the same reason, the selected Senate case reflects minimal collaboration on the part of both factions, as is typical for the upper chamber. Finally: majority status. Here, as noted in chapter 1, I examine only leaders whose party is in the majority at the time of the relevant episode. This is in part to ensure comparability across cases. Perhaps more important, it is when a party is in the majority that divisions within it are most apparent, making it easier to observe what different actors wanted and to evaluate how close they came to getting it.

I am also attentive to more subtle variation across factional configurations. As discussed in chapter 1, symmetric factional configurations can reflect minimal collaboration by both factions or extensive collaboration by both factions. For that reason, I include cases of both. And in the chapters that profile factional asymmetry, I take care to select cases that vary with respect to the spatial position of the collaboratively ascendant faction.

We might also wonder whether it is only certain leader goals that are advantaged by party symmetry or disadvantaged by party asymmetry. Accordingly, the chapters in this book chronicle the efforts of leaders who pursue a variety of aims, including traditional legislation, procedural reform, and long-term party branding.

Finally, one might reasonably worry that a leader's historical era shapes their capacity to exploit their party's factional configuration in ways that are not captured by the analysis presented here. To mitigate this concern, the book's cases span nearly a century of congressional history—beginning with legislative politics today, moving backward in time through the post-Watergate era, and ending in the mid-twentieth-century "textbook" Congress.

Notwithstanding all this variation, what these cases have in common is that each represents a "hard" case for my claim that leaders of divided parties can sometimes exercise real power. Each leader profiled in this book governed a party with sharp and persistent divisions. Those splits concerned the most critical questions of the day, from civil rights and anti-communism in the mid-twentieth century to the politics of healthcare and climate change in more recent times. Not only were these issues exceptionally salient, but they also became extremely visible, as factional differences of opinion hardened into deeper animosities and ensured that wavering members were drawn into the fray and forced to choose sides. These are the very conditions that we have been told compel leaders to exercise limited agency and eschew confrontation. That each leader profiled in the chapters that follow defied this expectation (albeit with differing results) should give us greater confidence not only that the core arguments of this book have merit but that they have the power to help us better understand some of the most consequential policy and procedural fights of the postwar period.

CHAPTER THREE

How Nancy Pelosi Built Back Better

Speaking to a throng of supporters gathered in downtown Chicago to celebrate his historic 2008 victory, President-elect Barack Obama promised that "change has come to America."[1] Back in Washington, few were more eager for that change than incumbent Speaker Nancy Pelosi. With Obama in the White House and sixty Democratic votes in the Senate, the Speaker would have the rare opportunity to see some of her party's boldest proposals become law.

As Pelosi well knew, however, there was little agreement within her caucus over how ambitious Democrats could afford to be. On the left, progressive representatives were agitating for immediate action on big-ticket issues, from healthcare to climate change. Guided by the conviction that "power is perishable . . . [and] when you get it, you must use it," Pelosi shared their sense of urgency and disdain for incrementalism.[2] Yet the Speaker's "majority makers"—moderate members who had won right-leaning districts with promises to steer politics "towards the middle"—worried that prioritizing a left-of-center agenda would alienate their constituents.[3] Over the next two years, these battles would break out into the open as the two factions sparred over the scope and content of their party's reform agenda and Obama's signature legislative initiative: the Affordable Care Act (ACA).

Throughout the drive for healthcare reform, Pelosi worked strenuously to get progressives the "best possible bill."[4] But in confrontations over key features of the ACA, it was the party's moderates who consistently prevailed, advantaged in negotiations with the Speaker by their extensive collaboration. Smaller in number and typically more junior than their progressive colleagues, moderate Democrats had long been committed to collective action and had worked over the preceding two decades to sustain it.

Crucial to that effort was the founding of the Blue Dog Coalition in 1994. From the outset, the Blue Dogs adopted a variety of organizational mechanisms to structure their collaboration: a hierarchical leadership structure, a vetting process for new members, annual dues, norms encouraging the exchange of information, and rules binding members to a common course of action and authorizing leaders to bargain on their behalf. In the ensuing years, moderates continued to commit their time and resources to collaboration, using the Blue Dog Coalition as a vehicle to articulate a centrist policy agenda, raise campaign funds, and recruit a new generation of like-minded candidates to run for Congress. Their robust intraparty organization empowered moderate Democrats, whether in the minority or majority, to have "say . . . in what passes and what doesn't."[5]

Progressives, too, had taken steps to organize their ranks, establishing the Congressional Progressive Caucus (CPC) in 1991. But from its inception, the CPC lacked much of the Blue Dogs' collaborative capacity. Helmed by Vermont's Bernie Sanders, the group cultivated a "kaffeeklatsch character" that tolerated—and some worried, even encouraged—members' intermittent participation. Moreover, the CPC conferred no authority on its elected leadership to direct members' activities or negotiate on their behalf, with progressives largely preferring to be "noticed as individuals, rather than as a caucus."[6] On the eve of Obama's election, the nearly twenty-year-old group remained little more than "a signaling device for [the progressives'] political base" and an occasional forum for members to "sit around and talk with each other."[7] Nor was there much interest in changing the status quo, as progressives hoped to capitalize on the fact that they now constituted close to a majority of the House Democratic Caucus and counted among their ranks some of the chamber's most senior members, including the three committee chairs (and Pelosi allies) who would help draft the ACA.

As we will see, this collaborative asymmetry limited Pelosi's ability to deny moderates what they wanted. Although broadly supportive of enacting healthcare reform, moderates were collectively troubled by core elements of the leadership-backed plan and, after launching a coordinated campaign to change them, threatened to withhold their votes unless they were accommodated. Progressives, by contrast, failed to identify a common set of negotiating redlines, with individual members of the faction going so far as to disavow the CPC's suggestion that they, too, would collectively defect if moderates were appeased. Given the reality of moderate collaboration and its absence among progressive Democrats, the

Speaker had little choice but to capitulate when moderates demanded that the ACA lose its "robust" public option and sharply restrict access to abortion.[8]

As House Democrats' factional configuration evolved, however, the Speaker would find greater freedom to push back against what she dismissed as the moderates' "namby-pamby approach."[9] When Democrats were again relegated to the minority after the 2010 midterms, progressives "began soul-searching."[10] Determined to help recover their party's majority and play a greater role in shaping its politics, they began to collaborate with greater consistency. Seeking to emulate the tactics that had made moderates so successful, progressives worked to revitalize the CPC, tightening its governing rules and strengthening the hand of its leadership. By the time House Democrats regained their majority in 2018, progressives' collaboration had come to rival that of moderates.

Predictably, this emerging symmetry exacerbated Democratic infighting. While emboldened progressives used the CPC to push for additional representation on power committees and in the ranks of leadership, moderates—whose commitment to collective action remained strong notwithstanding their diminished numbers—staged rearguard efforts to preserve their influence. But far from derailing her speakership, conflict between better-matched foes offered Pelosi new opportunities to hew more closely to her vision of "progressive pragmatism."[11] As we will see, with progressives newly capable of articulating a consistent bargaining position and holding to it, the Speaker was able to resist calls for incrementalism. She instead pushed her moderate flank to waive their pay-as-you-go (PAYGO) budget rule and back unprecedented investments to reduce carbon emissions and promote renewable energy, ultimately codified in a legislative package dubbed the Inflation Reduction Act of 2022 (IRA).

Assessing Pelosi's Legacy

Given the relative recency of these events, the task of assessing Pelosi's legacy has only just begun. To date, journalists and biographers have done the lion's share of the labor, typically identifying indelible features of the her personality—an unparalleled work ethic, extreme self-discipline, and extraordinary energy—that, they argue, contributed to her assertive leadership style and enviable win rate.[12] This chapter's aim is different. Consistent with the principled commitments of institutional political science scholarship, it seeks to sharpen our collective understanding of Pelosi's tenure by studying the structural conditions that facilitated her success.

What, then, might foregrounding House Democrats' emerging symmetry teach us about Pelosi's remarkable career? For one, it should lead us to anticipate—correctly, this chapter shows—that Pelosi's power would measurably evolve over the course of her two stints as Speaker. For readers eager to take stock of her legacy, this evolution complicates the standard depiction of Pelosi's mastery of the House. Notwithstanding her undeniable political acumen, the Speaker's growing capacity to compel her party's moderate faction to accept progressive interventions she believed essential cannot readily be explained by unchanging features of her biography or personality.

Nor can more traditional structural variables—for instance, whether government was divided or unified, or whether national politics became more (or less) polarized over time—provide much analytic traction. Both the ACA and the IRA were passed under unified government. And both bills were negotiated under conditions of high polarization, with little expectation that members of the Republican minority would contribute their votes to passage. Indeed, none did. In fact, absent attention to factional politics, we might well get the story backward. Pelosi, it is worth remembering, commanded a substantially larger majority in early 2009 than she did in 2021.[13] And it is perfectly plausible to think, as many political observers predicted, that the Speaker's smaller vote margin would limit her capacity to realize her agenda. Yet, the record suggests otherwise, validating this book's emphasis on a party's factional configuration as a key variable that helps explain shifts in leader power over time.

Foregrounding Democrats' evolving factional configuration also allows us to better situate Pelosi in political time. As outlined in chapter 1, leaders who encounter a similar factional configuration but inhabit different slices of secular time may be productively, and even provocatively, compared. By the same token, leaders who encounter a different factional configuration but exist in the same historical era may be helpfully distinguished. For those of us interested in pinpointing Pelosi's place in the congressional pantheon, this way of thinking makes clear that she shares more than superficial resemblance to that other Democratic titan of the postwar Congress, Sam Rayburn. Both are renowned for their longevity and legislative achievements. Both reached the apex of their success late in their long and distinguished careers, and both proved to be critical lieutenants to younger, more charismatic, presidents.

But beneath these results-centered benchmarks lies a deeper structural commonality. As we will see in this chapter and in chapter 6 (profiling Rayburn), both Democratic leaders made the most of a favorable factional configuration when they encountered it, each exploiting their party's emerging symmetry to get what they wanted at a time when divisions were especially pronounced. It is in this sense that Pelosi is rightfully regarded as Rayburn's equal. As was true for that giant of mid-twentieth-century politics, it is indicative of her political genius that she was able to draw strength from her party's increasingly symmetric divide to achieve two of the twenty-first century's landmark legislative victories.

For similar reasons, we can distinguish Pelosi from her Republican counterparts, from John Boehner to Kevin McCarthy, who might otherwise serve as natural comparators. Unlike her contemporaries, Pelosi gave up the gavel on her own terms, relinquishing the speakership at the peak of her powers rather than falling victim to party infighting. As I argued in chapter 1, her consistent outperformance of her GOP rivals is difficult to explain with reference to modern trends, whether growing polarization or the increasing centralization of authority and information, which ought to redound to the benefit of Republican and Democratic leaders alike. And so it is by attending to her party's factional configuration that we can best begin to appreciate why Pelosi represents a congressional throwback, a most fitting heir to earlier masters of the House.

Alternative Explanations

As we will do throughout this book, it is worth considering alternative perspectives that might explain the events detailed here. One such perspective is that Pelosi exercised little direct influence over the content of the legislation that would define her career. On this account, the House resolutions that would become the ACA and IRA tracked the preferences of critical actors outside the House—be it the Senate's median voter or filibuster pivot, or the Democratic president who signed the legislation into law—more closely than the Speaker's. There is certainly little doubt that the drafting of these House measures was informed by what members and leaders believed would be acceptable to the Senate's pivotal players and the White House. As one leadership aide put it, "You always have to be worried about the Senate, even when [your party] has sixty votes. . . . It's a huge source of frustration."[14]

But, as we will see, the lower chamber had its own bargaining dynamics for Pelosi to navigate. On healthcare reform, for example, House moderates were willing to accept a weakened public option, unlike their Senate colleagues. But they maintained their own list of demands, not shared with Senate moderates, including special carve-outs for the rural communities they represented and limits on women's reproductive care. So, too, when it came to President Joe Biden's climate change legislation, while Senate moderates protested the bill's price point, those in the House opposed waiving the chamber's PAYGO rule and the bundling of funding for clean energy and economic stimulus with more generous social welfare programs. While moderates in the Senate ultimately prevailed in both encounters, Pelosi had her way on climate change but not healthcare.

A related possibility is that, in leading negotiations within the House Democratic Caucus, Pelosi consistently opted to strike Solomonic compromises between moderates and progressives, crafting deals where both sides lost (or won) by equal measure. Indeed, as one of her colleagues observed, "[Pelosi is] very good . . . at finding common ground."[15] The implication is that the Speaker, in splitting the difference between her party's rival factions, was not getting what *she* wanted but instead choosing the midpoint between the vying factions' positions. Alternatively, we might posit the opposite: perhaps the deals Pelosi struck throughout her tenure consistently favored one faction over the other. On this account, the claim would be that the House bills that became the ACA and IRA routinely and disproportionately advantaged moderates in recognition of their pivotal spatial position or, alternatively, privileged progressives by virtue of their larger numbers—all to the detriment of Pelosi's own priorities.

As we will see, however, neither possibility finds much support in the record. Across both legislative battles, interviews with moderate and progressive lawmakers (as well as with members of their staff) reveal a striking consensus about who prevailed in any particular negotiating encounter. And these assessments, while admittedly subjective, rarely deviate from how other observers—including Senate Democrats, Republican lawmakers, journalists, and representatives of relevant interest groups—characterized the same events. Taken together, they suggest that the compromises Pelosi wrought were not predictably evenhanded, nor did they consistently favor moderates over progressives, or vice versa. Instead, the negotiating pattern that emerged was temporal. Over time, Pelosi was more often able to push moderates to accept progressive interventions the Speaker deemed important or essential to pursue.

Still a third possibility is that, across all three legislative battles, Pelosi, ever the loyal partisan, had indistinct or abstract policy preferences such that she would have been content with any bill that passed the House. The implication is that any attempt to discern whether she got what she wanted in a given legislative drive is impractical—or, worse, meaningless—because we could never observe Pelosi dissatisfied. Here, too, interviews, as well as the Speaker's confidential communications, reveal what her public statements do not. While she may have preferred to speak in general terms when engaging with citizens, she was adamant and precise in private settings about the programs and regulations she wished to prioritize. As one longtime colleague put it, "Nancy knew everything . . . she was methodical and better than [anyone] on the issues. But it was easy to underestimate her because she was polite, she listened, and she left things unsaid."[16]

Progressive Decline

Throughout the 1960s and 1970s, progressive Democrats in the House were ably represented by the Democratic Study Group (DSG). "The most elaborately organized 'party within a party' in the history of the House of Representatives," the DSG kept progressives united in pursuit of civil rights in the 1960s; a decade later, the group served as the driving force behind critical party and procedural reforms that undercut the power of southern committee barons.[17] By the 1980s, however, the DSG was no longer the "central clearinghouse" for progressive members of Congress. As Julian Zelizer writes, "the proliferation of specialized caucuses . . . devoted to liberal causes . . . siphoned off support" from the DSG. Within a few short years, "every [progressive] issue seemed to have its own splinter group."[18]

With progressives fragmenting, moderate Democrats saw an opportunity to pull the caucus back toward the center. For too many years, they complained, "the Democratic Party in the House was not representing [their] interests." What was more, Republican president Ronald Reagan's immense popularity "made it clear that it was in the best interests of the Democratic Party . . . to achieve better representation for the conservative element."[19] Determined "to advance a more moderate outlook for . . .

House Democrats," the party's beleaguered centrists established the Conservative Democratic Forum (CDF) in 1980.[20] "We knew there was strength in numbers," one member recalled. "We were very unhappy with the treatment we were getting from the [Democratic] House leadership. We were going to be heard from."[21] And, as described in more detail in chapter 5, over the next two years the CDF made more than just noise, allying with the Reagan White House to implement many of the president's proposed budget cuts.

As the public soured on the administration's fiscal policies, however, the CDF saw its influence wane. "There was a fascination about going to the White House," one moderate recognized, but with voters believing "Reagan's program [to be] basically unfair . . . the glamour and glitter has worn off." Nor were the CDF's collaborative arrangements sufficient to keep the group relevant. By 1983, the organization had become a "kind of a come-and-go deal." As one member put it at the time, "People are backing off." And with members playing a less consistently active role in the organization, the CDF had too few "swing votes" to consistently deny Democrats their majority. While members continued to believe that they could, "on occasion, get a number of people organized to have an influence," they observed that most of the time the CDF was left with "nobody to talk to."[22] Among Democrats, the CDF was resented for collaborating with the Reagan administration and sometimes undercutting the Democratic majority, while Republicans had little interest in working with members they would as soon replace with candidates of their own party. Disenchanted with what they perceived to be the CDF's limited efficacy, many members left to join the newly established Democratic Leadership Council in 1985.

By the 1990s, progressives had similarly come to chafe at their lack of influence within the party and, as they had in the 1960s, sought to collaborate once more. "Progressive politics is [still] good politics," Sanders declared. "But if we do not organize, if we do not work at electing new [progressive] members, if we do not build links with progressive groups outside of Congress," then "it will be difficult to achieve real change."[23] The CPC, he hoped, would pick up where the DSG left off. But even as the CPC quickly doubled in size—counting close to fifty members just two years after its founding—the group remained "a pale imitation of its predecessor."[24] As one longtime CPC member recalled, "In the beginning it was pretty large, but it wasn't very cohesive. It was just a thing to put your name on. I don't remember us taking any sort of action or having strategy meetings. We were just kind of there, we weren't a factor."[25]

The CPC's hopes for greater influence dimmed with the Republican takeover of the House and Senate in 1994. For moderate Democrats, in contrast, the GOP's success was proof positive that their own party "would have to move back toward the center" if it were to regain a majority.[26] Determined to help their co-partisans make that move, moderates organized anew. "In groups of three, four, five, six, seven," they met to discuss "way[s] to band their numbers together," eventually agreeing to impose a suite of collaborative arrangements, including internal voting rules, a system of multiple whips, and an elected leadership empowered to negotiate with leadership when so designated by a majority of members.[27] In short order, the organization they named the Blue Dog Coalition notched some decisive victories, first compelling House Republicans to preserve a cornerstone of the welfare state—the Aid to Families with Dependent Children program—during the national debate over welfare reform and then in 1998 passing the House version of what would become the Bipartisan Campaign Reform Act (better known as the McCain-Feingold Act, after its Senate sponsors, Arizona's John McCain and Wisconsin's Russ Feingold).

Over the next decade, the Blue Dogs would layer on additional organizational practices as they sought to increase their representation on the chambers' power committees and recruit other moderates to join their cause. After being burned by members "going directly to House leaders [to] negotiat[e] their own interests . . . and giving up information intended for bargaining as a group," the Blue Dog Coalition adopted rules to penalize breaches of confidentiality.[28] To discourage members from "miss[ing] a lot of meetings or fail[ing] to participate in other ways," they insisted that individuals support the group financially and attend meetings regularly.[29] And in acknowledgement of members' often divergent preferences, the Blue Dogs instituted a two-thirds majority vote to determine whether the group would adopt an official position or authorize leaders to negotiate on members' behalf.[30]

These collaborative arrangements were essential to maintaining moderates' influence within the party. One staff member commented, "They have shown . . . that if the Caucus listens to them, and moves toward them, they are willing to follow through and deliver."[31] Indeed, as minority leader, Pelosi was often deferential to the Blue Dogs. According to one senior member of the group, "Nancy [has been] willing to lead in a way that is comfortable to me; the Blue Dogs are listened to."[32]

In 2006, however, after Democrats regained their House majority, Pelosi vowed to be less tolerant of the moderates' independence. In the

Speaker's view, there were just three reasons to break with the caucus: "conscience, constituents, or the Constitution."[33] One moderate observed that while it had once been sufficient to say "it's a hard vote in my district and let it go at that," Pelosi now demanded that members "come before the caucus and articulate a reason."[34] The Speaker's insistence that moderates toe the party line was attributable, in part, to her awareness that she needed at least some of their votes. With a majority of 233 members, at least two-thirds of the Blue Dogs' 35 members would need to vote the party line to maintain Democratic control of the floor.

But to the considerable frustration of progressive Democrats, moderates' robust and sometimes even physical collaboration proved resilient to Pelosi's pressure campaign. When facing a tough vote, "the Blue Dogs started surrounding the freshman members on the floor with the senior members, literally flanking the younger members with the old guard," so "by the time [party leaders] got through, the freshmen were able to gather themselves and stick to the caucus line."[35] As we will see, the moderates' collaborative ascendancy would fundamentally constrain Pelosi as she sought to deploy her party's "perishable power" to get what both she and Obama wanted from the House.[36]

Moderates Muscle in on Health Care

Early in his presidency, Obama named healthcare one of his top legislative priorities. "I suffer no illusions that it will be an easy process," the new president told a joint session of Congress, "but I also know that . . . healthcare reform cannot wait."[37] Behind closed doors, his message was much the same. While action on climate change had been the focus of the campaign, healthcare was "number one among equals."

Pelosi, for her part, had hoped that energy and climate policy would be "the flagship of [her] speakership" and the new administration. Nevertheless, she was optimistic that the House would deliver on healthcare.[38] "Everyone votes for health," she assured the president. But the Speaker had far less faith in the upper chamber. "The Senate must do more than complain they can't get sixty votes," she warned Obama. "I need your commitment to get it done in the Senate." With the president's assurance that he would not ask House Democrats "to walk the plank for the Senate," Pelosi directed the chairs of the three House committees with jurisdiction over healthcare (the so-called tri-committee)—Charles Rangel on Education and Labor, Henry Waxman on Energy and Commerce, and George Miller on Ways and Means—to develop a single bill for the chamber to consider.[39]

Almost immediately, progressive and moderate Democrats began to jockey for control of the proposal. In an open letter to the Speaker, the CPC urged Pelosi to structure reform around a single-payer model instead of the administration's proposed design, which would supplement private coverage with a "public option." In private conversations, the CPC's leaders were more direct. They informed Democratic leaders that an "overwhelming majority" of their seventy-seven members were committed to a single-payer model.[40] Now was the time to "go big" and "transform the system," they counseled.[41] But in meetings with rank-and-file members of the CPC, some progressives confided to Pelosi that what mattered more was achieving universal coverage, regardless of whether public or private entities would be responsible for filling the gaps.[42]

Moderates, for their part, were uniformly opposed to a single-payer model, believing that "people . . . don't want a government-run [healthcare] program."[43] Even Obama's proposed public option, intended as a compromise between a system of private coverage and government care, was "possibly a bridge too far."[44] The Blue Dogs cautioned Pelosi and the tri-committee chairs that if the committee went ahead with a public option without attending to their concerns, the Coalition would block the measure in committee.

The Blue Dogs' threat put Pelosi—now presiding over a decidedly asymmetric party—in a bind. On the one hand, she shared progressives' desire to seize the moment. Ever since the New Deal, Democratic leaders had tried and failed to create a national healthcare program. And Pelosi herself had helped introduce legislation to create a government-run, single-payer system when Congress took up healthcare reform during President Bill Clinton's first term in office.[45] On the other hand, the Speaker could not deny the administration's assessment that "no plan—no matter how elegantly designed or executed—[could] succeed unless [they could] convince Blue Dogs . . . to adopt an open mind."[46] To pass any reform measure, Pelosi would need the support of at least 218 of her 258 Democrats. And while progressives were the larger of the two factions, the Speaker was confident they would fall in line behind whatever bill emerged. The Blue Dogs, while smaller in number, would be a tougher sell. Having spent the better part of a decade honing their collaboration, moderates had made clear that their whip counts were reliable and their capacity to collectively withstand leadership pressure strong. The Speaker's verdict:

no single-payer provision. Both factions would have to settle for a strong public option that would peg government-run coverage to Medicare.[47]

But moderates, confident they had the upper hand, would not settle. In a letter to the Speaker and tri-committee chairs, forty-five Blue Dogs voiced their "strong reservations about the . . . direction of the . . . healthcare reform proposal." "From where we are today, significant progress . . . needs to be made in order to address our concerns," they warned. "We cannot support a final product that fails to do so."[48] As the Blue Dogs' chair, Mike Ross of Arkansas, articulated the group's position, members were primarily concerned that a strong public option would undercut private insurers in rural communities. If the government's insurance program were based on Medicare reimbursement rates, which were lower than what private insurers paid, practicing medicine in rural communities would no longer be financially viable. Physicians would seek higher salaries elsewhere and hospitals, which counted on higher private insurance payments to offset the lower rates Medicare paid, would shutter. "We could give people a real shiny insurance card, but that's not going to matter if they don't have access," he warned.[49]

Reiterating their threat to defect, Ross reminded Pelosi that the Blue Dogs were prepared to vote against the legislation in committee and on the floor unless it was "substantially revised."[50] The Speaker was initially dismissive: "They are overplaying their hands. They like to show off."[51] But the Blue Dogs soon made clear that they were willing to stick together. Those members seated on the three committees tasked with marking up the healthcare legislation either voted against the measure or backed Republican amendments in a show of strength. "There's no doubt in my mind that if the Blue Dogs join with the Republicans they can bring this bill down," Waxman conceded after one such vote.[52] The moderates' collective defection left the Speaker with little choice. The tri-committee would have to weaken the public option. "You'll have to do what we all have to do: compromise," she told the unhappy chairs.[53]

Instead of relying on Medicare rates as the basis for reimbursement for the public option, the tri-committee agreed to a provision establishing state commissions to set reimbursement rates for hospitals. Under the new plan, patients at any hospital would pay the same rate for treatment, regardless of their insurance plan, and the state commission would ensure that local hospitals remained open by negotiating "reasonable rates" with rural providers. Recognizing the party's collaborative imbalance, the chairs conceded, "It's what the Blue Dogs want, so we'll give them what they want."[54]

The change left progressives seething. "Many of us favor a single-payer system . . . but we have compromised. We want a plan with a meaningful public option, and we can compromise no more," CPC cochair Lynn Woolsey of California told reporters at a hastily convened news conference.[55] Cochair Raul Grijalva of Arizona agreed: "We're at a point where there's no retreat, and we can and must hold the line."[56] But when asked if progressives would actually vote down the president's signature legislative ambition were their demands to remain unmet, the CPC's leadership demurred. "We're telling you this time: it's different," Woolsey tried to explain. "Not that we're going to vote with Republicans, but if reform legislation comes to the floor and doesn't include a real and robust public option, we will fight it with everything we have."[57]

Pelosi shared their frustration. For weeks, the Speaker had urged Obama to defend a strong public option, hopeful that with pressure from the White House, moderates might be persuaded to back down. But she had little patience for the CPC's claim that the party's left flank was cut out of the negotiating process. "Progressives have been well represented," she reminded the CPC's leadership. "Progressives are represented on the committees of jurisdiction . . . [and] progressives are chairmen of those committees."[58] As one member put it, "Pelosi's problem was that centrists in the party knew what they wanted and were willing to fight for it. Progressives just talked."[59] Or, as the Speaker put it, in recognition of her party's asymmetry, "the liberals are not operational."[60]

Months later, after the Senate forced the Speaker and her progressive colleagues to accept a far weaker reform package, House moderates dealt progressives another blow. While the Blue Dogs had prioritized weakening the public option, a narrow majority of the group was also determined to tighten the legislation's language on abortion as a covered medical procedure. Working with other self-described "Democrats for life" outside the Coalition, they sought to negotiate a separate deal with Pelosi to bar any insurance plan purchased with government subsidies from covering abortions. Capitalizing on their intensive collaboration—and dismissive of their progressive colleagues' limited efforts to match it—the Blue Dogs' leadership informed the Speaker that a supermajority of members would withhold their votes from the healthcare bill unless their pro-life colleagues were given a chance to vote on the amendment on the floor.[61]

Progressive Democrats were outraged when they learned that the Speaker was being pressured to permit a floor vote on an amendment restricting abortion coverage. "This amendment will be the greatest restriction on a women's right to choose to pass in our careers," they told the Speaker.[62] Pelosi agreed. She had long advocated for women's reproductive rights and was a founding member of the lower chamber's Pro-Choice Caucus. "I couldn't blame them" for feeling betrayed, Pelosi told her staff. But she knew she lacked the votes. And, as she explained to her colleagues, "in the end, this is not an abortion bill, this is a health bill, and I will not allow this issue to kill healthcare."[63] After some further negotiations with the White House, the House passed a modified version of the abortion amendment, which prohibited the use of federal funds to pay for abortion services as part of the public option or in plans offered on state exchanges. The House then approved the healthcare measure with the support of twenty-eight Blue Dogs, fifteen of whom had also backed the antiabortion amendment.

But Pelosi's work was not done. The House would have to reconcile its healthcare measure with that approved by the Senate. This set off another round of vote wrangling, as the Speaker sought to renegotiate terms with both progressives and moderates. To progressives, Pelosi offered little. Even though the CPC deemed the Senate bill a "nonstarter," the Speaker was clear: "it was this, or nothing."[64] Moderates, however, had better luck. "To get the pro-lifers, the White House promised an executive order that would restrict abortion funds as sharply as the House bill had." And to secure the remaining Blue Dog votes needed to get to 218, Pelosi and Senate Majority Leader Harry Reid worked out a series of funding compromises to be included in the reconciliation bill.[65] In the end, it was enough. The House approved the Senate's healthcare measure, and then the agreed-upon reconciliation package, the Healthcare and Education Reconciliation Act in March 2010.

There can be little doubt that passing the ACA was a remarkable achievement. After decades of false starts, Democrats oversaw the most significant regulatory overhaul of the nation's healthcare system since the passage of the Medicare and Medicaid Act in 1965. We should not understate Pelosi's role in securing what would become Obama's signature legislative accomplishment. "She defied the odds and the naysayers . . . she made it look easy," one biographer observed.[66] But when we look to the deals struck, it is apparent that the Speaker's power over her caucus was not uniform. With progressives fragmented and moderates united, Pelosi had little choice but to accommodate her party's centrists even when it pained her most.

Progressive Reckoning

Enacting the ACA had been difficult. Persuading a majority of Americans that the healthcare law would measurably improve their lives proved next to impossible. Seven months after Obama signed the bill into law, House Democrats lost sixty-three seats in the 2010 midterm elections, handing Republicans their largest gain in more than half a century. That "shellacking," as the president put it, forced Pelosi back into the role of minority leader and occasioned much introspection throughout the party over its future. For progressives, in particular, the election returns conveyed a disquieting message. While Republicans had been buoyed by a mobilized base hostile to the president and his policies, Democratic turnout and engagement had been tepid. The problem, as progressives saw it, was that Obama had tacked to the center, taking for granted the support of his party's liberal base.[67]

The solution? Progressives would "need to play a bigger part" in the party's internal decision making. But to do that, they would first have to reckon with their own collaborative deficiencies, as the fight over healthcare reform had made plain that progressives were not competing on equal terms with moderates. As Minnesota's Keith Ellison, the newly elected CPC cochair, recalled, "[Battling the Blue Dogs] felt like we were trying to stop some big car from rolling down an icy hill. We were holding onto it, but it just kept dragging us."[68]

The CPC's new leadership attributed progressives' struggles to members' unwillingness to prioritize collective goals over individual interests. Some members on the left believed this recalcitrance was because the CPC was "not getting members' buy-in on agenda setting."[69] As one member recalled, "plenty of people didn't come to meetings, and when those that did made choices, they weren't respected [by those who hadn't attended]."[70] Others noted that it was difficult to reach consensus because many CPC members "weren't actually progressive."[71] The organization's "open door" policy made it easy for "any Democrat . . . [to] become an official member, regardless of their politics, their source of campaign funding, their voting record, or even their attendance at CPC meetings."[72] Any lawmaker who feared a primary challenge from the left could join the CPC and cite their membership as evidence of their commitment to progressive goals. The CPC's size posed an additional challenge. With more than seventy members, it was difficult to move quickly. Even issuing a press release could take an entire day, as the CPC's leadership sought to consult with every dues-paying member to gain their approval of the text. The group's large size and informality also made it easy for party leaders or opposing factions to "divide and conquer . . . by talking to [members] separately and seeing if they could pick . . . [them] off."[73]

For progressives to negotiate effectively with Democratic leaders, the CPC's leaders believed they would need to find ways to cut down on their colleagues' dual tendency to free ride and to circumvent collective bargaining by negotiating their own side deals. According to Washington's Pramila Jayapal, Ellison's successor as CPC chair, "People got together, and they got mad at what was happening, but there wasn't infrastructure built for the caucus to be strong."[74] Or, as one longtime progressive staffer acknowledged, "[Throughout] Obama's first term, CPC members were viewed as doormats . . . they always took the bait [when offered by party leaders]."[75] House progressives would also need to formally empower their elected leadership to bargain on their behalf and commit to vote as a bloc when authorized by a majority (or supermajority) of their colleagues.

With Democrats back in the minority, however, these proposed reforms took a backseat to more immediate concerns: retaking the majority and recruiting new progressive candidates to run for Congress. Over the next five years, the CPC—in tandem with liberal interest groups across the country—engaged in a coordinated effort to identify qualified individuals to run for open seats in blue districts and, in some cases, even to challenge more mainstream Democratic incumbents in party primaries. When Democrats won back the House with a narrow majority in the November 2018 midterm elections, these efforts bore fruit, as the group saw its membership increase by more than a quarter.[76]

The influx of new members to the CPC reignited interest in collaboration. After some prodding, members began to meet more regularly for strategy sessions, and the CPC's leadership convened a series of orientation meetings for the organization's twenty first-time representatives. The group also designated a task force to study and draft stronger bylaws that would help progressives collectively maintain "a common purpose and vision."[77]

But to sustain progressive collaboration, the CPC would need to prove that collective action could pay dividends. To this end, the group's leadership persuaded its members to hold off committing their votes for or against Pelosi's third term as Speaker until they had negotiated a deal to secure better representation on House power committees.

Pelosi, also concerned about a mutiny on her right, agreed to reshuffle "seasoned" CPC members' assignments so that progressives would hold a greater share of seats on Ways and Means, Appropriations, and Energy and Commerce.[78] It was a significant victory for the CPC, but one for Pelosi as well. "The irony," one member noted, "was that offering Nancy 40 percent [of the caucus] for one price was a gift . . . she didn't have to spend as much time whipping and she could tell some of her majority makers they could walk. Plus when it came to legislating, she'd have progressives on those committees. It was win-win-win."[79]

Nearly two years later, days after Biden won the 2020 presidential election, the CPC completed its organizational overhaul. The group adopted the suite of rules recommended by its task force, including provisions that centralized decision-making authority in a single chair, now empowered to negotiate on members' behalf; required members to vote as a bloc on issues supported by two-thirds of the caucus; and stipulated that members who failed to abide by the rule at least 66 percent of the time would be expelled. Members would also be required to attend CPC meetings and respond to requests from the organization's whip.[80] More routine efforts to foster collaboration followed. The CPC began circulating weekly talking points and coordinating more closely with progressives in the Senate. Soon, members began meeting monthly with leaders of unions and progressive activist groups to coordinate grassroots messaging campaigns.[81]

The effect of these changes would reverberate beyond the CPC. For the first time in nearly three decades, progressives boasted collaborative arrangements that rivaled those of their moderate foes. Pelosi, once again Speaker with a co-partisan in the White House and a Democratic Senate, would have the opportunity to leverage the power this newfound symmetry offered as she set about passing the most ambitious climate change legislation the country had ever seen.

From Rules Runaround to Climate Change

Pelosi had long viewed addressing climate change as her central priority. But during her first stint as Speaker, she found it difficult to persuade moderate Democrats that it should also be theirs. While progressives had been enthusiastic, if idealistic, champions of climate legislation for decades, many moderate members were reluctant to support interventions that would meaningfully reduce carbon emissions or promote renewable energy sources. "We've got to find a way that we can accommodate our goals [on environmental policy] and not be seen as anti-business," the Blue Dogs implored their fellow Democrats.[82] With the Speaker, moderates were more direct. "What's the point of walking the plank on climate change," they reasoned, "if voters won't like it and the Senate won't pass it."[83] Even relatively minor efforts to cut greenhouse gases and carbon pollution were met with resistance, as anxious members sought to rein in associated costs and insulate their districts' agricultural and manufacturing industries from reform. "There's never a good time for energy," Pelosi acknowledged.[84]

By the opening of the 117th Congress in January 2021, however, times had changed. For more than a decade, progressives had urged Democratic leaders to remove the Blue Dogs' favorite deficit reduction mechanism, the PAYGO provision, from House rules. "PAYGO isn't only bad economics," New York's Alexandria Ocasio-Cortez tweeted on behalf of her CPC colleagues. "It's also a dark political maneuver designed to hamstring progress. We can't hinder ourselves from the start."[85] And a hindrance it was. In contrast to the statutory PAYGO provision—which aggregated the total cost of all legislation passed in a given year and sought to offset it with tax revenue and spending cuts—the House rule was more stringent, applying the same spending requirement to individual pieces of legislation.[86] This meant that *any* spending bill had to be deficit neutral, else it would trigger PAYGO's penalties and an automatic point of order to block the bill.

Notwithstanding the rule's conservative effects, Pelosi had faithfully backed moderates' defense of the provision for many years. Indeed, when the rule faced progressive criticism in 2009, the Speaker advised House liberals that ignoring the deficit was both politically and economically unsound. "We have a moral responsibility not to heap mountains of debt onto our grandchildren . . . [so] if we want to say that we want to increase entitlement spending, we must pay for that."[87] By 2021, however, her calculus had changed. With the CPC pushing for a full repeal of the House rule, and in light of the growth and maturation of their collaborative arrangements, Pelosi saw an opportunity to smooth the passage of climate change legislation on her own terms. She informed the Blue Dogs of the CPC's demand and their threat to vote down the rules package if they were not accommodated. Rather than risk losing the PAYGO rule altogether, she urged the group to compromise; accept a waiver that would exempt legislation on specific topics from its strictures and "live to fight another day."[88]

With the Blue Dogs' grudging support, Pelosi set out to draft the terms of the waiver. Many progressives (including the CPC's leadership) lobbied the Speaker to apply the waiver to healthcare legislation, in the hopes that it would prod the House to take up the group's Medicare-for-All bill. The Blue Dogs, for their part, urged Pelosi to limit the waiver to measures for additional pandemic recovery. The Speaker, however, went her own way. In addition to waiving deficit neutrality for COVID-19–related legislation, which neither progressives nor moderates objected to, Pelosi identified climate change legislation as deserving of a waiver. House Democrats, she vowed, would finally pass "legislation [that] is far-reaching, ensuring that the future economy is greener and cleaner."[89]

The Blue Dogs saw little to like in Pelosi's formulation. As they wrote to the Speaker and the Budget Committee chair, legislation responsive to a "climate emergency" was one thing, but it was something else entirely to exempt a large-scale climate bill from PAYGO's strictures. Moreover, they worried that progressives might "misapply or misuse the . . . exemptions," folding into the climate bill other social reforms that moderates opposed. Nevertheless, with the CPC united in its demand to end PAYGO altogether, the Blue Dogs agreed to the deal, warning only that they would "vigorously monitor the use of . . . waivers to ensure they are being utilized appropriately and sparingly."[90]

With the rules question resolved, negotiations turned to the content of the climate bill. As moderates had feared, progressives hoped to model the bill after their Green New Deal proposal, calling for a $6 trillion investment in "hard infrastructure"—roads, bridges, and broadband—and "human infrastructure" across five policy areas, including child and elder care, affordable housing, healthcare, climate investments, and immigration reform. In a series of coordinated press releases, members of the CPC defended their expansive approach to climate change.[91] "As we deal with a devastating climate crisis caused by decades of unchecked corporate greed, we need to [ask]: Do we want to continue building a world based on militarization, incarceration, poverty, and destruction of resources?" Internally, the CPC's leadership cautioned members to stand by the group's framework, saying, "We can't have a situation where the Speaker gets you to come out for something when the Progressive Caucus is still trying to negotiate."[92]

Pelosi had other plans. First and foremost, there would need to be two bills. One would deal with infrastructure, while a dedicated climate bill would help Americans invest in renewable energies and reduce their carbon emissions. While the Blue Dogs blanched at the Speaker's suggested price point for the climate legislation, the Energy and Commerce

Committee approved Pelosi's $550 billion target for climate-related spending. As for other progressive goals, the Speaker agreed that the ACA needed tweaking but saw little reason to relitigate the single-payer fight as progressives wished. Instead, she urged House Democrats to concentrate their energies on lowering the costs of prescription drugs, reducing the burden of healthcare premiums for working families, and expanding eligibility for low- and moderate-income Americans who would otherwise be denied Medicaid coverage.[93] She also backed a host of subsidies for families with children to lower the costs of childcare and education.

Moderate Democrats reiterated their opposition to Pelosi's proposed course of action. In conversations with House leaders and the Biden administration, the Blue Dog Coalition balked at the bill's ballooning cost—$3.5 trillion over ten years—and expressed frustration that reforms only "tangentially" related to climate change were being included.[94] Moreover, they worried that this would be another instance where moderates were "BTU'd"—that is, pushed to vote for "messaging bills that cannot pass both chambers and that are unpopular at home"—just to make progressives happy.[95] But the Speaker was unyielding: the climate bill *would* pass, and it would not be another "eensy-weensy" attempt to solve the climate crisis.[96] The party's growing symmetry had given her new leverage to push back against moderates' penchant for incrementalism.

What remained to be seen was how the House would compel the Senate, with only fifty Democrats, to pass its climate bill. The CPC thought it had the answer. Tie passage of the climate measure, which would need to pass the Senate by reconciliation, to the pending infrastructure bill, which had drawn considerably more bipartisan support in the upper chamber. As the CPC's leadership briefed its members, absent pressure from the House, progressives in the Senate thought it unlikely that the upper chamber would pass a climate bill of any magnitude.[97] The Speaker was of a similar view. The House position had to be "there ain't no infrastructure bill without the reconciliation bill"; otherwise, the Senate would have no incentive to negotiate with the lower chamber on either measure. And as Pelosi reminded her leadership team, she wanted to see both bills enacted.[98]

Moderates, however, strongly objected to the idea of holding the infrastructure bill "hostage." In a statement to Pelosi, the Blue Dog Coalition said its members "remain[ed] opposed to any effort to unnecessarily delay consideration of these critical infrastructure investments." Another letter soon followed, signed by nine moderates—enough to deprive the Speaker of a floor majority—stating their intent to vote against the climate bill unless and "until the ... Infrastructure [bill] passes the House and is signed into law."[99]

Pelosi's hard line with the moderates hinged fundamentally on progressives' improved collaboration. Throughout the summer of 2021, the Speaker held firm, citing the CPC's public statements that more than twenty progressives would vote down the infrastructure bill were it decoupled from the climate measure, more than enough to scuttle the moderates' legislative priority. But as Jayapal, the CPC's chair, well knew, "Pelosi's commitment to the dual-track strategy was only as dependable as the CPC's whip count."[100]

Progressives were not the only ones counting votes. Moderates, too, were consulting their members and reassessing how likely individuals were to stick together if Pelosi were to begin to actively whip for either bill. As they had in the past, the Blue Dogs claimed they held the pivotal votes. As one moderate described the group's strategy, "We're organized and willing to say no."[101] What remained unclear was whether either faction would be able to maintain that resolve if the Speaker called a vote and began to turn the screws.

For many Capitol Hill observers, the brinksmanship between House progressives and moderates seemed likely to compromise Pelosi's goal of getting both bills passed. But in the CPC's intransigence and the Democratic Party's concomitant symmetry, the Speaker saw an opportunity. For decades, progressives had folded when pushed by their moderate colleagues. Now was an opportunity for those on the left to demonstrate that they, too, were "operational."[102] Indeed, moderate Democrats were adamant that "a small faction on the far left" would not have the fortitude to employ "Freedom Caucus tactics . . . to destroy the president's agenda"—and they saw little reason to accept left-of-center proposals as a result.[103] For Pelosi to muscle through more progressive legislation, her majority makers needed to appreciate that they could not overpower their more liberal colleagues as they once had.

In September 2021, Pelosi decided the best path forward was to call for votes on both bills, with infrastructure proceeding first and the climate bill second. As one former leadership aide recalled, "this was a chance to see where the chips would fall . . . who had their numbers right and who was overcounting."[104] If progressives were wrong about their whip count, the infrastructure bill would pass—notching Biden a much-needed victory. And if they were right, moderates would learn that progressives could not always be "steamrolled" and would either decide to compromise on the climate bill or find the votes needed for infrastructure across the aisle.[105] If the Speaker was lucky, they would do both. It was hardly an ideal situation, another longtime committee staffer observed, but it was not without some upside: "Of course the Speaker never wants to schedule a vote without knowing the outcome . . . but the centrists just didn't believe the CPC would hold out. In that way, it was certainly instructive."[106]

As the CPC's leadership had warned, the progressives who declared themselves opposed to decoupling infrastructure from climate change held firm, forcing Pelosi to first extend the infrastructure vote and then push it off to allow her party to regroup.[107] Over the course of the next month, moderate Democrats scrambled to negotiate with the CPC, but they could not offer progressives what they really wanted: an agreement that moderate Democrats in the Senate would move on the climate bill once it was voted through by the House. What they *could* offer was the prospect of Republican votes on infrastructure, which the Speaker herself had struggled to find and which would permit some progressives to continue their protest without scuttling the bill's fortunes.[108]

With the end of October in sight, a deal materialized. After much moderate legwork, thirteen Republicans agreed to join Democrats in backing the infrastructure bill, enough to win passage if some progressive holdouts agreed to vote for it, too. The Speaker was initially wary: what was to stop the breakaway Republicans from retreating once their colleagues started applying pressure? But her own members were adamant they had the votes and assured Pelosi they would collectively back the climate bill once the infrastructure bill passed, something they had previously refused to do.[109] Confident in the moderates' whip count, the Speaker agreed to call a vote. Twelve hours later, the infrastructure bill passed with the support of all thirteen Republicans and seventeen of the progressive holdouts.

After subsequent negotiations with the Senate, Pelosi scheduled a vote on the climate measure. The bill had changed considerably since its original drafting to accommodate the smaller $1.5 trillion price tag envisioned by Senate moderates Joe Manchin of West Virginia and Kyrsten Sinema of Arizona. But the Speaker refused to allow the Senate to fully dictate terms to the House. Despite pressure from the Biden administration, she declined to remove several provisions that were unlikely to pass the upper chamber, including a mandate for four weeks of paid family and medical leave.[110] With moderates whipping their members to support the bill as promised, the $2.2 trillion climate measure passed the House, 220–213, handing the Speaker the second half of her legislative wish list.

The fate of the climate bill now rested with the Senate, where it would be considered under the rules of reconciliation to avoid a Republican filibuster. But even immunized from a filibuster, the bill's prospects were uncertain, as Manchin and Sinema would both have to back it to assure passage. For months Manchin hedged, at times telling Democratic leaders, "I can't vote for it."[111] But in the summer of 2022, Manchin agreed to support a more modest version of the bill, one that retained provisions focused on climate and energy and reducing healthcare costs but that stripped away more expansive social welfare guarantees like subsidies for college tuition and Pelosi's family leave plan.

The Senate bill, dubbed the Inflation Reduction Act, passed the upper chamber in early August 2022. Days later, House Democrats approved it, 220–207. The Inflation Reduction Act was not as ambitious as many progressives had hoped it would be, and for some moderates it was still too pricy. But the act, for all its challenges, contained many of the Speaker's core priorities: hundreds of billions of dollars to address climate change and significant steps to make healthcare more affordable for more Americans. As she reminded her caucus, "This legislation is historic, it's transformative."[112]

Conclusion

Even now, with some remove from the end of Pelosi's speakership, it is hard to grasp the full magnitude of her accomplishments. Over the course of her long career, she amassed a near-unprecedented legislative record, all the more remarkable given the challenges of legislating in an era of polarized parties and insecure majorities. And given her consistent record of achievement, it is easy to imagine that her power over the House was both foreordained and unchanging, driven by the sheer force of her willpower and work ethic.

But as we have seen, the reality is more complicated. Notwithstanding her political acumen, Pelosi's capacity to get her party's majority makers to accept the progressive policies she deemed essential varied over time. During the fight over healthcare reform, it was moderate members of her caucus who prevailed in clashes over key features of the healthcare law, despite Pelosi's undeniable skill and savvy. But that same skill and savvy yielded different results when her party's factional configuration became more symmetric. With progressives coordinating in ways that rivaled moderate Democrats, Pelosi found greater freedom to insist that when it came to climate change moderates accept her priorities over their own.

CHAPTER FOUR

How John Boehner Lost His Party and Then His Job

The 2010 midterm elections left Republicans feeling exultant. Flipping more than sixty seats—the party's largest gain in any congressional election since 1938—the GOP seized control of the House and fell just short of securing a majority in the Senate. Across the country, jubilant candidates declared, "We've come to take our government back!"[1] Predictions that the Republicans' resurgence would yield a durable shift in the partisan balance of power soon proved overwrought, as they lost their majority within the decade. But the 2010 midterms did herald a significant change in the internal composition of the Republican Party. Of the eightysome Republicans newly elected to Congress, roughly a third were affiliated with the "Tea Party"—a loose if passionate network of populist conservative voters, activists, and donors mobilized around personalized, and often racialized, antipathy toward President Barack Obama and his signature legislative initiative, the Affordable Care Act (ACA).[2] Likening their victories to a "hostile takeover of the Republican Party," the class of 2010 arrived "with a hard-charging, often unruly governing style that bucked convention . . . and in many ways set the stage for the rise of Donald Trump."[3]

It would fall to Speaker John Boehner to manage the renegades—a task made more difficult by House Republicans' pronounced factional asymmetry. For much of the 1960s and 1970s, moderate Republicans had been a vital force in Congress and the nation at large. By the 1980s, however, the party's course was "increasingly . . . determined by the right, not the center."[4] Energized and organized, conservative members of the House served as the vanguard for Newt Gingrich's Republican revolution. A decade and a half later, the rise of the Tea Party would deepen the right's commitment to collective action, spawning a range of collaborative initiatives to amplify the voices and promote the ambitions of a new cohort of conservative legislators.

Meanwhile, moderate Republicans struggled to keep pace with their colleagues' collaborative momentum. Perhaps unwilling, as one member put it, to be "visible" in a party increasingly hostile to compromise, they declined to reinvigorate their own collaborative infrastructure, preferring to "keep their heads down and serve their districts."[5] Thus, while conservatives rushed to coordinate their activities, scaffolding their collaboration through an alphabet soup of intraparty organizations—first the Conservative Opportunity Society, then the Republican Study Committee, and later the House Freedom Caucus—Republican moderates retreated, reluctant to respond in kind by further developing their own collaborative machinery.[6]

As this chapter argues, this factional asymmetry fundamentally shaped Boehner's speakership, severely restricting his capacity to exercise power and ultimately curtailing his time in office. It begins by tracing the evolving collaborative choices made by moderate and conservative Republicans in the House over the last quarter of the twentieth century, which set the stage for the pronounced asymmetry Boehner encountered as Speaker. It then chronicles the 2013 confrontation between the Speaker and his party's "hard-core" conservative faction over its insistence that House Republicans use a pending budget bill to temporarily strip the ACA of funding.[7] Boehner, we will see, had little confidence in the plan, believing it to be bad policy and worse politics. As he counseled his conference, the Senate's Democratic majority was sure to reject any challenge to the new healthcare law. And even if they were willing to endure cuts to ACA funding to avert a government shutdown, the gambit was unlikely to have its intended effect, as the White House would find ways to cover the funding shortfall until a final budget agreement could be negotiated. Worse still, blame for any lapse in government services would fall squarely on Republicans, giving Democrats the chance to play the "adults in the room."[8]

But the Speaker soon found there was little he could say to deter his mobilized right flank. Itching for a fight, these members continued to believe they had a viable strategy: "shut the government down and ultimately Obama would repeal Obamacare."[9] Unable to use moderates as ballast in this contest of wills—and seemingly disinclined to spur them to organize to better match their factional rivals—Boehner gave in, agreeing to let conservatives have the fight they so desperately wanted. Now, he confided to aides, the party's best hope was for the experience to be educational. The shutdown's eager boosters would either learn to listen to leadership or else find themselves sidelined when the GOP's approval ratings inevitably plummeted. As it turned out, Boehner was half right. The shutdown was immensely unpopular, but the fallout failed to weaken his adversaries. Just the opposite. Internalizing the lessons of party asymmetry, the conservative rebels recognized that the Speaker was ill equipped to resist organized pressure from the right. Two years later, secure in their power, they would seek his ouster. Unable, and perhaps unwilling, to make further concessions to a group he deemed the "crazy caucus," Boehner ceded the gavel to Paul Ryan, a successor the right believed at that time to be worthier of their support.[10]

A Relational Basis for Conservative Power

Given our present politics, it is increasingly difficult to imagine a time when the Republican Party was not moving inexorably rightward. For much of the twentieth century, however, the GOP's internal politics reflected a homeostatic push-and-pull relationship between the party's moderate and conservative factions. Emboldened by upwellings of grassroots activism, conservatives would periodically seek to purge competing strains of Republicanism from the party.[11] Moderates, in turn, would "stage . . . furious efforts to retake control" whenever conservatives pressed too far or too fast.[12] This intraparty dynamism fostered a salutary and generative ecosystem for both factions, helping to refine the ideas and policy prescriptions that animated generations of Republicans in Congress and the electorate.

Things look quite different today. Since the beginning of the twenty-first century, the GOP has undergone an "unprecedented transformation."[13] In place of this factional give-and-take, conservatives now reign supreme, particularly in the House. And, despite their growing marginalization, moderates have shown little inclination or capacity to restore a natural balance to their party. Many observers have pointed to the success of the Tea Party in the 2010 midterms as a key inflection point in the GOP's shifting politics. Yet, for Boehner and his leadership team, it was the lead-up to, and fallout from, the 2013 government shutdown that provided the clearest evidence that the right was likely to be ascendant for the foreseeable future. It was then, the Speaker would later recall, that a new class of conservatives began to organize and "buil[d] up their own power base" in the House, laying the collaborative groundwork to dictate terms to their co-partisans, regardless of whether their party was in the majority or minority.[14]

Boehner is not alone in crediting House conservatives for helping to assure their present dominance. Legislative scholars, too, agree that the Republican Party's right wing has by and large forged its own destiny. For some, the key point is that hard-liners, buoyed by the results of the 2010 midterms, have been willing—in contrast to their predecessors—to defect from legislative bargains that give them some but not all of what they want.[15] This tendency to behave as if "half a loaf is basically no bread" is thought to make conservative threats to reject compromise more credible, significantly advantaging them in talks with leaders.[16] Others suggest that the conservatives' organizational strategies—as Boehner put it, their efforts to "build up a power base"—have amplified their influence within the party. As I have argued elsewhere, in forming intraparty organizations like the Freedom Caucus, conservatives successfully adopted and adapted institutional practices geared to facilitating their collective defection, binding members to a common plan of action and empowering them to bargain without divulging areas of disagreement.[17]

This chapter approaches the question of conservative dominance from a different angle. Rather than focus narrowly on conservatives' own organizational choices or their orientation to compromise, it considers the relational dynamic between the GOP's moderate and conservative factions, exploring how House Republicans' factional asymmetry has incubated and perhaps entrenched right-wing power in the lower chamber. As we saw in chapter 3, factional mobilization on its own is not sufficient to guarantee like-minded lawmakers power within their party. It also matters whether a faction's level of collaboration exceeds that of its rivals. Recall that early in Nancy Pelosi's tenure as Speaker, moderate Democrats boasted substantially more muscle in intraparty deliberations because their progressive adversaries were disorganized and thus unable to sustain comparable levels of collective action. That advantage dissipated as progressives began to join forces more regularly. As applied to the contemporary Republican Party, the core insight is this: conservative power is conditional not just on hard-liners' increasingly sophisticated efforts to work together but also on moderates' failure to respond in kind. That decision, whether conscious or unconscious, to cede the collaborative field and refrain from pursuing moderate aims collectively has redounded to the benefit of conservatives and systematically hamstrung the party's leaders.

Alternative Explanations

The core empirical claim of this chapter is that Boehner, constrained by his asymmetric party, had little choice but to let conservatives pursue their shutdown scheme rather than impose legislative strategies he preferred. Perhaps the most obvious—and easily dismissed—alternative to this account is that Boehner believed in (and wanted to pursue) the gambit favored by his right flank. As we will see, there is no indication that the Speaker wished to use a government funding bill as a vehicle to repeal the ACA. On the contrary, there is abundant evidence that he believed holding federal spending hostage was doomed to fail.[18] Throughout the summer of 2013, Boehner cautioned that Senate Democrats and the White House were unlikely to give conservative Republicans the win they were hoping for. Indeed, the consensus within the Speaker's inner circle was that "you're not going to repeal Obamacare while a guy named Obama is President of the United States."[19] Both publicly and privately, Boehner reiterated his view that House Republicans' best option was to bargain with Obama over the particulars of the ACA's implementation. Such negotiations were possible only if Congress raised the debt ceiling and kept the government funded without drama. To behave otherwise would be "crazy . . . just fucking stupid."[20]

Alternatively, it might be that Boehner's hand *was* forced, but not by asymmetries in the extent of conservative and moderate collaboration. Perhaps the Speaker was constrained by the size of the conservative faction. With fewer than twenty votes to spare, Boehner would need some of the thirty conservative members who vowed to vote against a "clean" continuing budget resolution (one that lacked language mandating cuts to the ACA's discretionary funding) to forsake their commitments and back him. But while the conservatives' numbers might have jeopardized the Speaker's ability to rely solely on Republican votes to pass a clean budget resolution, assuming they could successfully hold together and defect en masse, he did not lack for alternatives to make up the shortfall. After all, there were forty-five moderate Republicans who were just as vehemently opposed to the shutdown plan as conservatives were for it. And many of them were eager to help Boehner forge a cross-party coalition were he to decide to work "directly with the Democrats" to get Republicans out of their funding jam—a strategy he had successfully pursued on several previous occasions.[21]

A final possibility is that Boehner, despite his own misgivings, pursued the shutdown strategy because it was favored by a majority of his conference. As we will see, the evidence on this score is mixed. It is true that informal nose counts taken in the summer months preceding the shutdown surfaced general enthusiasm for a confrontation with Obama. And in August, eighty members (a third of the conference) penned a letter to the Speaker encouraging him to "affirmatively defund the implementation of Obamacare in any relevant appropriations bill."[22] But as the Speaker's team underscored in discussions with one another, those advocating such a strategy were articulating a broad strategic vision rather than making an explicit commitment to vote down appropriations bills that included funding for the healthcare law. Perhaps more important, as the prospect of a shutdown loomed, the party's whips reported a notable softening in support for such an aggressive bargaining position. The members most determined to force a shutdown were increasingly outliers, "crazy, crazy people . . . who just want[ed] to fight."[23] With many in the conference willing to "go either way," this chapter argues that House Republicans' collaborative imbalance helped to tip the scales in favor of the conservatives' preferred approach.[24]

Organizing the "Vital Center"

Throughout the 1960s and early 1970s, moderate Republicans were a vital force in Congress. Critical partners in the cross-party coalition that secured civil rights for Black Americans, they would in later years champion a range of liberal causes, including efforts to ratify the Equal Rights Amendment, expand access to higher education, strengthen clean air standards, and provide medical care for the uninsured. In the House, their advocacy was facilitated by an intraparty organization: the Wednesday Group, so named because members met every Wednesday evening to "discuss pending legislation, committee activities, and long-range policy interests." "The group," one lawmaker recalled, "represented . . . GOP progressives," offering "a forum for discussing and developing their views . . . [away from] the largely conservative GOP."[25] Although members eschewed rules and procedures designed to achieve strict "internal conformity"—for instance, refraining from insisting that members vote together on the floor—the invitation-only group actively encouraged members to "join as individuals in taking specific actions" favored by the collective. Members would not be forced to coordinate their activities, but the strong expectation was that they would "work together on an ad hoc [basis]."[26]

And work together they did. In 1965, the Wednesday Group was instrumental in helping Gerald Ford, a fellow moderate, depose the conservative Charles Halleck as House minority leader. Up against Halleck, "a veteran gut fighter" who leveraged "every political I.O.U. he could" to forestall rebellion, Ford depended on members of the Wednesday Group to provide the necessary organizational capacity to whip votes and lobby wavering members in support of his insurgent candidacy.[27] He would pay moderate Republicans back in kind as minority leader and later as vice president and president, consulting the Wednesday Group on matters of policy and modeling many of his own proposals after those outlined by the moderate faction throughout the late 1960s and early 1970s.[28]

By the time Ronald Reagan was elected to the White House, however, moderates' collaborative momentum had slowed. Although the Wednesday Group continued to provide a forum for self-described "progressive" and "liberal" Republicans to discuss alternatives to the policies articulated by the administration, "considerable differences of opinion within the group" soon emerged over "how aggressive [members] want[ed] to be."[29] Believing the president's vision of conservativism to be dangerous, some hoped to challenge Reagan's hold over the party and, as one member put it, "impress with the force of [our] ideas."[30] But a majority of the group saw little value in confrontation, preferring to "be in step" (at least publicly) with the rest of the party, else risk being labeled as "incorrigible liberals" or "marginally Republican."[31] In consequence, the Wednesday Group drifted rightward over the course of Reagan's two terms, with those moderates determined to resist the White House leaving the organization and a small number going so far as to decamp across the aisle.[32] These departing members were soon replaced by more mainstream recruits eager for the fellowship and additional staff support the Wednesday Group provided.[33]

It would not take long for moderates to regret abandoning the collaborative machinery they had worked so hard to create and maintain. Increasingly aggrieved that they lacked a regular voice in intraparty deliberations, members appealed to Minority Leader Bob Michel, an old Ford ally who, like his predecessor, prized collegiality and compromise. Michel's advice was simple: "You guys need to get organized."[34] With the minority leader's blessing, a handful of former Wednesday Group members led by Connecticut's Nancy Johnson and Wisconsin's Steve Gunderson began to discuss how they might create a new, more durable organization to structure moderate Republicans' collaboration in the House. Agreeing to gather for pizza lunches in the basement of the Capitol, the leaders of the new Tuesday Group (née Tuesday Lunch Bunch) recruited a dozen of their colleagues to take part in weekly strategy and discussion sessions. On the eve of the 1994 Republican revolution, the group was thirty members strong.[35]

Conservatives in Flux

While the 1960s were a heady decade for moderate Republicans, the same could not be said for the party's conservatives. "Unorganized and utterly powerless," they were "isolated, discouraged, [and] defeated" by successive losses on civil rights, environmental regulation, and social welfare policy.[36] Richard Nixon's election in 1968 promised change. With their "own man in office," conservatives were confident that they could finally beat back the spread of "secular liberalism."[37] They were soon disappointed. Despite burnishing his conservative credentials on the campaign trail, Nixon was keen to work with congressional Democrats to rack up a positive legislative record. Together with Minority Leader Ford, the White House championed a range of moderate policies—including significant environmental and workplace protection legislation—and evidenced little regard for the president's right-wing backers.

Nixon's turn to moderation elicited a range of emotions from the thirty-some conservative Republicans in the House. Some remained supportive of the new administration, placated by the president's private assurances that he was still committed to conservative principles. Brushing off suggestions that Nixon was tacking hard to the left, they defended the president and reiterated their confidence in the White House. "I'm pro-Nixon all the way," declared Ohio's Sam Devine, who had first made his name investigating suspected communists in the state legislature. "I believe he is moving [conservatives] back into the mainstream of basic Republican policy."[38]

Not everyone agreed. Roughly a third of the conservative faction balked at what they perceived to be the administration's ideological "flexibility," warning their colleagues against "blindly following Mr. Nixon's leadership."[39] Determined to hold the president to the agenda he had outlined as a candidate, they committed to a strategy of collective resistance. To facilitate their collaboration, they—much like their moderate colleagues—created an intraparty organization, the Republican Study Committee (RSC). As one of the group's founding members recalled, "Nixon's record looked consistently left . . . [so] we said, 'If Jerry Ford isn't getting any pressure from the right, the only way he's going to go is left.'"[40]

Recruiting others to join their fight proved difficult. Many of their colleagues "felt no need to coordinate with others of their philosophy."[41] Not only did conservatives habitually disdain "group activities and pressures to conform to someone else's position or vote," but they were leery of upsetting the party hierarchy. "The senior members were worried about what the leadership would think [and] the freshmen were worried about what the senior members in their state delegation would think," recalled a founding member of the RSC.[42] Recognizing that collaboration was in and of itself an insufficient draw, the RSC began to offer new recruits research and campaign support. The carrots worked: "When other conservative members saw the sharp materials RSC researchers produced, they asked to join."[43]

By 1980, amid a national sea-change in conservative mobilization, a majority of House Republicans were clamoring to join the RSC. Within a year, three-quarters of the conference claimed membership. But such exponential growth proved a mixed blessing. On the one hand, it was clear that many lawmakers "wish[ed] to be perceived as conservatives" even if they had not previously "adopt[ed] conservative positions."[44] On the other hand, the RSC's expanded ranks made collective action in pursuit of those conservative positions more difficult, as "an enlarged membership . . . [brought] about . . . a dilution of principles."[45] With the group divided over just how conservative it should be, the RSC struggled to define a positive agenda or mobilize against those initiatives a majority of members opposed.

Though Reagan is today valorized as a conservative true believer, his administration proved a mixed blessing for the growth of right-wing collaboration in the House. Determined to build a durable legislative majority, the administration directed House conservatives to seek out common ground with their moderate colleagues. "We must recognize we have to convert those people of a more liberal view," Reagan insisted. "We don't win elections by destroying them or making them disappear."[46] The question of whether or not to embrace their moderate foes split the RSC, with some members applauding the president's efforts to work across the aisle and others expressing frustration that he took their votes for granted.

Recognizing that the RSC was no longer "at the cutting edge" of conservative politics anymore, those on the right began to drift.[47] Some joined Newt Gingrich's fledgling Conservative Opportunity Society (COS), a smaller and less formal organization. Others opted for more ad hoc arrangements, coordinating with colleagues on a short-term basis or participating in the RSC's strategy sessions as it suited them. Although the RSC's leadership expressed disappointment that these divisions made collaboration difficult, the reality was that a Democratic majority in Congress made it unlikely that conservative Republicans would make substantial gains. They would need a Republican takeover for collaboration to pay policy dividends.

Revolution for Whom?

The 1994 midterms provided just such an opportunity. Flipping more than fifty seats, House Republicans seized control of the lower chamber and, with it, the chance to pursue their own legislative priorities for the first time in four decades. Conservatives, for their part, expressed confidence that *they* would finally be in charge. "We've only been waiting forty years for this!" declared Henry Hyde of Illinois.[48] But the new Speaker of the House had other plans. Determined to consolidate power over his conference, Gingrich sought to undercut the influence of organizations like the RSC and the Tuesday Group (as well as his own COS). In an effort to eliminate rival power centers, he implemented a ban on public financing for all such groups, forcing both moderates and conservatives to raise private funds for their collaborative operations. Working with half the membership and a shoestring budget, the conservatives relaunched the RSC under a new name, the Conservative Action Team (CAT).[49] Another group of thirty mostly junior conservatives opted to collaborate separately, calling themselves the "New Federalists."[50]

Given their shared political outlook, conservatives quickly developed a productive working relationship with Gingrich and his leadership team. In the early months of 1995, members of CAT and the New Federalists joined forces to help draft legislation to fulfill the budget and tax commitments outlined in the Republican Party's Contract with America. In return for their support, the Speaker agreed to give serious consideration to proposals to abolish the National Endowment for the Arts and to defund the Department of Education. But the right's relationship with the Speaker soon soured.

Defying his carefully cultivated reputation as a rabble-rouser, as Speaker, Gingrich was determined "to prove that [the GOP] could govern." He found an unexpected ally in the Tuesday Group. "We can be very helpful to our party and very constructive," members assured the Speaker. Crucially, they had the collaborative apparatus to deliver on the priorities they shared with House leadership, including regulatory reform. In contrast to conservatives who found themselves divided between two organizations operating at half power, moderate Republicans had opted to stick together. Reflecting on their relative unity, moderates saw only upsides: "Our group is growing in strength; our group is going to be important."[51]

And they were right. In the fall of 1996, members of the Tuesday Group persuaded Gingrich to support two of their key priorities: a bipartisan minimum wage bill and a progressive-backed healthcare measure.[52] The group's influence soon extended to core planks of the Republican agenda, including fiscal and regulatory policy. Finding Gingrich greatly chastened by the public backlash to his forced government shutdown the previous winter, moderates convinced him to accept their proposal for a balanced budget bill. Validating their enhanced collaborative activity, the measure represented a compromise between moderates in both parties, coupling a substantial tax cut with increased spending on education and children's health.

As was perhaps inevitable, the détente proved unstable. Gingrich may have been willing to work with the "moderate, liberal enemies" who constituted the Tuesday Group, but other members of his leadership team were not. Conservative Majority Leader Dick Armey of Texas was particularly outspoken, telling reporters that he hoped the conference would soon "be strong enough" to reject the moderates outright.[53] For their part, conservative backbenchers expressed outrage that the Speaker had been "wagged" by the party's liberal "tail," while at the same time, admitting a grudging respect for the moderates' hustle. "They organized," one conservative groused, "and they won."[54]

The situation reached a boiling point in the summer of 1997. Believing they could oust Gingrich if they, too, could better organize their ranks, nearly half of CAT's members and several New Federalists joined a handful of top party leaders in an unsuccessful drive to unseat the Speaker. The failed coup exposed the limits of conservative collaboration as much as it weakened Gingrich's hold over the party. Some CAT members and New Federalists remained loyal to the Speaker, crediting him for their electoral success. Others believed the rebellion justified. They dismissed Gingrich as "all talk" and complained he had "yet to lead a real fight on issues dear to conservatives."[55] Still others were caught in the middle, sympathetic to their colleagues' complaints but unwilling to publicly question the Speaker's leadership.

To paper over their differences, conservatives sought a common enemy: moderate Republicans. Intent on curbing if not eliminating the Tuesday Group's influence, CAT and the New Federalists called on Republican leaders to "weed . . . out moderates" from positions of power and blasted their colleagues for "going squishy."[56] They also pressed the Republican conference to pursue conservative policy goals they knew had little chance of passage but would surely put moderates in a jam. As then Senator Joe Biden recalled, they put "enormous pressure on moderate Republicans to walk away from anything remotely approaching compromise."[57] Under sustained pressure from the right, the Tuesday Group's leadership struggled to maintain a critical mass or support members' collaboration.

But the moderates' challenges did not redound to the conservatives' clear benefit. The 1998 midterms—widely seen as a referendum on the party's legislative performance—thinned the Republican majority. Their disappointing showing at the polls put pressure on conservatives to "produce spectacular legislation" before the 2000 presidential election, but there was little agreement about what that would entail.[58] Gingrich's decision to resign the speakership posed additional problems. Unable to agree on a suitable replacement, conservatives were marginal players in the speakership race ultimately won by Dennis Hastert of Illinois. Dismayed by their lack of influence, the right's two organizations pursued divergent strategies. While the New Federalists disbanded, CAT rebranded—adopting the old RSC name and with it, the group's combative style.

Conservative Resurgence

After eight years out of power, the return of a Republican to the White House presented both obstacles and opportunities for the GOP's rival factions. For moderates, George W. Bush's narrow victory in 2000 prompted early optimism that the president would govern from the center. But it soon became clear that Bush and his principal advisors intended "to steer... legislative initiatives... as far right as possible." This approach left moderates to debate whether and how aggressively to resist a president of their own party. Some thought it best to embrace the administration and urged greater conformity to party orthodoxy. Others were highly critical of such a strategy and refused to blunt their barbs, accusing the administration of jettisoning the compassion that was supposed to be the centerpiece of the president's conservative agenda. Pursuing fringe right-wing politics, they argued, was both "stupid and gross."[59] Split over whether and how to engage the White House, moderates saw their influence ebb yet again.

Their fortunes took a brief turn for the better after Democrats regained control of Congress in 2006. Eager to pitch bills that would raise the minimum wage, overturn Bush-era restrictions on stem cell research, and cut interest rates on college loans as bipartisan efforts, House Democrats courted sympathetic votes across the aisle. Moderate Republicans appreciated the attention. Said one of the Tuesday Group's forty members, "For a pro-labor Republican like me, it's been very beneficial." Noting that "Democrats basically grabbed the center and ran with it," another member observed that working with Democrats made it possible for moderate Republicans to be more productive than when their own party controlled the House. "Under the Republican majority, those bills would never have gotten to the floor. Now they have been brought to the floor and I've voted for them."[60]

But a durable cross-party alliance proved elusive. With the 2008 presidential race underway, Democratic leaders were eager to flip moderate Republican districts to their side, and pressure to squelch bipartisan initiatives increased on both sides of the aisle. Ratcheting down their organizational activities, the Tuesday Group set aside the pursuit of legislative priorities that had the backing of moderates across the aisle and fell in line behind their congressional leadership in opposing the Democrats' agenda. In so doing, the leaders of the Tuesday Group conceded that they were sacrificing influence. They would aim, instead, to achieve something more modest: "We might be able to provide some balance and perspective" for the Republican conference.[61]

Conservatives, by contrast, experienced something of a revival during the first decade of the twenty-first century. The "new," post-Gingrich RSC proved as popular as its predecessor, and by 2002 it had doubled in size, counting seventy members. Emboldened, the group loudly, if unsuccessfully, protested the Bush administration's Medicare and education initiatives. After Republicans lost control of the House in 2006, the RSC renewed its attacks on the president's agenda, accusing his administration of working too closely with congressional Democrats. And in Bush's last months in office, House conservatives handed the White House and Boehner, then minority leader, "the worst defeat any party leader ha[d] suffered on the floor in decades."[62] Refusing to support the president's bipartisan initiative to rescue Wall Street in the aftermath of the subprime mortgage crisis, the RSC twice rallied its members to vote against the measure, forcing Boehner to renege on his commitment that Republicans would help pass the unpopular bailout plan. Dubbed by Jeb Hensarling of Texas "the keeper of the conservative flame," the RSC was burning brightly indeed.[63]

By 2009, with Obama in the White House and a Democratic-controlled Congress, conservatives forged ahead with even greater energy, while moderate Republicans stuck to the sidelines. On the House floor, at podiums on the Capitol's steps, and in prime-time spots on cable news channels, the RSC relentlessly hammered the new president's economic policies and vowed to obstruct his plans for healthcare reform. The group also butted heads with Boehner, believing "the job of the RSC . . . is to move the Conference to the most conservative position."[64] The conservatives' restlessness alarmed the minority leader and prompted *Politico* to observe that "there is no place in the Republican Conference that presents a bigger long-term threat to Boehner than the RSC."[65]

Led by Hensarling, the RSC also redoubled its recruitment efforts, encouraging members eager "to fight to pass conservative policy into law" to attend their weekly strategy sessions. Meeting every Wednesday afternoon in the Gold Room of the Rayburn House Office building, they discussed how to "blunt many of the horrendous policies coming out of the administration" and drafted a conservative action plan they hoped would move the GOP into the majority.[66] The outreach paid dividends. A year into Obama's presidency, the RSC had doubled in size and, with it, the group's operating budget. The influx of new dues-paying members enabled the RSC to expand its staff to ten aides, who were tasked with issuing a steady stream of press releases and legislative bulletins on conservative agenda priorities. The exposure only heightened the group's appeal with participants in the grassroots Tea Party movement, who welcomed "that hardcore group of small-government Goldwater conservatives in the RSC" to their town halls.[67]

But the RSC's rapid expansion engendered some growing pains. Whereas the "new" RSC had previously recruited only committed conservatives, the popularity of the Tea Party prodded others in the GOP to join the group in the hopes of burnishing their conservative credentials. In practice, little about the RSC's day-to-day activities changed; the group's regular meetings remained the province of the thirtysome conservatives who attended them and coordinated its operations, now with the benefit of a bigger budget. But on paper, at least, the organization was going mainstream, an impression Boehner reinforced when he tapped two of the RSC's former chairs to serve on his leadership team.

Elevating Boehner to the speakership, the 2010 midterms exacerbated the collaborative asymmetry between conservative and moderate Republicans. The sudden influx of so many new lawmakers spurred the RSC's conservative core, now led by Jim Jordan of Ohio, to expand the group's operations further to "go after obvious targets [like] healthcare, energy, cap and trade" and other "signature Democratic initiatives."[68] The Tuesday Group, by contrast, resolved to keep a low profile until the Tea Party fever broke, hopeful that in the meantime Boehner would recognize that "without centrists, Republicans wouldn't have a majority."[69]

Unhappy Warriors

Early in his speakership, Boehner projected confidence that he could heal the GOP's rifts and transform his conference into a team of "happy warriors."[70] "We will welcome the battle of ideas, encourage it, and engage in it—openly, honestly, and respectfully," he declared.[71] An experienced dealmaker, the Speaker believed he could give every Republican some of what they wanted.[72] Conservatives would get the messaging votes they craved—as one member put it, the "red meat to take back home"—while the rest of the party pursued substantive, if incremental, policy gains. Together, Boehner promised, they would "change . . . the debate here in Washington and the direction of our government."[73]

But it soon became clear that conservatives wanted more. And their party's factional asymmetry put them in a prime position to get it. In February 2011, they scuttled legislation to renew the Patriot Act, surprising Boehner and McCarthy, then party whip, who had assumed the measure would sail through. Smarting from the setback, the Speaker vowed to "listen harder" to his right flank. Nevertheless, his aides conceded that their strategy remained the same. "He sort of ignored [the party's conservatives] . . . and hoped they would go away."[74] They did not. Several weeks later, the RSC released a framework that insisted on sizable spending cuts and major budget reforms as a condition of their agreeing to raise the statutory debt ceiling. Known as "Cut, Cap, and Balance," the plan committed Republicans to reducing the federal budget by an additional $100 billion beyond what Democrats had agreed to in preliminary negotiations. In a show of force, thirty-nine of the RSC's most conservative members signed a public pledge affirming they would not vote for any alternative legislation that raised the debt ceiling without similar cuts or spending caps, or a balanced-budget amendment.[75]

While members of Boehner's leadership team—foremost, Majority Leader Eric Cantor of Virginia—voiced support for the proposal, the Speaker had his doubts. He told Jordan and the plan's signatories that Democrats in the Senate and White House would never agree to cuts without offsetting increases in government revenue. Nor, he confided to aides, were they likely to negotiate over the debt ceiling with members they perceived to be "a bunch of angry amateurs with no clue."[76]

Moderate Republicans echoed the Speaker's concerns. "This is ridiculous," one member of the Tuesday Group complained to Boehner. "You know this is not good . . . for those of us in moderate districts and . . . is never going to become law. There is no endgame." Best case scenario, the conservatives' unrealistic targets would give Republicans better leverage to negotiate a more favorable compromise with the Democratic Senate. But more likely, "we'll just shut the place down. And [Senate Majority Leader] Harry Reid has no reason to give us anything."[77] Perhaps more important, moderates wondered why leaders were "indulging the right flank" when it was the "squishies and bedwetters and RINOs [Republicans in name only]" who had given Republicans their majority.[78]

Given the conservatives' intransigence and their collaborative dominance, the Speaker recognized that he would have to seek a cross-party compromise. Opting to negotiate directly with the White House, Boehner "began to talk to the president about the need to deal with our budget problem."[79] By July, the contours of a bargain were beginning to take shape. "It was clear that we had an agreement, that there was $800 billion in revenues [for Democrats] and more than that in reductions and reforms on the spending side [for Republicans]."[80] But time was running out. While Boehner's aides were hammering out the details with their counterparts in the White House, conservatives were clamoring for a vote on their proposed framework. Hopeful that he could buy himself some breathing room, Boehner relented, and the House voted the plan through. As conservatives celebrated, the Speaker went back to the president only to find that the terrain had shifted. A bipartisan "gang of six" senators had floated their own budget plan by Obama, and he found their terms more agreeable.

The prospects of a bargain uncertain, Boehner began to consider alternatives—a "plan B"—settling on a two-step plan to raise the debt ceiling while capping annual appropriations to reduce the deficit. Reminding his conference that Cut, Cap, and Balance was "DOA [dead on arrival] in the Senate," the Speaker ordered conservatives to "get your ass in line" and back "the only real deal on the table."[81] But Jordan and his colleagues resisted. Sharing the chair's strategy in an email to conservative activists, an RSC aide wrote, "If we keep this [i.e., Boehner's plan B] from ever coming to the floor, we have a greater chance of victory. Now is the day to kill the Boehner deal."[82]

With conservatives actively pushing back against Boehner's proposal and the threat of a government shutdown looming, the Speaker and president returned to the bargaining table. At the last hour, they negotiated a compromise that included steep cuts but fell well short of the conservatives' budget framework and the targets Boehner had set for himself. "This isn't the greatest deal in the world," he told members, "but it shows how much we've changed the terms of the debate in this town."[83] All that was left was to muscle the bill through the House. Buoyed by Pelosi's commitment to provide Democratic votes to offset conservative defections, Boehner informed his conference that a vote was imminent. Several hours later, the House passed the Budget Control Act. It was, by Boehner's own admission, a pyrrhic victory. Sixty-five Republicans—including those who had pledged to exclusively back Cut, Cap, and Balance—had voted against the plan. Asked what he planned to do the next day Boehner replied: "Hopefully hid[e] somewhere."[84]

Coordinating "Legislative Terrorism"

But the right wing's collaborative advantage left little room to hide. A month later, conservatives rolled the Speaker for a second time, repeating their Patriot Act success by defeating a short-term government funding bill in what one lawmaker described as "Groundhog Day, all over again."[85] "It was the lowest I've ever seen Boehner," another recalled. "He just walked away that night, alone, hands in his pockets, head down."[86] The situation did not improve with time. After the 2012 election, the Speaker tried again to cut a spending deal with Obama, and when that failed, conservatives joined forces to tank the alternative he proposed. His frustration palpable, Boehner pressed the dissidents to explain themselves. "Now what?" he asked.[87]

The answer, it seemed, was some organizational housekeeping. Although delighted by their ability to push Republican leaders to the right, Jordan and the RSC's conservative core were increasingly disenchanted with the organization itself. The fight over the debt limit had exposed divisions among the group's hundred-plus members over how aggressively to pursue their policy priorities, leading conservatives to hope that "maybe some members will resign and step down." As one lawmaker mused, "if the positions are too strong for them, then they can leave. It would be a natural shift."[88] But, because the RSC had no formal mechanism to expel Republicans sympathetic to Boehner from its ranks, the organization's most conservative members began to collaborate outside the group's formally established meeting schedule and refrained from reporting their discussions back to the broader membership. "It created a different dynamic," another member acknowledged. They could still use the RSC's considerable operating budget and sizable membership when it suited them, but they would not be captive to more mainstream colleagues' priorities when they diverged from their own.[89]

While conservatives tightened the bonds of their collaboration by insisting on greater secrecy within their circle, cultivating a "do or die . . . fight club" mentality, and meeting on a weekly basis, moderates in the Tuesday Group continued to lay low.[90] Like the Democratic minority, they had learned from their party's successive fights over fiscal policy: "The big lesson was that Boehner did not come to the table with any particular strength. He wasn't able to cut deals" with Obama that reflected what centrists in either party wanted.[91] But, leaders of the Tuesday Group reflected, Boehner was not entirely to blame. Their own refusal to collectively challenge the RSC limited the Speaker's ability to tack to the middle. As one member observed, "They'd like to use us [the Tuesday Group] as a foil with the right-wing guys, so they'd be able to say 'Oh, we can't do what you want to do because of them.'"[92] Another moderate noted that "[on occasions] when we did go public, saying 'this is a stupid idea' in the Republican conference or [in] the media, frankly they—Boehner and Cantor—appreciated that."[93]

Nor was the Tuesday Group alone in thinking that the collaborative imbalance between moderates and conservatives made the Speaker's job more difficult. "I wish the Tuesday Group were more active," one leadership aide admitted. "It would help fight the caricature that we are all a bunch of right-wing nutjobs."⁹⁴ Boehner was even more direct. With moderates looking out for themselves, he alone was stuck dealing with the "legislative terrorists" on the right. And "it's hard to negotiate when you're standing there naked."⁹⁵

From Showdown to Shutdown

Coming out of the tumultuous debt ceiling fight, Boehner was eager to avoid another battle over government funding that might result in a shutdown. At the Republican Party's annual retreat in January 2013, he cautioned members to "think more and fight less." Rather than threaten to default on the debt as some right-wing members were advocating, he argued that the best course of action was to pass a short-term debt limit extension and series of continuing resolutions in exchange for meaningful spending cuts and a better debt limit deal in the fall. Determined to shore up support for his proposed course of action at the outset, Boehner negotiated directly with the RSC's self-described "Jedi Council"—Louisiana's Steve Scalise, Georgia's Tom Price, Ryan, Hensarling, and Jordan. It was Ryan who really sold the plan.⁹⁶ "[We] must recognize the realities of divided government," he advised his colleagues. "A short-term debt limit extension" would give Republicans "a better chance of getting the Senate and the White House involved in discussions" over government spending.⁹⁷ Deferring to Ryan's judgment, the Jedi Council agreed to follow Boehner's lead. With the conservatives in tow, Boehner was able to deliver what he promised. By early spring, the House had passed a temporary extension of the debt and a continuing resolution to lock in lower spending levels.

As summer approached, however, support for the Speaker's plan was starting to melt away. Moderates said little publicly, but privately they groused that Boehner had negotiated with conservatives and not them.⁹⁸ Conservatives, too, were talking—with one another and with sympathetic groups like the Heritage Foundation and Americans for Prosperity—about whether Boehner might be wrong. Perhaps government funding *was* a hostage worth taking. The problem, one conservative conceded, was that "in any negotiation, it's very difficult to get very far if you're not willing to live with the consequences of not having a deal."⁹⁹ If they were to use government spending to force Democrats to make painful cuts, they would need to be collectively committed to the possibility of a shutdown.

By August, conservatives were increasingly open to the idea that they could use the threat of a shutdown to repeal the ACA and thereby shrink federal spending. North Carolina's Mark Meadows, a new member of the RSC's conservative clique, drafted a letter "urging" Boehner to "affirmatively de-fund the implementation and enforcement of Obamacare in any relevant appropriations bill brought to the House floor."[100] Seventy-nine of his colleagues, including Meadows's thirty-nine allies in the RSC, added their signatures to the letter. Boehner was nonplussed. "[The ACA] is the law of the land," he reminded members on a conference call, and any effort to impede its implementation by cutting off government funding was bound to fail.[101] Nor was it clear that most of the letter's signatories actually wanted to use appropriations bills as vehicles to kill the ACA. Even Meadows's tone, the Speaker's deputies observed, was "very soft"—there were no redlines drawn or threats made to block legislation that did not include the defund language.[102]

Still, it was clear that the accord reached in January was fraying. As Boehner's team acknowledged, it didn't help that so many members were spending the summer back in their districts. "Somehow out on the campaign trail, the representation was made that you could beat President Obama into submission to sign a repeal of the law with his name on it," Cantor observed. "That's where things got . . . disconnected from reality."[103] It would be up to Republican leaders to bring members back to earth before the federal government ran out of money on October 1—the same day that the ACA's healthcare exchanges would open for enrollment.

On a conference call in late August, the Speaker reiterated his belief that another funding fight would distract from what everyone expected to be a rocky rollout of the healthcare exchanges. Let Americans see what the ACA looked like in practice, he advised. Republicans would be better off passing a short-term spending bill and ceding the spotlight to Democrats. But conservatives disagreed. They noted that Senators Ted Cruz of Texas and Mike Lee of Utah were counseling House Republicans "not to blink" in the face of a shutdown.[104] Bring a continuing resolution to the floor that included language eliminating funding for the ACA's implementation, they instructed.[105] Boehner tried again to head off conservatives in early September. Herding four to five members into his office at a time, the Speaker warned, "Don't do this. It's crazy." Offering up a new alternative, Boehner and Cantor suggested to members that they hold two votes, one to defund the ACA and the other to fund the rest of the government.[106] That plan, too, was shouted down.

At this point, the Speaker weighed his options. He could give in to conservatives, include the defunding language, suffer through the inevitable shutdown, and squander the opportunity to make Democrats squirm when their healthcare exchanges stalled out. Or he could bring a clean resolution to the floor, rely on Democratic votes to offset what would surely be at least two dozen conservative defections, and spend the next six months reminding Americans how badly Democrats had fumbled the ACA's implementation. It was clear to Boehner what *he* wanted to do, but also clear that he would have to pay dearly to get it. Seeing no great way out of the situation, Boehner folded, telling conservatives, "If you want to go fight this fight, I'll go fight the fight with you."[107]

With a shutdown only weeks away, moderates began making noise of their own. If House conservatives were intent on following Cruz over the edge, prominent moderates declared their intention to fight. In an interview on Fox News, Representative Peter King of New York told viewers that he and twenty-four of his colleagues were prepared to vote against the rule that would bring the defunding resolution to the floor—enough to prevent its consideration.[108] But with moderates lacking the collaborative mechanisms to collectively defect, Boehner wasn't worried. The general feeling in the Speaker's office was that "moderates always cave."[109] Sure enough, ten days before the government reached its borrowing limit, King and Pennsylvania's Charlie Dent, leader of the Tuesday Group, were the only moderates to vote against the rule. The problem, as King saw it, was that moderates "will talk, they will complain, but they never go . . . head-to-head" or "do what they say they're going to do."[110]

In late September, the House approved legislation to defund the ACA while keeping the government up and running through the end of the year. As expected, Senate Democrats stripped the House bill of its defunding language and sent a clean resolution back to the House. The House then passed another stopgap spending bill, this time with language delaying the ACA's implementation for a year. Again, the Senate removed the dilatory language from the bill and sent it back, at which point House Republicans passed another resolution that proposed to delay the ACA's individual mandate for a year. The Senate rejected that plan as well, and, on October 1, the federal government shut down.

Fighting the Good Fight

Moderates were not alone in expressing their concern about Boehner's chosen course of action. About a third of the conference pushed the Speaker to put a clean continuing resolution on the floor at once, before lasting damage was done. As one member recalled:

> He explained, 'There are about 85 of you guys I can count on to do the right thing. But you know, I got these 40 guys who just want to . . . blow this place up. Then there's like 110 other guys in between who can be pulled in either direction. Those are the guys I have to worry about.

In giving conservatives the shutdown *they* wanted, Boehner hoped "to break those guys" and in so doing undercut their influence over the rest of the conference.[111]

But when would they break? While the Speaker warned that public opinion was likely to turn against the Republican majority and tried to persuade members that defaulting on the debt would be catastrophic, his own deputies were more optimistic that the shutdown would "get something" from Democrats. In a strategy memo Cantor sent to House Republicans two days into the stalemate, he wrote, "I am confident that . . . Senate Democrats and President Obama will eventually agree to meaningful discussions that w[ill] allow us to ultimately resolve this impasse."[112]

With conservatives hell-bent on outlasting Obama, moderates saw another chance to gain an edge. If they could work with Democrats to get Republicans out of this mess, maybe everyone—the Speaker included—would see their value to the party. But rather than work through the Tuesday Group or more informally to coordinate their outreach, members floated proposals to reopen the government and courted Democrats on an individual basis.[113] The result was that no single measure won sufficient support to restart negotiations between the House and Senate. And all that their bipartisan outreach managed to elicit was the condemnation of their more conservative colleagues, who accused them (with no sense of irony) of undercutting the GOP's negotiating position.

Sixteen days into the shutdown, and with a default looming, the Senate brokered a truce: Congress would fund the government for another four months and extend the federal government's borrowing power to avoid a financial default. In return, the income verification rules for Americans using the ACA's insurance exchanges would be tightened. With every Democratic member voting to end the shutdown, Boehner passed the Senate measure through the House; 144 Republicans voted against it. The vote reflected what everyone knew. The deal, as one conservative put it, was a "goose egg... we got nothing." Boehner did not try to deny it. To his members assembled in a conference room in the Capitol's basement, he said, "We fought the good fight, we just didn't win." The only upside was that those on the right "had to have learned something from all of this... they saw their leaders fully engaged in the fight."[114] Perhaps now, they would trust him enough to let him do his job.

Walking Away

But the Speaker's asymmetric conference afforded him little peace. In early 2014, the chamber's most strident conservatives cut ties with the RSC, believing it was "no longer just [home to] the hard-core right wingers." As one departing member observed, "When working with likeminded people, you need something... that doesn't dilute its positions because of the size of the group."[115] Determined to keep their group "pure" where the RSC had not, the lawmakers adopted an invitation-only policy for new members and strict rules to govern how they would vote. They dubbed their new outfit the "House Freedom Caucus" on the belief that "it was so generic and so universally awful that... [there was] no reason to be against it."[116]

Although the conservatives' collaborative mechanisms were new, their aims remained the same. They wanted Republicans to advance conservative legislation on issues like taxation, welfare, and healthcare, and they wanted Boehner replaced with someone more tractable or sympathetic to their cause. Notwithstanding these shared ambitions, they divided over how aggressively to pursue their goals. Jordan, now de facto leader of the breakaway group, urged his colleagues to give the Speaker a chance; with his cooperation, it would be far easier to win over the rest of the conference. And if Boehner consistently bowed to moderate pressure or prioritized cutting deals with Senate Democrats, they would have ample ammunition to lobby potential allies in the Republican conference and entice a suitable candidate to run against him.

Meadows disagreed. Having made a name for himself in the 2013 shutdown fight, he was on the lookout for new opportunities to share the stage with more senior conservative heavyweights. He struck in the summer of 2015. Giving his colleagues only a few days' warning, Meadows filed a motion to vacate the chair with the House clerk in late July, days before Republicans were set to head home for the August recess. Win or lose, Meadows reasoned, *he* would come out ahead. If Boehner decided to hold a vote immediately, the Speaker might survive, but Meadows would burnish his antiestablishment credentials. And if by some miracle the Speaker lost, Meadows would get the credit.

Little did he know that Boehner had been planning for such an eventuality and had secured Pelosi's assurances that she would help him keep his post, should he need it. By voting "present," House Democrats would ensure that Boehner could prevail over any challenger with a simple majority of Republican votes cast. But the Speaker did not view the strategy as a fail-safe. Relying on Democratic votes would further enrage his conservative faction, and the turmoil that followed "would do irreparable harm to the institution." Moderate Republicans were unsparing. "You keep feeding the crocodiles and hope they're going to eat you last," they told Boehner. "But, see, they're still hungry."[117] Surprising nearly everyone—his leadership team, his conference, even Obama—the Speaker announced that he would relinquish his post and depart Congress at the end of October.

Aftershocks

In stepping down, Boehner thought he could "protect the institution of the speaker" and save his party from "prolonged leadership turmoil."[118] But House Republicans' continuing asymmetry meant his successors would face similar constraints. Ryan, Boehner's grudging replacement, was initially optimistic about his prospects. Sympathetic to some of the conservatives' policy goals—and believing, along with many on the right, that voters wanted "really clear choices"—he expressed confidence that he could forge a more productive relationship with the Freedom Caucus than Boehner had.[119] "The last thing we should do," he assured his right flank, "is point . . . our guns at each other."[120]

Eager to prove that he could be a more faithful ally than his predecessor, Ryan tacked hard to the right, announcing that his first priority as Speaker would be to repeal and replace the ACA. But as details of Ryan's replacement plan emerged, the Freedom Caucus loudly panned the proposal as "Obamacare lite" and vowed to oppose it.[121] Unable to muster a floor majority without the faction's support, the new Speaker went back to the drawing board. Edging out the committee chairs who had helped draft the original proposal, he invited the Freedom Caucus to revise the measure as its members saw fit. The Freedom Caucus's bill, which was far more sweeping than the one Ryan had initially envisioned, drew swift criticism from moderate Republicans, who worried their constituents were unlikely to appreciate the rollback in coverage the new proposal imagined. But lacking their rivals' reputation for collective action, their complaints did little to soften the legislative language. Faced with the choice of accepting the conservatives' preferred measure or voting to maintain the status quo, they gave in—just as Ryan and the Freedom Caucus had predicted they would.

When the conference turned to tax reform, little changed. Intent on avoiding another confrontation with conservatives, Ryan took pains to confirm at the outset that his tax plan would not cross any of the Freedom Caucus's "red lines." Satisfied, the group announced that most of its members were "lean[ing] yes . . . with the caveat that there is still much work that needs to be done."[122] Moderates, however, were unwilling to take a position either in support of or opposition to the plan. Said the chair of the Tuesday Group, "We haven't really gotten into [it] to the degree that I'm willing to stake out a position."[123] But having failed to take a position, moderates quickly found themselves excluded from subsequent negotiations, and their absence meant that Ryan had little choice but to partner with his right flank to notch the much-needed win.

As his speakership wore on, however, Ryan found it increasingly difficult to keep conservatives satisfied. Whenever they believed the Speaker had strayed too far from their own position, members of the Freedom Caucus—often backed by the Trump administration—threatened to withhold their support and vowed that Ryan would suffer "consequences."[124] Tired of pursuing a strategy of conciliation, Ryan in 2019 followed Boehner into retirement rather than work to rebalance the party's factional configuration. Given the growing friction between the Speaker and the Freedom Caucus, few House Republicans were particularly surprised, least of all the Tuesday Group: "We can all read between the lines . . . you don't have a lot of speakers surrendering power and walking away."[125]

Not every Speaker gets the chance to walk away, however. Ryan's eager successor, California's Kevin McCarthy, found it even harder than his predecessors to navigate the party's pronounced asymmetry. Burdened by a razor-thin majority, McCarthy was forced to accept nearly all the

Freedom Caucus's procedural and policy demands to secure the votes he needed to win the office in the first place (on a record-setting fifteenth ballot).[126] Having gotten the job, his task did not become any easier—though not for lack of trying. Like Ryan, the new Speaker was optimistic that skillful "member management" could prevent a mutiny on the right.[127] But yet another fight to secure a government funding deal would test his faith in that strategy.

Committed to keeping his right flank happy, McCarthy worked closely with the Freedom Caucus to draft a funding bill he knew would have little chance of becoming law. As one member involved in the process recalled, "Essentially, the leadership just picked up the House Freedom Caucus plan and helped us convert it into the legislative text."[128] By catering to conservatives on the front end, the Speaker hoped they would be willing to accept whatever he was able to extract on the back end during negotiations with the White House and congressional Democrats.

He was wrong. When word got out that a deal with the Biden administration was in the offing, members of the Freedom Caucus immediately called for the Speaker's removal, even as some acknowledged that the bargain McCarthy had struck represented "a directional shift" rightward. "It is inescapable," they told reporters. "It has to be done."[129] In a final bid to forestall the mutiny, McCarthy sought to defend his actions. In a conference-wide meeting he told members, "I do not regret negotiating; our government is designed to find compromise."[130] But a majority of Freedom Caucus members disagreed. "McCarthy . . . is somebody who we cannot trust," they warned. "We need a speaker who will fight for something, anything besides just staying or becoming speaker."[131]

Without a clear way to appease his right flank, McCarthy turned for the first time to Republican moderates. Perhaps they could help buy him enough time to renegotiate a truce. But lacking the conservatives' collaborative capacity, their efforts to persuade sympathetic Democrats to join them in the effort to save McCarthy came to little. Their would-be allies expressed skepticism that moderate Republicans would (or could) deliver on their promises to move bipartisan bills to the floor or negotiate more favorable committee ratios in return for minority party support.[132] Hemmed in by an ascendant conservative faction on his right and lacking the ballast of an equally capable moderate faction on his left, McCarthy found himself unceremoniously dumped—the first Speaker to be formally removed in the history of the House, though likely not the last.

Conclusion

It is understandable why House conservatives have been treated as primarily, and often solely, responsible for their party's repeated leadership shake-ups. The prevailing wisdom reflects a fundamental reality: dating back to the Gingrich–led Republican revolution, those on the party's right have adopted a variety of institutional practices that have empowered them to battle party leaders and win, notwithstanding their relatively small numbers. In isolation, however, these collaborative choices were not sufficient to assure conservatives such outsize influence. As we have seen, it also mattered that the right's increasingly sophisticated efforts to work together went unchallenged by their moderate peers. Time and again throughout the 2010s, moderate Republicans in the House failed to ramp up their collaborative activities or pursue their aims collectively. And conservatives were the net beneficiaries, as the absence of competition magnified their organizational capacity and conferred on them significant power to shape legislative outcomes—even where their wants diverged from those of leadership.

This relational understanding of conservative power has direct implications for our present politics. For those eager to restore the GOP to the more constructive factional equilibrium characteristic of earlier eras (or who simply wish to weaken the grip of the party's hard-liners) this book's diagnosis of the present state of Republican politics offers potentially good news. If, as the relational dynamic suggests, moderates have agency—if they can simply *choose* to collectively resist their more conservative colleagues—it is critical to encourage and aid them in that work. Implementing tried-and-true organizational techniques is surely easier to carry out than the difficult, if not impossible, task of persuading hard-liners to tack to the center. Promoting moderate collaboration is also likely to have productive downstream effects. In a more symmetric conference, we would expect that Republican leaders, too, would exercise greater power.

But there is reason for concern. It is plausible, perhaps even likely, that the collaborative imbalance between conservative and moderate factions is self-reinforcing, as conservatives have used their influence within the conference to devalue the moderate brand and impugn the virtues of bipartisanship and compromise. As one former leadership staffer put it, "There's no benefit to compromise. And if there is compromise, the willingness to vote for those things isn't there. Nobody wants to be accused of being a traitor, or be seen waving the white flag."[133] Because working together more overtly is likely to raise moderates' collective profile, it risks exposing them to greater criticism from colleagues, donors, and voters for deviating from the now-regnant conservative party orthodoxy.

Nor do moderates have the luxury of experimenting with collaborative mechanisms in a factional vacuum. Given their organizational head start, conservatives possess powerful institutional weapons to combat their rivals' nascent collaborative efforts. In practical terms, this means that creating the conditions for a fairer factional fight cannot wait. If moderates are to stand a chance, they must get their organizational act together—and soon.

CHAPTER FIVE

How Tip O'Neill Lost the Budget Battle but Won the Public Relations War

The 1980 election left little doubt that the Democratic Party was adrift. Frustrated by persistently high inflation and skyrocketing energy costs, voters handed Republicans control of the Senate for the first time in a generation. And despite holding on to their House majority, Democrats saw it shrink by nearly three dozen seats. Worse still, the party lost the White House in spectacular fashion, with Ronald Reagan beating out Jimmy Carter in all but five states. Heralding the maturation of a newly ascendant conservative coalition—a fusion of libertarian ideals, anticommunist rhetoric, and mobilized evangelical Protestantism—Reagan's victory raised questions as to whether the nation was on the precipice of a major electoral realignment. As the *New York Times* concluded, "[Democrats are] finally . . . out of gas. . . . The programs and philosophy that . . . sustained [the party] for a quarter of a century have ceased to work."[1]

Blame there was aplenty. Taking stock of their record under Carter, liberal and conservative Democrats in Congress offered dueling prescriptions for restoring their national majority. Framing Carter's loss as retribution for his embrace of the political center, liberal lawmakers urged incumbent Speaker Tip O'Neill—now the nation's most prominent Democrat and de facto leader—to conduct a "righteous scorched-earth campaign" against Reagan's proposed agenda.[2] The party, they felt, had lost its soul. And having betrayed the popular legacy of the New Deal and Great Society, Democrats were punished at the polls. The chamber's conservatives, by contrast, championed accommodation, believing that Reagan's victory exposed traditional liberalism's pathologies to devastating effect. As one

Texas Democrat recalled, "We [like most Americans] agreed that the tax system needed to be reformed . . . and that the Great Society programs should be cut back and eliminated."[3]

The terrain on which this factional debate would be waged was quite different from the one that had shaped the party's epic battles over civil rights in the 1950s and 1960s. As was true then, the party's liberal wing still hailed from the North and West, while the party's conservatives represented mostly southern constituencies. But by 1980, the liberals' numerical superiority was unquestioned. The passage of the 1964 Civil Rights Act and the 1965 Voting Rights Act occasioned not only the incorporation of formerly disenfranchised southern Black voters into the Democratic Party but also the exit of many conservative white southerners. That broad-scale political realignment left a rump constituency of approximately fifty conservative lawmakers in a caucus nearly five times that size. The party's right flank had been weakened in other ways as well. Most importantly, the 1974 post-Watergate midterms swept into office a "conquering army" of brash liberal reformers eager to take down the southern committee barons who had for decades stood in the way of liberal priorities.[4]

Notwithstanding their diminished numbers, conservatives' collaborative efforts would soon exceed those of their liberal colleagues. Determined to act as a unified bloc against their more numerous foes, they formed the Conservative Democratic Forum (CDF) in November 1980. Popularly known as the "Boll Weevils" in recognition of members' rural constituencies and disruptive tendencies, the CDF aimed to facilitate conservative efforts to "moderate the liberal leanings of the House leadership" and ensure its members a decisive role in chamber policymaking.[5] Liberals, by contrast, found themselves split between an older generation of dyed-in-the-wool New Dealers, a younger group of lawmakers who tended to emphasize the efficient (and not just the generous) provision of social services, and a cadre of more mainstream members eager to work with leadership to advance popular liberal priorities.[6] Thus divided, the party's left wing abandoned the institutions and organizing mechanisms that had once facilitated their collective action and brought them significant influence in the House.[7]

Predictably, O'Neill struggled to navigate this asymmetric factional configuration. As we will see, in his first major confrontation with the Reagan White House, the Speaker stood by as nearly three dozen Boll Weevils joined the Republican minority to enact the president's budget plan. O'Neill's apparent unwillingness to take a hard line in negotiations with Reagan, and his subsequent failure to discipline those Democrats who had backed the president, infuriated the party's liberal majority. Their outrage was understandable. Although increasingly "portly [and] white-haired," O'Neill was well versed in the art of legislative dealmaking and had demonstrated a knack for keeping southerners in line earlier in his speakership.[8] Yet here, liberals complained, the Speaker had effectively ceded control of the House to his right flank. Stranger still was what O'Neill *did* do. Turning away from the backroom politics that had guided his ascent to the speakership, he chose to battle the charismatic Reagan on television—a medium even his allies doubted would get him what he wanted.

Why, despite the backing of an increasingly liberal caucus, did the Speaker hesitate to turn the screws on those Democrats who had pledged their allegiance to Reagan? And why, at the very moment when Democrats' growing ideological homogeneity should have cemented his control over the legislative process, did O'Neill choose instead to wage a public relations campaign against a president whose communication skills were unrivaled?

To answer these questions, it is necessary to take stock of the factional configuration O'Neill encountered. Notwithstanding the advantages of his party's leftward shift, the collaborative asymmetries between liberals and conservatives substantially limited O'Neill's range of motion. As we will see, the Boll Weevils' sustained efforts to collaborate made them less vulnerable to threats of discipline and neutralized the Speaker's informational and procedural advantages. Unable to rely on House liberals to counter conservative Democrats' organizational might, the self-described "progressive liberal" was compelled to leverage his own standing as the implicit leader of the opposition to battle Reagan outside Congress.[9] It is ironic, then, that what O'Neill and others believed to be a second-best strategy proved quite so effective. Going head-to-head with the telegenic Reagan, the plain-spoken Speaker convinced the nation that the president's economic program was both dangerous and fundamentally unkind.[10] In the process, he elevated the profile and prestige of the speakership for a new century of political combat.

Reexamining a Transitional Figure

Although O'Neill was often described by colleagues as guileless—a "what-you-see-is-what-you-get kind of person"— his political biography reflects considerable political sophistication.[11] First elected to Congress in 1952,

O'Neill initially played the faithful scion of Boston's Irish Catholic political machine, the natural heir to John F. Kennedy's House seat. The young O'Neill understood that, in exchange for a seat on the powerful Rules Committee, his job was to serve as loyal lieutenant to Majority Leader (and, later, Speaker) John McCormack—"my man on the committee," as O'Neill's fellow Bostonian put it.[12] Despite his northern ties, the affable O'Neill soon earned the trust of the committee's senior southerners, becoming an effective liaison between the Democratic Party's conservative and liberal factions. A decade into his tenure, these skills would make him an important ally of Lyndon Johnson's presidential administration.[13]

But O'Neill was no ordinary machine politician or party lackey. Defying the counsel of his legislative patrons, he renounced his support for the Vietnam War in 1967, a move that prompted Johnson to accuse him of giving in to "all those guys at Harvard Square."[14] That decision proved critical to his subsequent political fortunes. O'Neill's early opposition to the war earned him the respect of the party's growing liberal faction, while his roots in right-leaning machine politics ensured the continued approbation of the party's powerful, if shrinking, conservative flank. Leveraging his status as a reliable factional intermediary to claim the post of party whip in 1970, O'Neill played an essential role in helping Democrats navigate the choppy waters of institutional reform. Like Nancy Pelosi several decades later, O'Neill was a firm believer in party responsibility. Faithful to these principles, he aided more progressive (and largely junior) colleagues by sponsoring their proposal to require secret-ballot votes for committee chair positions.[15] And yet, he consistently kept his distance from the party's liberal wing. Older than many of his new allies, O'Neill found their aggressive tactics anathema to his own more collegial approach. His core political instinct—"to take advantage of an association with the reformers without alienating the elder statesmen of the old regime"—proved impeccable.[16] Only six years after joining the leadership, O'Neill became Speaker by acclamation after Oklahoma's Carl Albert announced his retirement.

Much like the man himself, O'Neill's legacy has proven difficult to define. The first cohort of scholars to evaluate his time in office tended to cast him as the last of the "textbook" Speakers—a leader who favored compromise and backroom deals to achieve his ends.[17] Writing in 1980, Joseph Cooper and David Brady observed that O'Neill presided over a fractionalized caucus and so relied on a "highly personal, informal, permissive, and ad hoc" approach to leadership.[18] In consequence, they predicted,

O'Neill was unlikely to be an especially strong leader in the long run. This characterization mirrored the general perception of the Speaker by his contemporaries on Capitol Hill. As senior aides recalled, O'Neill was not a "strong-armer." His methods of "persuasion [were] very soft" and he "only took stands where there was consensus."[19]

A decade later, with O'Neill having transformed the public-facing role of his office, a new generation of scholars evaluated his legacy afresh, characterizing him as the first in a line of increasingly powerful modern Speakers. As David Rohde's landmark study of the postreform House highlighted, O'Neill presided over a homogenizing (if not yet fully homogeneous) party caucus that delegated to the Speaker considerably more formal authority than his predecessors ever possessed.[20] Thanks to reform efforts championed by the Democrats' liberal faction, O'Neill had the power, among other things, to play a more direct role in committee assignments (including appointments to the Rules Committee), make multiple committee referrals, and deploy restrictive rules to structure floor debate.[21] But O'Neill was not simply in the right place at the right time. He understood that Congress was changing and was prepared to change with it. He was, as Steven Smith describes, "an old-style politician who realized that the post-reform House called for a new style of leadership."[22] For this reason, O'Neill is often credited with "revitaliz[ing]" the speakership and thereby demonstrating the newfound power of the office.[23] It was O'Neill who brought the speakership "cautiously into the brave new world" forged by reform, creating a strong precedent for subsequent leaders on both sides of the aisle to exercise ever more control over House proceedings.[24]

Clearly, both accounts have merit. O'Neill *did* enjoy enhanced procedural prerogatives that far outstripped what any Speaker in the textbook Congress possessed. At the same time, it is undeniable that, in his first great confrontation with a partisan adversary in the White House, he failed to marshal those prerogatives to hold his balkanized caucus together. As this chapter argues, making sense of these seeming contradictions requires attending to the collaborative dimension of party divisions. As we will see, O'Neill's early losses to Reagan and his subsequent decision to "go public" resulted from the organizational ascendance of conservative Democrats and the concurrent decline of House liberals.[25] Indeed, the Speaker's access to a wide range of leadership instruments proved of little value in a political context marked by the liberals' collaborative lassitude and the conservatives' corresponding vigor. And so, recognizing the limits of his parliamentary authority, O'Neill turned outward, adopting an extrinsic public relations strategy that sought to exploit his standing as the nation's best-known Democrat.

From this vantage, O'Neill is a critical link in the speakership's evolution for reasons scholars have largely overlooked. The relative collaborative dominance of conservative factions in both parties—among the Democrats, first the CDF and later the Blue Dog Coalition; among the Republicans, first the Republican Study Committee and then the House Freedom Caucus—has been a fact of life for the past forty years. Against this backdrop, O'Neill's tenure is particularly notable because he was the first modern legislative leader to grapple with conditions that are now routine: a party leader granted considerable procedural power and privileged to preside over a homogenizing party caucus, who nevertheless proved unable to keep his troops in line because of his party's asymmetry.

Alternative Explanations

As in previous chapters, it is worth pausing to consider other explanations that might account for the developments described in the pages that follow. Perhaps the most obvious alternative appeals to "stark arithmetic."[26] As virtually every history of the budget fight makes plain, O'Neill's majority in 1980 was a relatively narrow one, at least in comparison to those enjoyed by previous Democratic Speakers. With only fifty votes to spare, O'Neill was vulnerable to threats of defection from the forty-member CDF. As one House Democrat said at the time, "Tip's got no control. He's got 180 votes and that's it."[27]

But arithmetic alone cannot explain O'Neill's deference to the Boll Weevils or his decision to abandon a floor fight and instead wage a public relations war with Reagan. For one reason, simply possessing the requisite votes did not assure the conservatives their leverage. Rather, the conservatives were pivotal because they bargained and defected collectively, a tactic made possible by the CDF's organizational efforts. Having institutionalized their collaboration, the Boll Weevils were able to resist O'Neill's entreaties and bargain directly with the White House. For another reason, the CDF's numerical might did not consistently deter the Speaker from sanctioning dissenters. When, for instance, the conservatives succeeded in rolling Democratic leaders on a procedural vote in the summer of 1980, O'Neill announced that he would oust two of the most senior defectors from their committee posts. "Those things," an observer commented, "get around" and the Speaker soon secured the culprits' assurance of future loyalty. In fact, even as the budget fight brewed, many House Democrats believed O'Neill fully capable of using his authority to hold the CDF in line and expressed frustration when he did not.[28] Nor is it clear why the Speaker did not attempt to solicit the support of liberal Republicans to offset conservative opposition within his own party, as he had done to good effect during Carter's presidency.[29] In short, understanding O'Neill's apparent inability (or unwillingness) to wage a successful floor campaign against the administration's budget plan requires more in the way of explanation than simply counting heads.

A related possibility is that the ideological overlap between the Boll Weevils and House Republicans was so significant that no amount of pressure could have averted passage of the budget bill. On this account, the combination of low polarization and "deep regional and ideological divisions" within the Democratic majority hamstrung O'Neill before he even got out of the gate.[30] But this account is difficult to square with the reality that House Democrats were trending toward greater interregional convergence. The steady exodus of southern conservatives from the Democratic Party meant that those southerners who chose to remain largely resembled their nonsouthern colleagues. As Lawrence Dodd and Bruce Oppenheimer observe, "since the full implementation of the Voting Rights Act, southern Democratic House members [became] more ideologically diverse; they [were] not all conservatives."[31] Representing economically struggling, largely rural districts, these lawmakers "did not necessarily see government as the enemy" as Republicans did, but instead believed it to be an engine of progress.[32] As one southerner explained, "Even conservative [Democrats] draw lines with Republicans. We believe that government has an obligation to help people less fortunate than we are."[33]

Across the aisle, Reagan's advisors were quick to acknowledge this ideological gap, underscoring how difficult it was to "construct . . . and hold . . . together a coalition that included a significant bloc of Democrats . . . prepared to defect."[34] Nor, for that matter, was there strong support among congressional Republicans for Reagan's bipartisan outreach. "If I were Reagan, I wouldn't have a thing to do with these guys," one conservative lawmaker told reporters. "You look at their districts, those ought to be Republican seats. I would say they can go ahead, vote with Tip, and then we'll go into every one of their districts . . . [and] elect a Republican. . . . And we'll have a majority in the next Congress."[35] Moderate Republicans, dubbed the "Gypsy Moths" by their peers, were no happier with Reagan's decision to seek votes across the aisle, complaining that "[southern] Democrats want to increase domestic spending . . . and Ronald Reagan [is going] along with it."[36]

A third possibility is that the president's immense popularity cowed House Democrats, leaving O'Neill without strong backing to confront the White House. Barbara Sinclair, for instance, notes that "many Democratic House members read the election returns as a signal that their constituents demanded support for the Reagan program." In consequence, she argues, "there was no way in which the Democratic leadership could defeat Reagan," regardless of how skillfully the leadership deployed its considerable resources.[37] But Reagan's own advisors doubted his ability to intimidate congressional Democrats, counseling him to "go forward expeditiously, while . . . at the height of your influence." Likewise, there is little evidence that most House Democrats sought to avoid confrontation with the White House. Quite the opposite. When O'Neill shied away from conflict—refusing, for instance, to delay consideration of Reagan's budget plan—he was pilloried by his party's rank and file. As a fellow member of the Massachusetts delegation recalled, "He was getting the shit kicked out of him."[38] With many House Democrats spoiling for a fight, it is hard to explain why O'Neill, either in concert with the CDF or backed by the caucus's sizable liberal faction, did not do more to blunt Reagan's agenda or reshape it into something the party could get behind.

Conservatives on the Defensive

By the late 1970s, conservative Democrats in the House were a downtrodden lot. Theirs had been a long fall from grace. Beginning in the 1960s, liberal Democrats had successfully weakened the seniority system (which disproportionately benefited long-serving southern members) and, together with party leaders, reanimated the Democratic caucus as an instrument for control.[39] The consequences of these efforts for conservative Democrats were catastrophic. In 1975, with incoming committee chairs newly subject to approval by a caucus majority, three southerners who had collectively served for more than a century lost their chair positions outright; a fourth—George Mahon of Texas, who had entered Congress at the height of the Great Depression—eked out the slimmest of victories.[40] These "seniority violations had a profound impact . . . greatly reduc[ing] the influence and independence of [mostly southern] committee chairmen" and obliterating the most important source of conservative power in the House.⁴¹

Other reforms pushed in the same direction. As party leaders gained direct authority over appointments to the Rules Committee—and with the power to make other committee assignments delegated to a newly constituted Steering and Policy Committee staffed by liberal members—conservatives saw their influence wane.⁴² Acknowledging the shifting power dynamics within the Democratic caucus, O'Neill recalled that "in those years," he and fellow party leaders "paid no attention to . . . the conservatives. We felt that there was no need."⁴³

Electoral changes wrought by the passage of civil rights legislation compounded the conservatives' difficulties.⁴⁴ Most important, the Civil Rights Act of 1964 and the Voting Rights Act of 1965 helped revive the Republican Party in the South after many decades of dormancy under Jim Crow. Exploiting southern whites' alarm at the Democratic Party's embrace of civil rights, Republicans began to mobilize them by emphasizing their own racial conservatism. As one House Republican explained, "We saw the southern conservatism emerging and took advantage of it."⁴⁵ Accordingly, the region's Democratic representatives—long accustomed to limited competition in low-turnout party primaries—now had to win general elections against high-quality foes with popular appeal.⁴⁶ In addition, the creation of majority-minority districts throughout the former Confederacy brought a new cadre of more liberal Black lawmakers to Capitol Hill, further thinning the ranks of conservative southern Democrats.⁴⁷

Though they had long been their party's institutional innovators, conservative Democrats did not redouble their efforts to collaborate. Just the opposite. The organizational infrastructure that had once structured their collective action in the aftermath of the Supreme Court's 1954 *Brown v. Board of Education* decision fell into disuse in the years following the party's great civil rights battles.⁴⁸

Little would change in the 1970s. When it came to the party's embrace of institutional reform, conservative Democrats never matched their liberal colleagues' collaborative momentum—best illustrated by their inability to forestall the unseating of long-standing southern committee chairs. On policy, these same dynamics obtained. Early in his speakership, for example, O'Neill was charged with shepherding an energy package through the House.⁴⁹ In selecting the members of an ad hoc committee he had established for that very purpose, the Speaker "quietly short-changed the [southern] oil-producing states," privileging "flexible wheeler-dealers ... over industry champions."[50] Absent collaboration, the southerners were largely passive witnesses to O'Neill's legislative savvy, as the Speaker muscled the measure through the House with the help of his liberal allies.

Nor was O'Neill averse to deploying the power of his office, at one point dramatically "bang[ing] a quick gavel" to defeat a measure favored by southerners and their Republican allies "as soon as he saw a majority in his favor."[51] In consequence, as their "numerical strength ... decreased, and as the electoral potency of the Republican party in the South grew," the conservative faction simply "became more and more frustrated," believing "that their voice was being ignored within the party."[52] As one member recalled, the liberals "thought they had these overwhelming numbers and could shove things down [the conservatives'] throat."[53] Or, as another lamented, "We've been treated like stepchildren."[54]

Liberal Infighting

Liberals, by contrast, seemed poised to dominate Democratic politics for years to come. Encouraged by their civil rights victories and emboldened by conservative losses, they set out to wage a coordinated attack on the "House establishment," believing that the committee system and many party rules were "owned lock, stock, and barrel by the conservative coalition of Republicans and southern Democrats." "We got into reform," one liberal aide recalled, "because it became very apparent that the deck was stacked against us and we had to unstack it."[55]

Determined to undermine the institutional levers that empowered a dwindling number of conservatives to intervene in party politics, the liberals turned to the organization that had brought them victory on civil rights: the Democratic Study Group (DSG). As it had then, the DSG served as the liberals' think tank, incubating a variety of proposals to reduce the power of the southern minority and "reinvigorate" the majority party caucus.[56] So too, the DSG provided substantial organizational muscle, whipping liberals to turn out for caucus votes on reforms that would weaken their southern opponents and "foster collective control" over the House.[57] Reflecting the liberals' pronounced collaborative advantage at the time, one observer remarked, "In the old days, the DSG was viewed as a band of Young Turks. Now its leaders are matured legislators with a sense of how power relationships work."[58]

And yet, House liberals' successful pursuit of institutional reform concealed growing dissent within their ranks. Perhaps the biggest challenge was the sheer size and diversity of the party's left wing. Bolstered by Democratic gains in the 1974 midterms, the DSG amassed nearly 225 dues-paying members by the mid-1970s, nearly three-quarters of the party caucus.[59] With such large numbers, differences in opinion and outlook soon cleaved the organization. Many of the DSG's founding members—lawmakers who remained committed to New Deal and Great Society–style interventions—continued to represent a powerful force within the liberal faction and the Democratic Party at large. As Rohde notes, these long-serving members shared a "preference for a large, activist federal government" and benefited disproportionately from a key reform: the devolution of committee power to congressional subcommittees, where their senior status afforded them the lion's share of authority.[60]

But old-school liberals were no longer the undisputed leaders of the party's left flank. The post-Watergate midterms heralded the arrival of a new generation of reformist, efficiency-minded lawmakers often critical of what they perceived to be their elders' "spend first" attitude. As Senator Gary Hart of Colorado declared, "We are not a bunch of little Hubert Humphreys."[61] A generation younger than many of the dyed-in-the-wool New Dealers, these "Watergate babies" viewed themselves as avatars of a new style of politics—one forged in the ferment of the 1960s-era counterculture rather than the smoky backrooms of party meeting halls. One member of the "Class of '74" recalled, "We were young. We looked weird. I can't even believe we got elected." This new cadre of reformers declared themselves eager to sweep away the "cronyism and parochialism" they believed had disabled the legislative branch and enlarged the power of the presidency. Numerous enough to constitute their own "class" and hire their own staff, the newcomers saw it as their mission to dismantle institutional practices like the seniority system they felt prevented Congress from addressing issues like healthcare, energy, and the environment that disproportionately motivated younger American voters.[62]

Still a third cohort of liberals, together with Louisiana's Gillis Long, then chair of the Democratic Caucus, founded a new organization known as the United Democrats of Congress (UDC).[63] "A loosely knit alliance" of mostly liberal members who resented the Watergate babies' individualism and influence within the DSG, the UDC's stated mission was to "strengthen the vital center of the Democratic Party."[64] But the group was little more than a front for Long's own ambitions. Under its aegis, he urged liberal Democrats to embrace party regularity and further elevate the Democratic Caucus as the center of party decision making.

Their ranks fragmenting, House liberals struggled to work together.[65] Absent the "glue" of civil rights and institutional reform, a "proliferation of specialized caucuses" like the Congressional Black Caucus and UDC diluted the liberals' numerical might and collaborative energy. As Julian Zelizer writes, the liberals largely "reverted to their habit . . . of emphasizing the parts rather than the whole."[66] Buffeted by these centrifugal forces and spurred by the entreaties of Long and others in the Democratic Caucus who were eager to co-opt the DSG, the group officially shifted course in the summer of 1977.[67] The organization would now focus "entirely . . . on providing research materials designed to brief—rather than lobby—Members on issues on which they must vote."[68] Only two years after orchestrating the downfall of southern committee barons, the DSG had abandoned the project of coordinating self-consciously liberal activity in the House.

Party Asymmetry and the Rise of the Conservative Democratic Forum

As the threads binding the liberal faction continued to fray, Reagan's election as president in 1980 galvanized conservative Democrats to organize anew. Their collaboration began with a series of conversations. "Seven or eight fellows would sit together during roll calls, toward the back of the House, [and] we'd have a cup of coffee during a break and talk about how disappointed we were with the way things were going," one conservative recalled. "Gradually [we] came [to] the idea, why not have an informal group? Maybe we could put pressure on the leadership."[69] In the fall of that year, those frustrated conservatives agreed to join forces for the long haul, establishing what they called the Conservative Democratic Forum.[70] The group, as one participant recalled, was "formed out of frustration, more than anything else," and their overriding intent was "to get the leadership's attention.'"[71]

Informally dubbed the "Boll Weevils," the group's membership was keenly aware that Republican gains in the House meant that collectively they were likely to be pivotal to legislative outcomes. As their de facto leader Charlie Stenholm of Texas explained, "It suddenly became very obvious that we could possibly affect the course of legislation."[72] Meeting with O'Neill and his leadership team shortly after Reagan's victory, Stenholm scolded the Speaker for taking conservative cooperation for granted. Presenting statistical analyses detailing conservative underrepresentation on key committees, Stenholm demanded that O'Neill offer CDF members better assignments and an additional seat on the party's Steering and Policy Committee. He also urged the Speaker to devote more room on the legislative agenda for "moderate" legislation.[73]

The Speaker, who had never before met with the party's conservatives as a group, privately acknowledged that the bargaining dynamic had changed. The CDF, O'Neill observed, "organized on the theory that the squeaky wheel gets the grease."[74] Their liberal counterparts, by contrast, evidenced "a lot of idealism and not much concern for production."[75] Indeed, the conservative group possessed many of the hallmarks of structured legislative collaboration. Although the CDF did not name a formal leader, Stenholm was its undisputed point man. As one legislative aide to Reagan recalled, "Stenholm was the one who corralled these guys. Stenholm was the one we would talk to about who we should go after."[76] The office of Mississippi's Gillespie "Sonny" Montgomery served as the CDF's "war room." And reflecting their solidarity, "members even committed to wearing a boll-weevil tie and pin."[77] Although the group did not bind members to specific policy positions, the CDF held regular meetings to discuss issues and work out common positions, reflecting members' explicit commitment to establishing a forum for debate.[78] "The whole purpose," one conservative explained, "is to determine whether there is anything we can do to . . . exercise . . . our maximum potential. Do we have access to all the information we need? Should we coordinate our activities better?"[79] Their organizational investment soon paid dividends, as party leaders agreed to appoint several CDF members to power committees. Almost overnight, one Capitol Hill observer noted, the CDF had become "the best organized and most cohesive of the informal groups on the Democratic side of the aisle."[80]

It was against this asymmetric factional backdrop that O'Neill and Reagan would battle over tax cuts and domestic spending. Although the Speaker presided over what appeared to be a healthy Democratic majority, conservatives' organizational momentum and liberals' increasing disorganization meant that, in truth, he had little leverage over his party's right flank. O'Neill knew what he wanted: "to resist the [president's] attack on key social programs, . . . to build his House majority in the 1982 election, and . . . to preserve his own power."[81] But he would prove unable to meet the challenge. Unlike Pelosi, O'Neill had no liberal army to help him bully his party's conservative bloc into submission. Instead, he would try, and ultimately fail, to deal with the CDF on his own.

Factional Asymmetry and the Battle over Reagan's Domestic Policy Agenda

With both parties' troops in position, the battle began. The White House moved first, proposing to cut more than $74 billion in federal spending and to significantly reduce both individual and corporate tax rates. Cognizant that the support of conservative Democrats would be critical to passing his spending plan, Reagan devoted considerable energy to lobbying members of the CDF—both individually and as a group. He made campaign-style appearances throughout the South, blanketed the region with radio and television advertising, and alongside his aides, spent hours cajoling members over the phone.[82] "We brought them down in droves to see the President in the Oval Office," Reagan's congressional liaison recalled. "We took them to the Kennedy Center presidential box and wined them and dined them. We took them up to Camp David for a weekend."[83] O'Neill understood the state of play. When a group of mostly conservative Democrats rose to applaud the president during his first congressional address, the Speaker whispered to Vice President George H. W. Bush, "Here's your forty votes."[84]

Phil Gramm of Texas, a CDF member and former economics professor, would play a key role in the conflict's denouement. Appointed to the Budget Committee over the reservations of many high-ranking Democrats, Gramm had promised Majority Leader (and fellow Texan) Jim Wright that he would support the committee's budget resolution on the House floor. Gramm, however, had secretly reneged on that commitment, working directly with senior administration officials to craft a substitute amendment.[85] When news of the amendment broke, liberal Democrats were apoplectic. O'Neill should have anticipated Gramm's duplicity, they groused, and the Speaker, who had opted to travel abroad on a long-scheduled diplomatic mission, should have been there to stop it. "He gave [the CDF defectors] a free ride," a New York Democrat told the press. "He should have called them in and said, 'If you're not with us on this, don't come into my office and ask for anything. . . . You know that chairmanship you're after. Forget it.'"[86] But absent the kind of structured collaboration that had made possible their assault on the seniority system, there was little the party's fragmented left wing could do but fulminate that O'Neill had "no game plan."[87]

Despite the efforts of Democratic leaders to "activate... every pressure group that we could," their internal whip counts made clear they had little chance of preventing conservative Democratic defections.[88] Acknowledging that he did not have the votes to block Gramm's proposal (dubbed Gramm-Latta to acknowledge its Republican cosponsor) on the floor—and critical of what he called a "telephone [lobbying] blitz like this nation has never seen"—the Speaker publicly conceded to the president.[89] "The congress goes with the will of the people, and the will of the people is to go along with the President. I know when to fight and when not to fight."[90] Privately, O'Neill raged. "He would stomp and rave and snort against [the CDF defectors] . . . threatening to run opponents against them in their districts [and] . . . withhold congressional campaign money."[91]

The party's factional asymmetry would soon deal O'Neill another painful loss. Consistent with the institutional machinery created by the Legislative Reorganization Act of 1970, the Gramm-Latta budget resolution represented a spending blueprint, with individual committees retaining jurisdiction over how to implement its goals. As liberal critics argued, this structure provided an opportunity for Reagan's newfound allies to have their cake and eat it too—that is, to vote to restore some of the most popular programs set to be cut while nevertheless claiming to have supported the president's budget. As one staffer put it, "We don't want these bastard Democrats who voted for Gramm-Latta to come in here and be able to vote for a couple of programs and be able to go home and say, 'See, I saved your impact aid.'"[92]

But when the administration proposed its own, more draconian, package implementing Gramm-Latta (known as "Gramm-Latta II" to distinguish it from the initial budget resolution, now called "Gramm-Latta I"), the CDF seized on a different opportunity: traditional legislative horse trading. As Reagan's congressional liaison recalled, "Being politicians, they saw an opportunity. 'Reagan wants my vote, I need some peanut subsidies, and if the vote became really crucial, they might give me those peanut subsidies.'"[93] As with Gramm-Latta I, the CDF held strong, coordinating efforts by conservatives to extract what they could from leaders on both sides of the aisle. O'Neill's efforts to "stroke . . . the boll weevils" sowed even more discord among his already divided liberal wing. While some appreciated the importance of securing the conservatives' support, others resented that doing so was necessary. Divided and disorganized, the liberals found themselves shut out of negotiations altogether.[94] In the end, Reagan's budget reconciliation bill narrowly passed the House, 217–211; twenty-nine Democratic defections had made the victory possible. "The Democratic cloakroom had all the earmarks of a tobacco auction," the chair of the Budget Committee observed, and the conservatives were the clear winners.[95]

The fight over Reagan's tax plan played out in similar fashion. As with the budget, the CDF's collaboration made it possible for the group to extract key policy concessions from the White House in exchange for members' agreement to break party ranks. Kent Hance of Texas—like Gramm, a member of the CDF whom O'Neill had appointed to the Budget Committee—declared that as long as the Reagan administration needed the group's votes, "we're a political faction that's going to have to be dealt with. . . . The only reason the White House called on our group is because we've got the swing vote."[96] Democratic leaders sought to respond with sweeteners of their own, offering tax cuts for independent oil producers in exchange for the CDF's support.[97] But Reagan ultimately outcompeted O'Neill's team. "The White House," suggested an industry publication, "developed its own Christmas tree version that matched [Democratic leaders] on most items and outdid [them] on breaks to oil and farm interests—the key to the Southern vote."[98]

As with the battles over the president's proposed budget, the Democrats' factional asymmetry created the structural conditions for the conservatives' success. Collaboration put the CDF's members at the center of a bidding war, while the liberals' inability to mobilize their forces as they had in the heyday of their struggles for civil rights and institutional reform rendered them largely marginal players. "For a change," Stenholm celebrated, "we're on the winning side of the votes." Taking stock of O'Neill's losses, one commenter observed that all the Speaker's "power, experience and resourcefulness were inadequate to the task of bringing to heel the renegade 'boll weevils' within his own party."[99]

A Speaker for the Small Screen

Humiliated by the twin losses, O'Neill retreated. Notwithstanding the range of procedural tools at his disposal—including greater control over the chamber's agenda and key committee appointments—he had failed to keep his party's conservative flank from backing Reagan's economic agenda. And though House liberals boasted superior numbers, their decision not to collaborate had left him without an effective counterweight. So while loath to leave the familiar tactics of House combat behind him, the Speaker could not deny that his asymmetric party demanded a change in strategy.

His career depended on it. As the *New York Times* grimly observed, "The suggestion that [O'Neill] may face a challenge for re-election as Speaker may be academic. Democrats in the House of Representatives may not be electing anything higher than a minority leader."[100] Congressional colleagues were no kinder. Impugning the Speaker's leadership, Long expressed "frustration" that House Democrats had "collapsed in the face of President Reagan's opposition and rhetoric."[101] Still others wondered aloud whether O'Neill's struggles were the result of his advanced age, questioning whether he had the mental acuity to keep up with the times. The Speaker, one member opined, was "a white-haired ghost of Congress past, struggling to adjust to the Reagan era like a dinosaur confronting evolution."[102]

Defying the counsel of his leadership team and his own instinct that "you never attack a man when he's as popular as this president," O'Neill decided to risk it all.[103] Declaring at a meeting of the House Democratic Caucus that "an old dog can learn new tricks if he wants to learn new tricks," he promised to "take off the gloves" and battle Reagan over the airwaves.[104] Abandoning the legislative arena, he would make the case directly to the nation that the president's domestic policy agenda had left most Americans worse off than they had been during the Carter years.[105] As O'Neill later described the strategy, "Somebody had to stand out there and stay with the basic creed of the Democratic Party, the concern for the needy and the handicapped and the golden ager. Somebody had to . . . stop being an apologist."[106]

But after a lifetime in Congress, cultivating a more television-friendly public persona would not be easy. When the Speaker agreed to appear on an ABC News program in the summer of 1981, it was not only his first network TV interview during Reagan's first term—it was his first network TV interview in three years.[107] O'Neill's longtime secretary recalled that he was "scared to death of [television]. . . . He was so afraid he would say something wrong. He was afraid of being embarrassed. He lacked confidence."[108]

In truth, the Speaker was an unlikely candidate for media success. Sixty-eight years old, he was six foot three inches tall and weighed nearly three hundred pounds. And as his newly minted communications advisor, future cable host Chris Matthews, described him, "Tip's already imposing self was topped with a head of hair that remained defiantly thick for his age and always sent dandruff flaking onto his giant shoulders."[109] O'Neill was conscious of these perceived deficiencies, "frequently worry[ing] about his appearance and just as frequently say[ing] so."[110] Worse still, O'Neill—though quick-witted in conversation—was wooden when delivering prepared remarks. Stiff and awkward, he was known to read press releases in their entirety, including the words "Statement of Thomas P. O'Neill, Jr." printed at the bottom of the page.[111] Television, colleagues feared, would make the Speaker appear old and out of touch.[112]

Those close to O'Neill also understood that he had a generational remove from television as a cultural presence. Instead of watching television, Matthews reflected, "[O'Neill] and his buddies were out at dinner every night. . . . The old-timers didn't appreciate the TV culture because they weren't in on it."[113] One lawmaker noted that O'Neill had "operated all these years in the back room, making deals. Now he [found] himself thrust out there on the point of controversy, and it's a very hard problem for him."[114]

Yet despite O'Neill's apparent limitations and private doubts about the wisdom of his new approach, the decision to go public proved to be a good one. On camera, it turned out, the Speaker's physical size and distinctive mane conveyed both warmth and political gravitas. A Republican congressman commented, "You put all the House members in a line and bring in a Martian to pick out the speaker, and the Martian goes straight to Tip. The girth, the breadth, the height, the whitest hair in the House. The man just looks like a speaker."[115] Whatever O'Neill lacked in charisma and polish, he made up for in authenticity. One member of the Democratic Caucus suggested that the Speaker's disheveled look provided a particularly effective contrast with the debonaire Reagan. "The Republicans thought they would take Mr. Smooth and Tip and show Tip as the old pol. But nowadays, I think people kind of like that old pol. They sense he's a fighter."[116] For Matthews's part, he came to believe that "this big, overweight guy with his shock of white hair had the goods in a way we just hadn't been seeing. The truth was, many people *liked* his looks. What was the Speaker of the House *supposed* to look like, anyway?"[117]

O'Neill's success was by no means assured. He and his staff took pains to smooth his transition from rumpled floor captain to media darling. Determined to match Reagan's apparent vitality on camera, the Speaker slimmed down and switched from his preferred powder blue suits to darker ensembles that sharpened his image on screen.[118] And to match the grandeur of the Oval Office and White House Rose Garden, where the president often gave his televised addresses, O'Neill insisted that his own media appearances take place at the House rostrum or in the Speaker's formal office. It was not wasted effort. As one Republican contemporary recalled, "All of a sudden it was Tip not just being in the Speaker's office . . . but taking the microphone and becoming the voice to challenge Ronald Reagan."[119] Years later, no less an authority than Newt Gingrich would observe that "if you were to study Tip . . . you saw a man who had learned a great deal about television as the dominant medium in the game."[120]

The Speakership, Transformed

It is often said that O'Neill's decision to go public modernized the speakership. His embrace of television "elevated the national visibility" of the institution and, with it, "the office's potential to articulate and establish the House's agenda."[121] His successors—perhaps most notably, Gingrich and Pelosi—would become well-known public figures themselves, dueling with presidents of the opposing party and serving as the targets of opposition campaigns. One of their number, Washington's Tom Foley, observed that while "[Sam] Rayburn could have walked down the streets . . . without anybody noticing him, Tip O'Neill couldn't do that, and it is very unlikely that any future Speaker will be anonymous to the country."[122] O'Neill also achieved significant short-term political gains, leveraging a downturn in the economy and growing doubts about whether the administration's optimistic budget projections had been made in good faith to increase the Democrats' House majority in the 1982 midterm elections by twenty-six seats.[123] And, as the Speaker's leverage improved, he managed some measure of retribution against the CDF, ultimately stripping Gramm of his post on the Budget Committee and denying other CDF claimants their requests to serve on power committees.[124]

Yet, while legislative scholars have been right to emphasize these institutional and policy consequences, the Speaker's media turn, coupled with his inability to manage his divided party, reveals an equally important developmental legacy. A short four years after his 1977 elevation to the Speakership, conservative Democrats—tired of taking their lumps at the hands of their liberal opponents and buoyed by the resurgence of mobilized conservatism in the country at large—renewed their efforts to collaborate, determined to benefit from the same collective strategies that had effectively magnified the power of southern conservatives a generation earlier. And despite the liberals' considerable achievements from the mid-1960s to the mid-1970s, they would prove unable to match this level of sustained cooperation. From this vantage, O'Neill's tenure marked the beginning of a pattern that has endured ever since: a legislative leader compelled to manage a resurgent conservative faction without the benefit of a similarly organized liberal flank.

While O'Neill is often grouped with his Democratic predecessors and successors in a line of increasingly potent leaders running from the compromising Rayburn to the czar-like Wright, the account developed here suggests he has more in common with a later generation of leaders, including John Boehner, Paul Ryan, Kevin McCarthy, and Mike Johnson. Like these latter-day Republican Speakers, O'Neill struggled to impose his will on his increasingly mobilized conservative faction. As Ronald Peters puts it, it was O'Neill's "fate . . . to bring his sharp political instincts and strong liberal views to office during a conservative period in American politics."[125] And like his Republican successors, the Speaker found himself adopting strategies to keep his rank and file in line that relied on nontraditional sources of leverage—most often, an appeal to the broader electorate, "an external strategy" that sought to "influence public opinion in members' districts as a way of getting their support on the House floor."[126]

So what can O'Neill's experience teach us about leading divided parties in the modern Congress? At a minimum, his turn away from traditional legislative politics suggests that contemporary congressional leaders who find themselves burdened by asymmetric factional configurations will find little recourse in the array of procedural prerogatives they now possess. O'Neill himself intuitively grasped this point. Despite enjoying considerably more institutional authority than his predecessors, he often commented on how different—and more constrained—his own tenure was than that of Rayburn. "Sam Rayburn," he reflected, "could do things that I could never think of doing today. He didn't know 20 guys in Congress, but he was an amazing power."[127]

Rather, as O'Neill's decision to adopt a public relations strategy makes clear, Speakers encountering asymmetric configurations may be compelled to seek alternatives to the exercise of traditional legislative authority. How effectively they will be able to identify and exploit these alternatives depends on a contingent array of structural and individual factors well beyond the scope of the analysis developed here. What we can say with confidence is that in O'Neill's case circumstances proved unexpectedly propitious for reasons largely unrelated to his party's asymmetry. By the fall of 1982, an economic downturn, coupled with the Speaker's serendipitous public reception as a frumpy throwback, yielded surprisingly high returns on what seemed at the outset to be a Hail Mary strategy that even he put little faith in.

Conclusion

The tale of the 1981 confrontation between O'Neill's House Democrats and the Reagan White House over budget and tax policy is an oft-told one. This chapter has sought to retell it by focusing on factional dynamics within the Democratic Party. While scholars have long recognized the CDF's crucial role in facilitating members' decision to break ranks with their party and side with the opposition, they have missed the collaborative imbalance that made it possible. As this chapter has shown, what mattered was the party's factional asymmetry—the conservatives' decision to work together, coupled with the liberals' inability (or unwillingness) to do the same. That asymmetry not only limited O'Neill's ability to cajole and discipline his party's wayward members, but it propelled the veteran politico, most comfortable in the back rooms of the Capitol, into the public eye.

Comparing O'Neill's struggles to those of Boehner and contrasting them with Pelosi's late-stage successes underscore the central thesis of this book. In and of themselves, party divisions do not necessarily constrain leader power. Rather, it is the relative collaborative might of rival factions that fundamentally shapes leaders' capacity to get what they want. What curtailed O'Neill's ability to make full use of the speakership's expanded authority was not the fact that he inherited an ideologically divided Democratic Caucus. Rather, it was the collaborative dominance of the conservative faction. Their commitment to work together and the liberal faction's comparative disorganization insulated conservatives from the Speaker's influence, making it nearly impossible for him to discipline individual CDF members or buy them off. The liberals' organizational failures, in turn, left O'Neill without auxiliary troops to force the conservatives into line. As we will see in chapter 6, these aspects of O'Neill's tenure distinguish him from Rayburn and help demarcate the boundaries between the two factional configurations at the heart of this book.

CHAPTER SIX

How Sam Rayburn Tamed the House Rules Committee

The Democratic Party responsible for enacting the New Deal and steering the United States through the Second World War famously confederated "two radically disparate political systems."[1] It brought together liberal lawmakers from northern and western cities, whose constituents were prounion, working-class Catholic and Jewish immigrants, and conservative lawmakers representing southern, often rural, communities where nativist, Protestant whites relied on legal barriers and state-sanctioned violence to prevent Black residents from participating in politics. In the New Deal's earliest years, this coalition held strong. After all, "a flat broke Southern dirt farmer [was] . . . in the same difficulty as a flat broke Northern workman."[2] But as the pressures of the Great Depression eased, the party's two great factions began to fight over labor-management relations, social welfare programs, and most important, civil rights.

Controlling the pivotal votes in nearly every congress from the New Deal to the Great Society, southern Democrats consistently found themselves on the winning side of these confrontations.[3] It was their propensity to collaborate that enabled them to sustain this decisive role in national policymaking. By working together, they "exercised power and influence far beyond their mere numerical strength."[4] Structuring their collaborative activity through formal intraparty organizations—the Southern Caucus in the Senate and the Southern Delegations in the House—the region's senators and representatives worked together to identify threats to the South's racial order and collectively rebuff them using an array of obstructionist parliamentary tactics. In the lower chamber, these activities tended to run through the Rules Committee, which became notorious for blocking liberal initiatives and promoting conservative policies opposed by a majority of Democrats.

Their lack of control over the most important committee in the House would become a persistent source of frustration for the Democratic Party's leadership.[5] Though sometimes sympathetic to the southerners' agenda, Speaker Sam Rayburn was adamant that the Rules Committee should not be used to subvert majority opinion within the party or to promote narrow sectional interests. Yet with liberal lawmakers outnumbered and disorganized, the Speaker had little recourse but to rely on what he deemed second-best strategies—evasive parliamentary maneuvers and short-term compromises—to counter the southerners' obstruction and shepherd key policy initiatives through the House.[6]

As this chapter shows, it was only when House liberals began to collaborate in earnest, shifting their party's factional configuration from asymmetric to symmetric, that Rayburn decided the time was ripe to confront his wayward southern flank. Relying on liberals' newly created collaborative arrangements to aid his cause, the Speaker set out to enlarge the Rules Committee in a concerted effort to undercut the southerners' gatekeeping power, while simultaneously providing himself with additional committee seats he could dispense to members he deemed worthy of reward. Leveraging the liberals' collaborative capacity to extend his reach over the House, Rayburn whipped votes, corralled Republican support, and directed the lobbying activities of John F. Kennedy's presidential administration and sympathetic interest groups to win what he would later describe as "the worst fight of my life."[7] As he expected, that fight proved deeply consequential. Enlarging the Rules Committee weakened the South's dominant position within the Democratic Party and ushered in an era of sweeping legislative reform.[8]

Rayburn, Reconsidered

Rayburn's nearly two decades long tenure as House Speaker (1940–47, 1949–53, 1955–61) has offered generations of legislative scholars a template to understand how party divisions shape leader power. In the "textbook" Congress, where southern and nonsouthern Democrats found little common ground, we are taught that Rayburn exercised limited authority, instead prioritizing "restrained partisanship and conflict resolution."[9] Seizing on his ostensible preference for accommodation, scholars have characterized Rayburn as the prototypical "caretaker" Speaker, often citing his time in office as powerful evidence for the idea that "[ideologically] cohesive parties are the main precondition for strong leadership."[10] In keeping with this view, Rayburn's ascension to the speakership in 1940 is said to mark the moment "where the organization of the House passed from hierarchy to bargaining."[11] Presiding over a caucus where members harbored radically different ideas about what was good for the country, Rayburn seemingly had little choice but to be "more permissive and consensual" than his czarist predecessors.[12] This impression is one that Rayburn deliberately cultivated, often reassuring colleagues that "the old days of pounding on the desk and giving people hell are gone."[13]

But this picture is overdrawn. Rayburn, we will see, was not a committed accommodationist. As he confided to associates, "I like power, and I like to use it."[14] Lawmakers like Tip O'Neill who came of age under the Speaker's tutelage tended to agree. The Rayburn they knew preferred to be "dictatorial," a stark contrast to the "friend Sam" image he nurtured in the public's view.[15]

This chapter explains why Rayburn was at first compelled to play the role of party conciliator and why he was finally able to transcend his party's ideological divisions to exercise real power in the twilight of his speakership. As we will see, Rayburn had few opportunities to promote his own wants over those of his party's rival factions for much of his tenure. But it was not House Democrats' significant ideological fractures that limited his power. Rather, the challenge was that those differences of opinion were asymmetrically mobilized. Indeed, for most of Rayburn's reign, southern conservatives worked to identify and enforce a collective "strategy ... for the Southern Group."[16] House liberals, by contrast, struggled to collaborate in kind. As one liberal put it, "there [was] ... a great inability to exercise a collective will."[17] Only in 1959, with the formation of the Democratic Study Group (DSG), did liberals' collaborative capacity come to rival that of the Southern Delegations.[18] It was then, as Missouri's Richard Bolling later observed, that "liberal Democrats [emerged as] a ... cooperative group."[19]

Rayburn, we will see, rushed to exploit this increasingly symmetric configuration. Determined to get the Rules Committee *he* wanted, the Speaker commandeered the liberals' collaborative arrangements to serve his own ends, using the DSG to frame his desired intervention, count noses, lobby wavering members, and whip votes. As Nancy Pelosi would do many decades later, he deployed the liberals' growing organizational capacity to counterbalance the power of conservative Democrats. In so doing, he effectively co-opted the liberals' organizational strength, deploying their resources to lengthen his own reach within and beyond the House.[20] So critical was this collaborative ballast that one of Rayburn's contemporaries observed, "Had there not been a DSG in 1960, the Speaker would have had to promote the organization of such a body."[21]

Alternative Explanations

As in previous chapters, it is worth considering plausible alternatives to the history detailed here. Some observers have suggested that the south's growing intransigence forced Rayburn to initiate his reform drive.[22] In this telling, the Speaker did not want to confront his southern brethren but ultimately concluded that he had little choice in the matter. As we will see, however, Rayburn did not immediately pursue reform upon concluding that the southerners' use of the Rules Committee to obstruct legislative action posed a grave threat to his party—or that it demanded a durable resolution. Rather, he waited until the liberal DSG was sufficiently organized that it could provide a counterweight to the formidable Southern Delegations. Moreover, the fact of southern intransigence does little to explain why Rayburn chose to expand the Rules Committee, when many Democrats, including members of the DSG and those closest to the Speaker, advocated reducing its size or purging its most perfidious members.

Others have posited that Rayburn's hand was forced not by southern intransigence but by pressure from liberal Democrats.[23] Yet here, too, the timing and nature of the Speaker's intervention suggests a more complicated reality. Undoubtedly, the party's most liberal members—frustrated by the southerners' success in stymieing legislation they favored—had long urged Rayburn to discipline the Rules Committee's errant members and reassert party control over this key gatekeeping apparatus. But for much of his tenure, the Speaker resisted their entreaties, preferring to guide his favored initiatives through the chamber using his considerable guile and parliamentary sophistication. Only when Rayburn judged that his left flank possessed the necessary organizational capacity to support his intervention did he take decisive action. And while the Speaker relied heavily on the liberals' collaborative arrangements, the DSG's confidential records and correspondence with House leadership make clear that

Rayburn was securely in command. Indeed, dictating the substance of the reform, the Speaker explicitly rejected the DSG's preferred approach to curbing the conservatives' influence—purging the committee of some of its disloyal southerners.

Still another possibility is that Rayburn agreed to reassert control over the committee not because he wanted to, but at the behest of the incoming Kennedy administration.[24] There is certainly ample evidence that the Speaker believed it imperative for the new president's program to receive a full hearing in the House. But neither Rayburn's nor Kennedy's papers give credence to the idea that Rayburn acted at the White House's direction. The record makes clear that Kennedy expressed concern that, absent Rayburn's action, his bold New Frontier agenda would founder. But he did not presume to suggest how or when the Speaker should intervene.[25] In fact, for much of the fight, Rayburn urged the White House to keep to the sidelines, believing the president's involvement would be detrimental to their shared cause. So, while Rayburn's actions undoubtedly benefited Kennedy (just as Kennedy's victory buoyed Rayburn's fortunes), it would be a mistake to conclude that the Speaker was acting as the president's agent.[26]

Rules Reform in the "Textbook" Congress

Emerging late in the New Deal era, an increasingly powerful alliance between conservative southern Democrats and the Republican minority posed a significant threat to the Democratic majority's iron grip on the House. This "conservative coalition" relied principally on the chamber's Rules Committee to block consideration of initiatives supported by mainstream Democrats and "actively promote . . . conservative initiatives over the objections of Democratic leaders."[27] Most famously, the coalition repeatedly blocked liberal efforts to advance civil rights legislation. But its members also ensured passage of damaging antiunion legislation and greenlit investigations of the executive branch under Democratic presidents Franklin Roosevelt and Harry Truman.[28]

Increasingly extensive collaboration undergirded the southerners' ability to maintain this sometimes precarious cross-party alliance. They began to mobilize their forces in the late 1930s—a period that witnessed renewed bipartisan interest in federal antilynching legislation, which southern lawmakers came to see as an initial salvo in the battle to dismantle Jim Crow.

Though southerners in the House would initially eschew the formal collaborative arrangements of their Senate colleagues, they nevertheless began to pool intelligence and collectively discuss how best to implement the Southern Caucus's instructions. As alarm grew that Democratic leaders were doing "everything in [their] power to bring about the passage of anti-southern bills," the region's representatives began to impose more formal collaborative arrangements, ultimately founding the Southern Delegations in February 1948.[29] Seventy members strong at the outset, the group deputized an executive committee, appointed a whip, and elected Mississippi's William Colmer as its leader.

The escalation in southern collaboration created new burdens for Rayburn. No longer able to secure individual southern votes through charm or patronage, the Speaker had to negotiate with the entire southern bloc every time legislation he deemed essential to the national welfare or Democratic agenda came up for a vote. The Speaker's ostensible reluctance to "bind" or "crack down" on the Southern Delegations won him considerable praise from his colleagues and journalists. *Time* called him "the best compromiser" since Henry Clay. But Rayburn rejected the honor, insisting, "I try to compromise by getting people to think my way."[30]

Democratic gains in the 1948 elections provided Rayburn and those in his inner circle the opportunity to consider more durable interventions. Notably, his determination to undercut the power of southern committee members was not driven by a particularly liberal outlook on racial issues.[31] Rather, the Speaker's frustration stemmed from his conviction that Democratic members of the Rules Committee, regardless of their regional or ideological "prefix or suffix," owed their loyalty to leadership, first and foremost.[32] And discomfited by the southerners' efforts to collaborate with greater intensity, the Speaker solicited "advice and counsel" from House confidantes about how to curb their influence.[33] Reflecting on his continued "trouble with the Committee," Rayburn determined that he would "not make mistakes this time."[34]

Purge or Pack?

The letters Rayburn received outlined two paths forward. For some correspondents, the surest way to curtail southern influence was to change "the complexion of the Rules Committee" at the opening of the Eighty-First Congress in January 1949.[35] Wilbur Mills of Arkansas—chair of the powerful Ways and Means Committee and a member of the Southern Delegations—advised the Speaker to prioritize "Democrats who have manifested a high degree of loyalty." "In my opinion," he wrote, this would "prevent [the Rules] Committee from being controlled . . . by a collation [sic] of some of our Democrats and the Republicans."[36] Jere Cooper of Tennessee echoed Mills's recommendation, urging Rayburn to keep Colmer, who had been the committee's most junior southern member, from returning after being exiled during the previous Congress. "I just don't see how you can figure on putting Colmer back on," he wrote.[37]

But for others, changing the Rules Committee's "complexion" by removing southern members or refusing Colmer's "right to return" would antagonize moderate southerners and precipitate a costly battle. Better, they argued, to expand the committee's size, thus diluting the southerners' vote share. Rules Committee chair A. J. Sabath articulated the logic in a letter to Rayburn: "I feel that the Committee should be increased to thirteen members, we having nine and the Republicans four so that we would have nine . . . that will go along and won't [make] yours and my life miserable." Were this plan to meet with the Speaker's favor, he would need only to "use [his] influence" to "elect . . . members that will cooperate . . . [and] not inflict upon the Rules Committee and me reactionaries."[38]

Responding to these missives, Rayburn declared himself eager for a fight. "I will not favor the return of Bill Colmer to the Committee on Rules," he wrote Cooper. Denying the congressman his former seat on the committee would send a clear warning to all that disloyalty would not go unpunished. Only Democrats who were "one-hundred percent with us" would be allowed the privilege of regulating House procedure. But before the Speaker could "ask . . . the Committee on Committees to give a place . . . on Rules" to the two "loyal and fine" Democrats the Speaker had identified (one of whom would replace Colmer), Majority Leader John McCormack interceded on the Mississippian's behalf.[39] Believing he owed his leadership post to the support of southern segregationists like Colmer, who was also a friend and "poker pal," McCormack urged Rayburn to let the congressman return to his old seat. The majority leader's support for Colmer created a new complication for Rayburn. With his own forces divided, the Speaker feared he had little chance of defeating whatever coordinated defense the Southern Delegations was sure to mount.[40]

An Interim Solution: The Twenty-One-Day Rule

Rueful, Rayburn relented: Colmer would return to the Rules Committee. With the southerners collaborating in earnest—and liberal Democrats showing no sign of countermobilizing to force Colmer's ouster—the Speaker would need to identify a parliamentary vehicle to circumvent the committee's obstruction that much of the party could back. Emphasizing that he did not wish to force through civil rights legislation per se, Rayburn cast the issue in majoritarian terms. "The rules of a legislative body," he declared, "should be such at all times as to allow the majority of a legislative body to work its will."[41] Accordingly, he instructed the House parliamentarian to draft a new rule that would empower committee chairs to call up for consideration bills that had stalled in the Rules Committee for more than twenty-one days.[42]

Predictably, the committee's conservative majority opposed the new rule, charging that it "meant . . . a return to czarism."[43] But many liberal and moderate Democrats, including southerners not on the committee, were more enthusiastic, as many initiatives broadly favored within the party had been stalled by the conservative coalition's obstruction. The proposed "twenty-one-day rule" also found favor with Rules chair and Rayburn ally Sabath, who had been widely criticized for his inability to keep the committee's southern members in line. With strong Democratic support, including a score of southern moderates, and the blessing of President Truman, the new rule was swiftly adopted, 275–143.[44]

Armed with this new parliamentary tool, the Speaker was confident he could move much of the Democrats' legislative agenda through the House. This sentiment was widely shared. As one commentator observed in the *New York Times*, "Mr. Rayburn . . . has received a power and a responsibility not given in generations to a Speaker of the House. He will be in command . . . not . . . whatever bloc of rebellious southern Democrats can be marshalled."[45] And indeed, during the remainder of the Eighty-First Congress (1949–51), the twenty-one-day rule was used to bring anti–poll tax legislation to the floor and to force votes on controversial housing and minimum wage bills.[46] But the Speaker soon came to doubt the rule's virtues. "Irresponsible" committee chairs who had not "cleared" their bills in advance were threatening to discharge unwelcome legislation to the floor without his say-so.[47] For the price of limiting southern obstructionism in the Rules Committee, he had ceded greater control of the floor. Unwilling to pay that price in perpetuity, he grudgingly backed a successful bid to repeal the rule two years later.[48]

Republican control of the House during the Eighty-Third Congress (1953–55) temporarily eased Rayburn's frustration with southerners on the Rules Committee, but after the Democrats regained their majority following the 1954 midterms, trouble was soon afoot. For the next several years, the Speaker relied on a combination of ad hoc parliamentary maneuvers and aid from his old friend, Minority Leader Joe Martin, to break the southerners' blockade and move priority legislation to the floor.[49] But "Judge" Howard Smith, who had replaced Sabath as Rules chair, soon found a clever way to obstruct liberal proposals: he simply declined to convene committee meetings when liberal initiatives were to be considered.[50] Adding to Rayburn's troubles was Martin's departure as minority leader in 1959. He was replaced by Charles Halleck, a partisan brawler who refused to honor Martin's commitment to support the Speaker when he needed spare Republican votes.

The Factional Configuration Shifts

As Smith's intransigence grew increasingly bold, House liberals began to mobilize their own ranks to counter the southern bloc's influence. Motivating their efforts was the recognition that Smith and his allies were at a considerable collaborative advantage. Pointing to the Southern Delegations' thick organizational ties, the liberals concluded that their own "lack of success . . . has been [the result of] a breakdown of communication."[51] To fight on equal terms, "it was necessary to organize so that they could communicate, plan strategy, and coordinate the efforts of like-minded Democrats in the House."[52] Thus, members of the liberal faction began meeting in the winter of 1956 to map out how they might better collaborate to advance a shared set of legislative priorities. By spring 1959, they had established a formal organization—the DSG— replete with a steering committee, designated whips, issue-specific task forces, and a leadership board.[53] Though this effort marked the bitterest stage yet in relations between the party's southern and nonsouthern wings, it would prompt Rayburn to take the most decisive action of his speakership.

From the outset, the DSG made clear that it aimed to support Rayburn's efforts to promote liberal legislation. In return, one member recalled, "we were assured the Leadership would welcome such organization" though it "could not present us with [a] formal blessing."[54] Determined to cultivate a productive relationship with their party's leadership, the group sought to "contain" the "bomb throwers" and "irresponsible liberals" who counted themselves as members, but who "made it impossible to do anything."[55]

Rayburn, however, was initially skeptical that the liberal faction would hold together, echoing the concern harbored by the DSG's own leaders that their "loose-knit coalition . . . ha[d] the tendency to go their own separate ways."[56] Believing the group did not yet possess the thick, time-tested collaborative arrangements necessary to outmuscle southern conservatives on the floor, the Speaker resisted the DSG's calls for a vote to reinstate the twenty-one-day rule.[57] Nevertheless, he was sympathetic to the liberals' complaints that Smith and his Republican allies were holding up action on education, civil rights, the minimum wage, and urban renewal — all issues Rayburn now thought central to the Democratic Party's future.[58] On civil rights, in particular, the Speaker's views had plainly evolved. As he told his wary deputies, "It will not just help the party . . . these people are entitled to this."[59]

Determined to bring the Rules Committee to heel, Rayburn began to scheme. Confronting the committee would be easiest, he reasoned, if public opinion demanded an intervention. Within the Democratic Caucus, the Southern Delegations would likely oppose any reform, but the rest of the party might be persuaded to take action if the Speaker sufficiently "dramatized . . . the case against the Rules Committee." A rump session of Congress following the 1960 Democratic Convention would be his stage; the DSG his star. Rather than seek to minimize divisions within the party, Rayburn instructed the group to clamor for action on civil rights and other liberal priorities. And the group responded. Agreeing to put the DSG's organizational mettle to the test, its leaders pledged to keep "members on the floor during the . . . procedural wrangle and roll call votes by which . . . opponents . . . sought to block consideration."[60] If the liberals could make good on that commitment, the Speaker would see to it that their desired measures reached the Rules Committee in "rapid succession." Counting on Smith's intransigence and the DSG's support on the floor, Rayburn would then use a variety of procedural maneuvers to discharge the legislation from the committee — demonstrating, in the process, the need for a more permanent solution.[61]

Pack, Not Purge

But what would that solution be? For DSG leaders, the answer was clear: purge the committee of its troublesome southerners and replace them with liberals willing "to implement a legislative program consistent with [the] Democratic program."[62] The virtue of this approach was that it could be executed within the Democratic Caucus, where Rayburn commanded a certain majority.[63] The Speaker's leadership team, including Majority Leader McCormack and Democratic Whip Carl Albert of Oklahoma, proposed an alternative. If Rayburn thought purging southerners would appear too punitive, he could instead shrink the committee by one seat. This would give the Speaker the opportunity to remove one southerner of his choice, effectively neutralizing the conservative coalition without precipitating a caucus bloodbath. In a leadership meeting at President-elect Kennedy's Florida compound in December 1960, Albert made the case that Colmer should once again be Rayburn's target, predicting that few in the party would rise to defend him, given that Colmer had bolted the party's ticket a month earlier.[64] Vice President–elect Lyndon Johnson seconded Albert's suggestion, still smarting over Colmer's defection.[65]

Rayburn liked neither plan. Moderate southerners, he recognized, might not rally to Colmer's aid, but they would surely defend the seniority system. Exiling him from the Rules Committee, either by purging him or shrinking the committee's size, would be rightfully perceived as an assault on that system.[66] For days the Speaker brooded. As Albert recalled, "On tough decisions, Mr. Rayburn almost became a loner. He didn't say anything for four days on the Rules Committee dilemma. Then he said that purging Colmer was going too far."[67] Returning to the plan Sabath had proposed in 1948, the Speaker decided he would instead seek to expand the committee's size by three, explaining to allies that "it was always better politics to give than take away."[68]

But expanding the Rules Committee would require the Speaker to move the fight out of the Democratic Caucus, where support for reform was assured, and onto the chamber floor, where he would need at least 218 members to back the intervention. Rayburn remained undeterred. The success of the incoming administration and the future of the Democratic Party, he said, depended on taming the conservative coalition.[69] "The issue is very simple," he explained to a wary McCormack and Albert. "Shall the elected leadership of the House run its affairs, or shall the chairman of one committee run them?"[70] All the same, Rayburn acknowledged that waging a successful floor battle required some cunning. He would need moderate southerners to join liberal Democrats in backing reform, and even with some southern votes, he would be short a majority without Republican support.

Preparing for Battle

Rayburn would use the DSG to achieve both objectives. To win over moderate southerners, the Speaker leveraged the liberals' close relationship with the Capitol press corps. In a meeting on January 2, 1961, Rayburn informed the DSG that he intended to purge Colmer from the Rules Committee and instructed the group's leaders, including New Jersey's Frank Thompson and Missouri's Bolling, to get their members in line. Albert recalled, "Almost instantly the liberals (never known for their secret-keeping capacity) leaked the word to the press."[71] As Rayburn had anticipated, news that he was considering a purge brought moderate southerners to his office in droves.[72] Would he not consider a compromise? After much discussion, Georgia's Carl Vinson, one of Rayburn's closest friends and an influential member of the Southern Delegations, offered the deal the Speaker had been fishing for. If Rayburn made peace with Colmer, Vinson promised to deliver a bloc of southern votes to help pass the expansion plan.[73]

Whipping Republican votes would be another matter. Here again, Rayburn deployed the DSG to lobby moderate Republicans who had previously helped pass civil rights legislation in 1957.[74] He also turned to his old ally Martin to help drum up additional support. These efforts became more difficult once Minority Leader Halleck learned that Rayburn was trolling for votes. Warning his conference to steer clear of Democratic entreaties, Halleck threatened to withhold patronage and deny favorable committee assignments to any Republican who backed the expansion plan. The Speaker responded by vowing to reward Halleck's victims with patronage of his own, reminding the minority leader that this was "a game that two c[ould] play."[75] Rayburn was well aware that this was more bluster than credible threat, as even those Republicans who thought Rayburn had the right of it were facing intense pressure from leading conservative interest groups to oppose the enlargement plan.

In the week preceding Kennedy's inauguration, the Speaker accelerated his reform drive, directing the DSG to coordinate with the party's whips to count noses and corral wavering Democrats.[76] By the liberals' estimate, Rayburn had between 190 and 200 of the 218 votes he needed.[77] To win, he would need to keep southern defections to a minimum and secure close to two dozen Republican votes. When the Speaker learned he was within range, he demanded even more from his liberal auxiliaries. The DSG's Bolling and Thompson were asked to work with Kennedy's legislative liaisons and liberal interest groups—including the AFL-CIO, National Education Association, and NAACP—to determine what patronage the White House could offer "shimmying" members "to stiffen [their] backbone[s]," as Rayburn put it.[78] Meanwhile, Vice President-elect Johnson and southern members of the president's cabinet were ordered to appeal directly to their home state delegations.[79] Rayburn, for his part, made clear to new Democratic members of the House that he would look favorably on those who backed his reform when making committee assignments.[80]

When Smith learned that Rayburn was coming close to securing the necessary votes, he and his lieutenants approached the Speaker with several compromise proposals. Bolling's records, as well as those of the DSG, reveal that Smith was willing to trade "substantial limitations on the power of the committee" in exchange for Rayburn's decision to abandon his reform effort. "There was an offer to yield the right to prevent bills from going to conference . . . [and] a suggestion of a change in the rule regarding tie votes—which presently prevents a bill from going to the floor." After Rayburn rejected both options, Smith made his final plea: he would refer Kennedy's first five bills to the floor so long as Rayburn backed off.[81] As the DSG noted, this was a significant concession intended to preserve "the heart of it—control of the Committee itself."[82] But the Speaker was unmoved, telling the chair, "Shit, Howard, Kennedy may have forty bills in his program before he's through."[83]

On January 17, the Democratic Caucus formally endorsed the Speaker's expansion plan by a voice vote. Even after Rayburn rejected the proposal to purge Colmer, many in the party, including the members of the DSG, had long assumed that Rayburn would secure passage of his expansion proposal on the House floor by first holding a "binding [internal Caucus] vote . . . a rarely used device which [if successful] would compel the southern Democrats either to vote for his proposal [on the floor] or absent themselves altogether."[84] But, as Rayburn explained to his deputies, a precommitment vote of this kind would only lend credence to the concern raised by opponents that he intended to "pack" the Rules Committee by unjust means. If he truly had the courage of his convictions, he would not try to push the changes through without permitting the southerners to vote freely on the House floor. Moreover, by promising Smith that he would not insist on a show of force, the Speaker secured the chair's "assurance that the [Rules] committee would meet with reasonable promptness" to report the proposed change. At the time, however, there were whispers that the Speaker chose not to impose a binding vote because he thought he would lose it.[85] The DSG's whip reports suggest otherwise. Just as Rayburn would have won the support of the Caucus in effect[ing] . . . a purge" of Colmer, "it is equally clear," the group maintained, "that he had enough votes in [the] caucus to bind all the Democrats to support his enlargement plan" on the floor.[86]

Four days after the Democratic Caucus backed Rayburn's expansion plan, the Republican conference voted overwhelmingly to oppose it.[87] Many who would later support the Speaker on the House floor confessed that Halleck had shaken them down.[88] Although the minority leader denied applying pressure, Rayburn did not believe him. "Somebody sure as hell is," he complained.[89]

Everyone, it seemed, knew the floor vote would be a close one. Indeed, bravado aside, even the Speaker conceded that he might well lose. After completing a final whip count, the DSG determined that only 216 members were likely to support the proposed committee expansion. McCormack and Albert were slightly more optimistic, believing they would get the 218 votes the Speaker needed. Fearing Rayburn's plan might ultimately fail, a delegation of Democrats broached the possibility of a last-minute compromise with Smith. But the Speaker was adamant: "Hell no. We're going to vote. . . . The only way to avoid a vote is for me to abdicate and I won't do it."[90]

In the final days before the vote, Rayburn left no stone unturned, directing the DSG to further ramp up its public relations campaign. The liberals "distributed literature explaining the fine points of House procedure to new members and providing arguments for the Rayburn position."[91] Meanwhile, the Speaker checked and double-checked with his supporters that they would be on the floor when he needed their vote. One Democrat recalled that upon learning he would be out of town, Rayburn (not known for his penchant for oratory) promised, "If you'll cancel . . . I'll come to your district and make two of the damnedest speeches for you."[92]

Endgame

Five minutes before noon on January 31, Rayburn convened his usual gaggle with the press. As reporters jostled inside the Speaker's office, Rayburn radiated confidence. "We have the votes if all of them honor their promises," he said. Then, as was his custom, he marched across the hall onto the House floor and up to the Speaker's rostrum. From the packed press galleries above the floor, observers noted that the lawmakers below—Democrats and Republicans alike—broke into loud applause, a violation of custom but an acknowledgment of Rayburn's mettle.[93] Indeed, it was not lost on the body that Rayburn's show of force had required great effort from an aging Speaker whose health was in significant decline (and who would die less than a year later). After gaveling the House into session, a quorum call revealed that 427 members were present. Among those absent was the Speaker's old friend Martin, whose own failing health kept him from the floor.[94]

Debate began with a speech from Smith. "I have no quarrel with the Speaker," he solemnly declared. "If there is any quarrel between the Speaker and myself it is all on his side. I'll cooperate with the Democratic leadership as far as my conscience will permit." This comment was met with smiles and then laughter when the Speaker joked that the chair's conscience was prodigious only when it suited him. Not appreciating the ribbing, Smith retorted that "some of the gentlemen who are laughing ... do not understand what a conscience is." With that, the chair quickly got down to business. He denied that the Rules Committee was ever an impediment to realizing Democratic priorities: "If this committee did something that the House thought it should not do, then you would have cause to complain." It was liberals, he said, who were responsible for the real "ruckus," noting that "those of us who oppose this packing scheme have offered every honorable solution for the sake of harmony."[95]

Halleck soon followed with a speech of his own. The minority leader accused Rayburn of taking premature action. "Why is it not the better part of wisdom and good judgement to wait and move along in this Congress and see how the Committee on Rules performs?" The House, he noted, had been plenty productive in the last legislative session. There was little reason to take such drastic measures, particularly when Smith had pledged to move the incoming administration's program to the floor. Turning to the Republican minority, Halleck closed with a warning for those members sympathetic to "our great Speaker," stating that "I have an avalanche of mail, most of it handwritten, from people opposed to this resolution. . . . They are afraid the floodgates will be let down and we will be overwhelmed with bad legislation."[96] With this, all eyes turned to Rayburn.

The final nine minutes of the debate would be the Speaker's. "This issue, in my mind, is a simple one," he said. "We have elected to the Presidency a new leader. He is going to have a program that he thinks will be in the interest of . . . the American people. . . . I think the House should be allowed on great measures to work its will, and it cannot work its will if the Committee on Rules is so constituted as not to allow the House pass on those things." Dismissing the charge that his enlargement plan was backed only by "long-haired radicals," the Speaker delivered his closing argument. "The only way that we can be sure that [Kennedy's] program will move . . . is to adopt this resolution today."[97] Cheers broke out as he walked back to his rostrum.

With debate concluded, Rayburn ordered the House clerk to call the roll. As names were called, members spread tally sheets across their desks to keep track of who was ahead. No one roamed the hallways or engaged in idle chitchat as was the custom during roll calls, although a few members stepped into the cloakroom for a nervous smoke. At the three-hundredth name, the vote was tied. Thompson, sitting with Albert at the Democratic leader's desk, checked the votes cast against the DSG's tally sheet. In the press gallery, reporters compared the ongoing roll call to their own whip counts, signaling their predictions to the lawmakers pacing below. As the clerk neared the bottom of the list, the Speaker was leading by just one vote. When he finished, Rayburn was ahead, 214–209.[98]

But eleven members—more than enough to change the outcome—had failed to respond to the clerk's initial call. As the House parliamentarian whispered the tally to the Speaker, the eleven names were read again. The chamber was abuzz. With bated breath, the House waited as each name was called. Only six responded. They were evenly split: three voted against the expansion proposal, three in favor of it.[99] Gripping the official tally card in his hand, Rayburn declared, "On this vote, there being 217 ayes and 212 noes, the resolution is adopted."[100] His announcement was met with shouts of triumph from reformers and growls of frustration from conservatives.[101]

While elated supporters congratulated the Speaker, Smith left the chamber chewing an unlit cigar. Reporters trailed him, asking why he thought the southerners had lost. The chair responded, "We didn't have enough votes." Rayburn, for his part, was all smiles. As he walked back across the hallway to his office, he was asked to comment on his victory. Winking, the Speaker replied, "I always feel good when I win."[102] Rayburn felt even better the following day. At his direction, the Democrats' Committee on Committees named two DSG members, Carl Elliot of Alabama and B. F. Sisk of California, to the two newly created committee seats. The Rules Committee was now to be governed by a slim but decidedly liberal majority.[103]

Policy Gains and Developmental Implications

The policy gains from Rayburn's victory were considerable and immediately felt.[104] In quick succession, the major planks of Kennedy's New Frontier program were reported by the Rules Committee to the floor and, in most cases, passed by both chambers. First was the administration's minimum wage bill, which gave wage and hour protection to an additional four million workers and represented the first significant extension of the Fair Labor Standards Act in thirty years. Soon thereafter, Rayburn, together with Vice President Johnson, successfully maneuvered the president's housing and redevelopment measures through the House and Senate. The new laws committed billions of federal dollars to rural conservation, urban renewal, public transportation, and public housing for elderly, disabled and low-income Americans, and it created low-interest mortgage loan programs for moderate-income families and job-training programs for the unemployed. Among Kennedy's greatest progressive victories, their passage led conservative Republicans to muse that "the southern wing of this [Democratic] coalition has been shot at and badly hit."[105]

Indeed, the Rules Committee held up only one of Kennedy's legislative priorities. This was a school construction bill that sought to deny federal funds to parochial and private institutions. At the outset, Rayburn warned Kennedy that targeting parochial schools would be unwise, a conviction shared by several members of the president's inner circle.[106] As the Speaker told the president in no uncertain terms, because many urban Democrats represented districts where parochial schools were prominent fixtures in the community, limiting funds to public schools was bound to be controversial. And with several Catholic Democrats on the Rules Committee, conservatives did not have far to look to find the votes they needed to scuttle the proposal.[107]

Perhaps more important than producing short- and medium-term policy gains for liberal Democrats, Rayburn's successful bid to expand the Rules Committee meaningfully reduced the power of the conservative coalition and strengthened the office of the Speaker. The move eliminated what legislative scholars agree was "the conservative coalition's most potent weapon for exercising negative agenda control." In so doing, Rayburn substantially increased the odds that the coalition would be rolled on the floor, helping to cement majority-party control over the chamber.[108] As one Senate conservative observed, beginning in 1961, "the combined votes of Southern conservatives and Northern non-urban Republicans, which from 1940 to 1960 won victory after victory . . . no longer function[ed] effectively [in the House]."[109]

While regaining control of the Rules Committee had been his proximate goal, Rayburn cast his victory in broader terms. True, he had successfully curbed the power of southern Democrats in the House. But, more important, he had augmented the prestige and authority of the speakership. As he told his closest aides, "When the House revolted against Speaker [Joseph] Cannon in 1910, they cut the Speaker's powers too much. Ever since I have been Speaker, I have been trying to get some of that power back for the office."[110] In what would prove to be his last great act as Speaker, Rayburn finally succeeded.

Conclusion

Students of Congress have long characterized Rayburn's years at the helm of the House Democratic Caucus as the apogee of the caretaker, hands-off model of party leadership. Seeking to keep an ever more precarious peace between restive northern and western liberals and defensive southern conservatives, Rayburn is said to have shied from conflict and sought conciliation wherever possible.[111] But this stylized account is misleading.

Throughout his fight to tame the Rules Committee, Rayburn plotted his course carefully. Undeterred by mounting tensions within the Democratic Party, the Speaker waited for his moment. Only when Democratic divisions were at their apex—with liberals successfully organizing their ranks to counter southern conservatives' parliamentary savvy and discipline—did Rayburn strike. Recognizing that the liberal faction "supported the same things he did," he commandeered their organizational apparatus, using the DSG as an auxiliary force against the entrenched defenses of the Southern Delegations.[112] Rayburn's successful bid to enlarge the Rules Committee makes clear that the Speaker was not averse to conflict, nor did Democratic divisions always constrain him. In fact, it was his party's increasingly symmetric factional configuration that empowered the Speaker to battle southern Democrats for control of House procedure.

Like Pelosi's successful bid to quash resistance to a once-in-a-generation climate bill, the timing and nature of the Speaker's intervention suggest that we have misunderstood the generative potential of party factionalism. Leaders of symmetrically divided parties are not consigned to a minimalist, supervisory role. Rather, symmetry can have a salutary effect, offering opportunities for leaders to consolidate power and set their party's direction. Rayburn's campaign to expand the Rules Committee makes clear that the collaborative arrangements of an amenable faction can be used as "a counterweight . . . by the leadership." As House liberals well understood, "probably the leadership would feel better without the DSG, but now that it is a fact, it must be used and dealt with, perhaps advantageously like all other political realities."[113]

CHAPTER SEVEN

How William Knowland Saved McCarthyism from McCarthy

The economic turmoil of the 1930s decimated the Republican Party. Blamed for the 1929 stock market crash and the ensuing Great Depression, the formerly Grand Old Party struggled to identify a program that would appeal to an enervated electorate. Hewing to tradition, conservative Republicans maintained that the old ways were still the best ways. Refusing to abandon the GOP's antistatist principles, they railed against federal efforts to stabilize the nation's economy and promote the welfare of its citizens. But with Americans only beginning to recover from the Depression, these broadsides against the New Deal proved exceedingly unpopular.[1] Vindicated that attacking social programs was a losing strategy, the party's moderates instead preached accommodation to the new order. But their program of "efficient social welfare" proved no more appealing.[2] Neither a rebounding economy nor the Allies' victory in World War II provided resolution.

In the Senate, moderates in the mold of self-described "New Deal Republican" (and New York governor) Thomas Dewey continued to back the New Deal's most popular initiatives, while advocating a restrained but interventionist approach in international affairs.[3] The conservative "Old Guard," led by Ohio senator Robert Taft, rejected this prescription. For the party to be "a going concern, vigorous, strong, solvent and powerful," they urged Republicans to redouble their commitment to austerity, limited government, and isolationism.[4] Evenly matched in size and evidencing minimal collaboration across the board, neither faction succeeded in gaining the upper hand.

Joseph McCarthy would redefine the terms of this long-simmering conflict. The Wisconsin senator's inflammatory search for suspected communists in government showcased a new, populist brand of conservatism, one that sought to stoke public hostility against elites and perceived outsiders while avoiding criticism of popular assistance programs.[5]

Conservatives, for their part, were quick to recognize McCarthy's electoral appeal and hoped his message would inspire voters to back other right-wing candidates. "It all comes down to this," one conservative party chair wrote his fellows. "Are we going to try to win an election, or aren't we?"[6] Despite their enthusiasm, however, conservatives showed little interest in deepening their collaboration to promote his agenda, relying on the senator's talent for generating headlines and Taft's prodigious appetite for administrative work to further their collective cause.

For Republican moderates, however, McCarthy's crusade threatened to consume the party with "fear, ignorance, bigotry, and smear."[7] Dwight Eisenhower's successful 1952 presidential campaign only heightened these concerns. With McCarthy giving the new Republican administration no quarter, his attacks imperiled moderates' opportunity to parlay Ike's victory into concrete policy gains. But like their conservative opponents, they remained disorganized, relying on the sporadic efforts of individual lawmakers to confront McCarthy—ever hopeful that their own champion, Eisenhower, would finally strike the senator down.

Taft's sudden death in the summer of 1953 left his handpicked successor, California's William Knowland, to chart the party's path forward as Senate majority leader. Favorite son of a powerful newspaper baron and an ardent anticommunist, Knowland saw value in the Wisconsin senator's rejection of traditional small-government conservatism in favor of a more populist approach. But while he, too, accused State Department officials of selling out the people, Knowland came to believe that McCarthy's rhetoric would have to be "toned down" if it were to serve the party's interests. As this chapter details, the fight to censure McCarthy provided an opportunity for the majority leader to separate the populist conservatism he thought had such promise from its erratic standard-bearer. McCarthy, he believed, had been right to accuse governing elites of betraying ordinary Americans in the fight against communism. But in failing to follow "normal procedure," the senator was a liability to their shared cause.[8]

Casting Knowland as a leading man in the Senate's confrontation with McCarthy is an admittedly unorthodox choice. More often than not, the majority leader is relegated to the back pages of congressional history, dismissed as a lightweight when compared to better-known contemporaries like Taft, Everett Dirksen, and famed master of the Senate Lyndon

Johnson.[9] But the evidence presented here suggests that Knowland played a far more decisive role than the conventional wisdom allows. Leveraging his party's symmetric factional configuration, the majority leader worked to deny conservative Republicans their preferred messenger, McCarthy, while rebuffing the moderates' demand that the GOP rid itself of his message. At a time when McCarthy's excesses—his increasingly unhinged personal behavior, incendiary allegations, and brazen use of the Senate's investigative powers—made populist conservatism vulnerable to attack from Eisenhower and his moderate allies, Knowland's intervention ensured its survival.

A Lost Hero of the Modern Conservative Movement

In the decades after McCarthy's censure and subsequent downfall, populist conservatives labored on the margins of a party increasingly committed to the twin ideals of laissez-faire economics and limited government.[10] By the end of the first decade of the twenty-first century, however, a cohort of Republicans were beginning to question this reigning orthodoxy. Rejecting their forebearers' opposition to welfare spending, a new generation of conservative activists declared their support for popular social programs like Social Security and Medicare. But this was not a return to Dewey's moderate Republicanism. Insisting that only *some* Americans were deserving of government assistance, these self-identified "Tea Partiers" framed their support in "us versus them" terms, invoking classically populist tropes that emphasized racial, ethnic, and class distinctions.[11] Donald Trump's stunning rise and continued hold over Republican voters make clear that this populist turn is no passing fad; it has come to define the party.

Naturally, scholars of American politics have been eager to explain the renewed appeal of this strain of conservatism.[12] Political psychologists, for instance, have identified a range of individual character traits, such as deference to authority or aversion to novelty, that might prompt the public to favor Trump's inflammatory rhetoric and that of the bevy of candidates who have followed in his wake.[13] Complementing these accounts, historical institutionalists have identified links between the today's accusatory populist conservatism and long-standing ascriptive forms of Americanism championed by groups like the Know-Nothing Party, Ku Klux Klan, and John Birch Society.[14] Common to both approaches is the view that this kind of conservatism is an inevitable, perhaps indelible, feature of American politics.

And yet, populist conservatism has not always dominated the right. Through detailed studies of the grassroots politics of the postwar Sun Belt and the mobilization of the Moral Majority, historians of postwar America have shown just how contingent the rise of populist conservatism was. On their account, it is the entrepreneurial creativity of activists—direct-mail pioneer Richard Viguerie, televangelist Jerry Falwell, and Equal Rights Amendment opponent Phyllis Schlafly, to name only a few—that best explains populist conservatism's fluctuating currency in Republican politics.[15]

But telling the full story of the contemporary conservative movement's origins and the sources of its influence also requires accounting for developments in traditional institutional venues.[16] After all, seizing control of government is generally a principal aim of grassroots activists and the movements they lead. Accordingly, this chapter foregrounds the legislative politics of the mid-twentieth century. By training our focus on Congress (and the Senate specifically), we will see that populist conservatism's survival required careful tending by high-level legislative patrons— lawmakers like Knowland who, without much fanfare or publicity, labored to protect it and facilitate its transmission to subsequent generations.

Alternative Explanations

Despite Knowland's central role in helping to orchestrate McCarthy's downfall, his efforts are rarely acknowledged. More often, it is suggested that it was Lyndon Johnson, then Senate minority leader, who masterminded McCarthy's prosecution. Some accounts focus on the decision to create a select committee to assess the senator's wrongdoing, suggesting that Johnson planted the idea in Knowland's head and citing an off-the-record conversation the minority leader had with reporters the year before the censure resolution was introduced. Johnson is said to have outlined how he would approach the McCarthy problem: "I'd appoint a bipartisan select committee, and I'd put on our side the very best men we have . . . and I'd ask 'em to make a study of McCarthy and report to the Senate. With the men I'd pick, the Senate would accept their judgment and that would be the end of it."[17] Other accounts center on the bespoke committee's composition, suggesting that Johnson "ma[de] Knowland think *he* had selected" McCarthy's jurors when in fact it was the minority leader who called the shots. As Robert Caro recounts, "Johnson would suggest some Republican he knew Knowland detested. He'd say, 'Now, Bill, I'm sure you want so-and-so.' Knowland would say 'Oh, no! Good God, no, I don't want so-and-so!' and he'd wind up naming the man Johnson wanted."[18]

But as we will see, there is little evidence to support either version of events. Though less charismatic than his Democratic counterpart, Knowland was a canny and successful politician in his own right—a "grim-visaged mastodon with convictions and the courage to back them up."[19] Anointed by Taft and possessed of powerful allies within the GOP, he had outpaced skilled contemporaries like Dirksen and Leverett Saltonstall of Massachusetts (who chaired the party's Steering and Policy Committee) to reach the pinnacle of legislative power barely a year into his sophomore term. Considered for the Republican vice presidential nomination in 1952, the majority leader would soon maneuver to credibly position himself as Eisenhower's heir apparent and a replacement for Richard Nixon were Ike to seek a new number two.[20] Nor did Knowland stumble on the technical aspects of the job of party leader. Despite his considerable disagreements with Eisenhower over the substance of the party's agenda, colleagues recalled that Knowland was "good" at keeping the Senate running by unanimous consent, effective at "testing the sentiment on a bill" and assessing "who's going to object."[21]

Moreover, whatever their respective skills and talents, Johnson had no special incentive to counter McCarthy.[22] While some Senate Democrats, particularly southern conservatives, were sympathetic to McCarthy's cause, others feared the electoral consequences of taking a public position against him.[23] Indeed, it was this dynamic that empowered Johnson to regularly insist that the senator was "a Republican problem," prompting McCarthy's opponents to complain that Johnson was "the root of all [their] difficulties on the Democratic side."[24]

Perhaps it is more plausible that Knowland simply steered Republicans in the direction they were already heading. Not so. As we will see, when the Senate began to debate the resolution proposing to censure McCarthy, contemporaneous accounts describe Senate Republicans as divided about whether and how to discipline McCarthy. Conservatives, predictably, rallied to his defense, though some acknowledged discomfort with the senator's caustic behavior. Speaking for colleagues who believed the Wisconsin senator deserved no punishment, Dirksen, for instance, charged that those who condemned McCarthy were "in bed" with the Communist Party.[25] Moderates, for their part, were no friends of McCarthy, but "preferred to avoid" taking a public stand.[26] Even senators who had publicly disavowed McCarthy were wary of prosecution; the party's whip counts reveal that they, too, needed to be "tactfully persuaded."[27] To the extent that most Republicans agreed on anything, it was that confronting McCarthy was bad politics. It risked "embarrass[ing] and undermin[ing]" the party by raising an issue that the Democrats could use to further their "political objectives."[28]

Alternatively, it could be that in pursuing McCarthy's censure as he did, Knowland—like any floor leader worth his salt—was simply seeking to minimize public displays of dissension within his party. On this account, creating a select committee to evaluate McCarthy's alleged misbehavior was a savvy play to move the Senate's deliberations into a less public forum in the hopes of keeping the party's internal wrangling out of the headlines. But the historical record makes clear that forming a special committee was not a popular choice. Nor did anyone appear to think that it would successfully bury the issue. Moderates loudly protested the proposal to delegate McCarthy's prosecution to a bespoke committee, arguing on the Senate floor that it was an unnecessary delay in bringing charges.[29] Conservatives were equally bitter toward the majority leader for "sponsor[ing] the appointment of a committee because they felt that McCarthy could do no wrong."[30] Indeed, they were so concerned about the prospect of a special committee that prominent conservatives urged McCarthy to make amends. Were he to apologize—whether to members of the select committee, as Arizona's Barry Goldwater recommended, or to the Senate itself, as Dirksen advised—chances were good, they thought, that their colleagues "would lose complete interest in the movement and . . . the censure attempt would die."[31]

Given these sentiments, it seems quite unlikely that Knowland's strings were being pulled by Johnson, or that he was acting as an agent for either of his party's rival factions. Rather, we will see that it was the GOP's symmetric factional configuration that enabled the majority leader to divorce the anticommunist cause he cared so deeply about from the spokesperson he had come to mistrust.

The GOP Adrift

The New Deal transformed partisan politics in the United States. For Democrats, the unprecedented opportunity to remake constitutional government brought with it not just a sea change in the party's electoral fortunes but also a restructuring of its internal composition. Liberals, trade unionists, Jews, and urban Blacks were durably incorporated into a party long dominated by the South's Bourbon elite.³² Notwithstanding its considerable internal tensions, that unlikely coalition dominated American politics for a generation. For Republicans, however, the New Deal was no less than a "political disaster."³³ The stunning popularity of President Franklin D. Roosevelt's ambitious social programs made clear to GOP leaders—long accustomed to holding the reins of national power—that Democrats had worked a seismic shift in the political landscape. How would the party respond?

Alf Landon's 1936 presidential campaign represented the conservatives' first salvo in the brewing battle for their party's future. Financed by prominent conservative businessmen, the former oil executive lambasted FDR's Social Security plan as a "gigantic fraud."³⁴ But after being hammered for his ties to the nation's now-discredited financial dynasties, there was little Landon could do to "stop the Democratic onslaught."³⁵ With Americans decisively rejecting Republican pleas for a return to business as usual, the party was desperate to moderate its message. So desperate that, in 1940, the GOP selected former Democrat Wendell Willkie as its presidential standard-bearer. But Willkie's efforts proved no more successful than Landon's.³⁶

The United States' entry into World War II in 1941 further compounded the GOP's troubles, "instill[ing] a sense of entitlement . . . the federal government increasingly would have to placate."³⁷ Whatever conservatism would mean to the millions now mobilized to fight in Europe and the Pacific, it would have to reckon with dizzying changes that further grew the government: among them, wage and price controls, labor arbitration, mass income taxation, and structural deficits. With the war and its aftermath as backdrop, Dewey replaced Willkie at the top of the party's 1944 presidential ticket. Intent on crafting a "forward-looking" program for the GOP, the popular governor embraced a variety of traditional Democratic priorities, including the right to strike. But moderate Republicans' second attempt to dislodge Roosevelt from office was no more successful than the first. More than a decade after ceding national power, neither wing of the party had articulated a vision or presented a candidate capable of building a new majority.³⁸

Not surprisingly, Republicans' halting search for political relevance did not yield an intraparty truce. Effectively locked out of the White House, the party's two factions waged war in Congress. In the Senate, conservatives rallied to Taft. Grandson of a cabinet official and son of a president and Supreme Court justice, the man famously known as "Mr. Republican" believed "in moving very slowly and changing almost never."[39] Accordingly, he staked his political reputation, and that of his fellow conservatives, on the idea that only continued opposition to Roosevelt's program of social democracy would reverse his party's fortunes. "There is only one way to beat the New Deal," Taft insisted. "And that is head on. You can't outdeal them."[40]

Taft's stature, however, concealed substantial dissension within conservative ranks. While there was general agreement that the New Deal represented a depraved vision of government involvement in the economy, Taft's acolytes differed over how much intervention was too much, particularly when it came to policies that benefited the nation's largest corporations. So, too, growing tensions with the Soviet Union scrambled the Old Guard's long-standing commitment to isolationism, with some on the right increasingly favoring muscular defense spending to fight communism abroad.[41] But the conservatives' disorder also reflected their overreliance on Taft's gravitational pull. With Taft taking on the role of factional impresario—the right's "intellectual and practical head"—there was little incentive for conservative senators to collaborate with any degree of regularity.[42]

Often falling prey to sectional divisions, the Senate's Republican moderates found it no easier to organize their ranks. Although guided by the shared conviction that the GOP should not "sa[y] no to all proposals for change," they struggled to articulate a positive legislative agenda.[43] Western moderates, for their part, continued to defend federal policies that aided agricultural recovery, but they wavered on measures they saw as unfairly advantaging urban communities. Easterners, by contrast, were more willing to back the New Deal's expanded social safety net—reassured by corporations back home that Roosevelt's program promoted economic stability—but hesitated to further subsidize the nation's farmers. Lacking a Taft-like figure to bridge these regional differences, moderate Republicans tended to advance their policy priorities haphazardly and with little coordination.[44] Moderate senators and their staff readily acknowledged this deficiency. As one legislative aide described the problem, "To achieve unity, we must work for it. Coordination is no gift of the gods."[45]

Even on bills that bridged the moderates' sectional divide, collective action proved difficult to sustain. For instance, Senator Wayne Morse of Oregon would later recall that, despite collaborating in committee to soften the initial draft of what would become known as the Taft-Hartley Act (formally, the Labor Management Relations Act of 1947), he and his fellow moderates failed to defend their preferred language from conservative attack on the floor. As Morse observed in the wake of their defeat, "Had those . . . who stood shoulder to shoulder during the long weeks of committee hearings and discussions . . . continued to stand together in support of the committee bill when it reached the floor of the Senate, the Taft-Hartley law would not be the law it is today."[46]

The Eightieth Congress (1947–49) represented a high-water mark for conservatives. With Roosevelt no longer in the White House (Vice President Harry Truman having been elevated to the presidency upon FDR's death in 1945) and Republicans making significant gains in the 1946 midterms, Taft—like many in the party—was certain he had a "popular mandate to cast out a great many chapters of the New Deal, if not the whole book."[47] But only a year after triumphantly enacting their long-sought labor law reform, Taft lost the party's 1948 presidential nomination to Dewey, a result that underscored the limits of the conservatives' appeal. Moderates would fare little better, finding themselves in a familiar predicament on the heels of Dewey's general-election loss to the incumbent President Truman. Lacking the numerical might and organizational wherewithal to realize their policy ambitions, they were left to snipe at the party's right wing. Still bitter, Morse minced no words in laying the blame for the GOP's electoral failures on Taft and the Old Guard. "Everyone knows that the Taft-Hartley Act was a terrific liability to the Republican Party."[48]

Enter Knowland and McCarthy

While Taft claimed the limelight in the years immediately following World War II, it was Knowland and McCarthy—both members of the 1946 freshman class—who would go on to transform the Republican Party. Of the two, McCarthy, whose last name has become a metonym for the frenzied populist conservatism he helped ignite, is surely the better known. His "casual disregard for custom and authority" quickly made him enemies in Washington.[49] Only two years into his term, the junior senator from Wisconsin was banished from the Banking and Currency Committee after his behavior so incensed colleagues that the committee's chair threatened to resign. Undaunted, McCarthy directed his contempt elsewhere, attacking another chair who was, at the time, investigating (and defending) American troops accused of war crimes.[50]

With support at home eroding, the senator cast about for an issue that would bolster his flagging reelection chances. Capitalizing on the country's nascent paranoia about perfidious elites, McCarthy found a message that catapulted him virtually overnight into the center of national power. In his infamous address to the Women's Republican Club of Wheeling, West Virginia, in early 1950, McCarthy eschewed both the antistatist diatribes of conservatives like Taft and the progovernment entreaties of moderates like Morse. As would come to define his rhetoric, the senator expressed "no problem with an activist government and never challenged the New Deal's social welfare programs."[51] Instead, he articulated a politics of grievance, calling attention to a generic sense of American decline—describing what he called "a position of impotency." In his telling, those responsible for "selling this nation out" were not ordinary "innocent" Americans but Washington's "warped" elites who had "the finest homes, the finest college education, and the finest jobs in government."[52] This accusatory message, and his claim to have a secret list of more than two hundred communists working in the State Department, captured the public imagination, generating headlines and turning the senator into a political celebrity.

Though Knowland, like McCarthy, chafed at the Senate's restrictive folkways, the two men could hardly have come from more disparate backgrounds. McCarthy's was a classically hardscrabble origin story. Born on a small farm in northeastern Wisconsin, the former Democrat painstakingly made his ascent: from farmhand to grocery store clerk, then to law school, a position in a prominent local practice, and ultimately an elected judgeship.[53] Knowland, in contrast, was the scion of a wealthy and well-connected California family. Having served in both chambers of the state legislature and the US House of Representatives, his father leveraged a controlling interest in the *Oakland Tribune* to emerge as one of the state's most influential Republican power brokers.[54] In 1928, the younger Knowland entered the family business, working briefly at the paper before winning a seat in the California State Assembly.[55] By 1934, he was a state senator and, four years later, the youngest member of the Republican National Committee—a position he obtained with the help of Earl Warren, then a rising star in the party who owed his own start in politics to the older Knowland's patronage.[56] A decade later, the bond between Warren, newly elected governor, and the Knowland family would prove critical. When California senator and progressive Republican icon Hiram Johnson died in August 1945, it was Warren who selected the younger Knowland—then in the army serving in the European theater of operations—as his replacement.[57] The future majority leader would win his seat outright in the 1946 midterms in a campaign that cemented his bona fides as an anticommunist hard-liner.[58]

Like Warren, Knowland occupied an enigmatic middle space in the Republican Party of the mid-twentieth century.[59] When it came to domestic politics, he (like McCarthy) was more moderate than Taft and his conservative brethren. Indeed, as a freshman in the California Senate, Knowland had pushed for a bill to create a state unemployment program. Several years later, he publicly condemned conservative Republicans for their "program of carping criticism" and urged the party instead to adopt a positive, progressive platform.[60] And upon arriving in Washington, the junior senator backed legislation to create a national Fair Employment Practices Commission to address racial discrimination in the labor market—a key priority of the Truman administration and an initiative that Taft, along with many other conservative Republicans, strongly opposed.[61]

Nor was Knowland willing to fall in line when it came to the GOP's internal affairs. Less than four years into his Senate career, he joined a heterodox group of junior Republican senators eager to loosen Taft's grip on the Republican Party. Dubbing themselves the "Young Turks," the dissidents shared little beyond a distaste for Taft's leadership; the group included moderates like Morse alongside others who, like Knowland and Henry Cabot Lodge Jr. of Massachusetts, defied easy categorization.[62] At the opening of the Eighty-First Congress in January 1949, the rebels made their move, proposing to replace Taft as chair of the Republican Policy Committee and threatening to block the Ohioan's preferred choice for minority leader. In a measure of the status he had gained in his short time in Washington, Knowland was put forward as the Young Turks' proposed floor leader.[63] Their challenge proved premature, as Taft quickly defused the conflict by taking on one Turk as party whip and adding two others to the Policy Committee.[64]

While Knowland may have resented Taft his power, the junior senator from California was no moderate. Despite his deviations from conservative orthodoxy, he was "never identified in the minds of the Taftites with 'the Dewey people.'"[65] And, as a westerner, he benefited from the Old Guard's sustained prejudice against the northeastern Republican elite. Most important, as the 1940s drew to a close and the Cold War pivoted to East Asia, Knowland positioned himself ever more firmly as a crusader against communism.[66] He would later reflect that, although McCarthy had been said to "overstate his case," it was clear the senator "had a case to state," declaring, "There is no doubt about it that there were espionage agents that had infiltrated the government."[67] Knowland would also join McCarthy in singling out the State Department for particular scrutiny, going so far as to condemn career-level bureaucrats by name on the Senate floor.[68] Blaming one department official, Owen Lattimore, for "losing" China, Knowland asked his colleagues, "Wherein do the end results [advocated by] Mr. Lattimore differ from the objectives of international Communists?"[69]

How Do You Solve a Problem Like McCarthy?

In reanimating a dormant strain of American conservatism, the junior senator from Wisconsin reshaped the GOP's internal politics, for both moderates and conservatives saw in McCarthy a vehicle to resolve the party's long-running civil war. Thrilled by McCarthy's popularity, conservatives rejoiced that an unapologetically hard-line politics could so captivate the public. While some expressed private doubts about McCarthy's character—Taft called his Wheeling speech a "perfectly reckless performance"—and embrace of welfare programs they had long opposed, the party's Old Guard saw in the senator a figure who could best express their agenda to achieve maximum public resonance.[70] Consequently, they tended to excuse McCarthy's excesses and deviations from traditional conservative principles and instead urged him to "keep talking" about the communist threat. As Taft advised, "If one case doesn't work out . . . proceed with another one."[71]

The headlines and acclaim that McCarthy soon garnered meant that conservatives could afford to support his crusade with minimal collaboration of their own. In the Senate, aid to McCarthy was limited to ad hoc efforts by individual lawmakers to reinforce the senator's claims on the floor and familiarize him with the nuances of State Department procedure.[72] Outside Congress, the senator's conservative allies provided his office with research support and helped ensure a friendly audience for hearings convened by the newly empaneled subcommittee to investigate State Department employees, chaired by Maryland's Millard Tydings.[73] But with McCarthy's place on the Tydings Committee offering a highly visible forum to air his allegations, the senator demanded little in the way of assistance from his fellow conservatives. Indeed, as the midterm elections of

1950 approached, it soon became apparent that the Republican Old Guard needed McCarthy more than he needed them.[74]

In those early days, because moderate Republicans generally shared their colleagues' enthusiasm for McCarthy's campaign, they found little reason to collectively oppose him. Substantively, most thought his allegations of communist infiltration of government agencies were well founded.[75] Even Maine's Margaret Chase Smith, who would eventually condemn McCarthy in her celebrated "Declaration of Conscience," admitted she was "impressed" by his Wheeling speech.[76] Instrumentally, moderates like Chase Smith recognized that the Wisconsin senator's talent for seizing headlines could help them win—and, ideally, retain—the legislative majorities that had largely eluded the GOP. Once in power, they hoped a mutually beneficial division of labor could be established. In exchange for a free hand to investigate alleged cases of communist subversion, McCarthy would support (or at least not oppose) their more progressive domestic policy agenda. Even those moderates skeptical of McCarthy's agenda regarded his fight as a passing fad, a sideshow in their decades-long war with the Old Guard.[77]

Though moderate misgivings would grow as McCarthy's attacks became ever more brazen, their efforts to restrain or hold the senator accountable remained sporadic and disorganized. Chase Smith's critique of the senator's tactics, delivered on the Senate floor in the summer of 1950, is instructive. Rebuking McCarthy for turning the upper chamber into "a publicity platform for irresponsible sensationalism," she accused him of seeking "selfish political gain at the sacrifice of individual reputations and national unity."[78] But while her fellow moderates cheered the speech, only six (out of nearly a dozen) agreed to back it.[79] Most refused, claiming they preferred "to convert McCarthy rather than get him reprimanded publicly."[80] Unwilling to take on a greater leadership role within the moderate faction, Chase Smith had little recourse. As her own biographer details, neither she nor her fellow signatories made any further "attempt to enlist supporters, organize active opposition to McCarthy, or continue the effort [initiated by the Declaration] in any manner."[81]

Over the next year and a half, McCarthy would give the moderates little reason to change course. His continued broadsides against the Truman administration and Democratic lawmakers held out the possibility that the GOP could retake Congress and the White House. Indeed, McCarthy was a featured speaker in congressional races across the country during the 1950 midterms, credited with helping to defeat several Democratic incumbents.[82] There was also fear that McCarthy would target those within his own party who stood in his way. As one lobbyist affiliated with the moderate faction advised, "Members are genuinely concerned . . . that the Wisconsin Senator might invade their States at election time and defeat them."[83]

As they turned their attention to the 1952 presidential election, moderates had yet another reason to eschew collaboration: Eisenhower's eagerly anticipated entry into the presidential race. Believing the beloved former general could match (if not exceed) McCarthy in popularity, moderates hoped the "McCarthy problem" might be solved without their aid. With McCarthy attacking wartime icons like General George C. Marshall—and Ike firing back, declaring he had "no patience with anyone who can find in [Marshall's] record of service . . . anything to criticize" and announcing that he would never campaign for McCarthy—moderates had good reason to think that, once in office, Eisenhower would do what was necessary to put the Wisconsin senator in his place.[84]

Knowland Steps In

Eisenhower's ascension to the White House did little to alleviate his party's factional strife. While Taft would be the first Republican leader to manage the escalating conflict between the executive branch and the junior senator from Wisconsin, the task would soon fall to Knowland.[85] After being diagnosed with terminal cancer in April 1953, Taft passed away three months later. Head of the party's Steering and Policy Committee after his own resounding reelection, Knowland was Taft's chosen successor.[86] Aloof and uncompromising, Knowland lacked the humor of rivals like Dirksen and the gravitas of Colorado's well-respected Eugene Millikin.[87] But Taft selected the Californian in part because he thought Knowland was best positioned to navigate the party's charged factional landscape. The new majority leader had bonds with both factions but was indebted to neither. His friendship with the liberal Warren and support for several controversial Eisenhower appointees could help bridge his differences with moderates, while his aggressive criticism of US foreign policy aided him in making common cause with conservatives.

There would be little room for error, as Republican control of the Senate rested on the thinnest of reeds.[88] Adding to the new majority leader's burdens were the parliamentary savvy and personal guile of

Johnson, his newly elevated Democratic counterpart, and his own increasingly fraught relationship with the president. While Johnson delighted in exploiting Knowland's fragile majority to partisan advantage, Eisenhower found him disagreeable, remarking to a friend that it was a "pity" Knowland's "wisdom, his judgment, his tact and his sense of humor lag so far behind his ambition."[89]

McCarthy, meanwhile, was in full flower. In addition to his seat on the powerful Appropriations Committee, the senator was promoted to chair of the Committee on Government Operations, which encompassed the recently constituted Permanent Subcommittee on Investigations, charged with exposing communist subversion.[90] From this redoubt, McCarthy assailed the executive branch anew, targeting allegedly lax security at the State Department, the content of its overseas libraries, and purported communist infiltration at the agency's flagship radio broadcasting network, Voice of America.[91] He then turned his attention to the Defense Department, investigating allegations of espionage at defense plants and communist sympathizers within the Army Corps of Engineers.[92]

Though their despair at the senator's power deepened, Republican moderates remained loath to criticize McCarthy publicly, let alone coalesce into a bona fide internal opposition. Indeed, their disarray was such that they could not even agree on a joint plan of action, squandering Knowland's declaration that he was open to curbing "one-man rule of Senate investigating committees."[93] While some moderates proposed to strip McCarthy's subcommittee of its singular authority to investigate communist subversion in the hope of dimming the senator's spotlight, others joined with Democrats in advocating for stronger minority rights in the hope that such rights would offset the senator's control of committee proceedings.[94]

As the moderates remained divided, neither proposal got off the ground. Instead, the task of checking the senator fell to a few Democrats and a new political action committee, dubbed the National Committee for an Effective Congress, and its McCarthy "Clearing House." Describing the "tremendous vacuum" in organized opposition to McCarthy in either party, the committee's founding director Maurice Rosenblatt recalled "men with good intentions . . . standing out in a no-man's land, attacking . . . and not making a dent."[95] With Democratic leaders studiously refusing to aid the anti-McCarthy cause and many of the party's southerners sympathetic to the senator, the moderates' disorganized approach left little need for the conservatives to collaborate themselves.[96]

It would be the Eisenhower administration that ratcheted up tensions with McCarthy. Angry at the senator's continued harassment of senior defense officials, the White House retaliated in March 1954 by releasing a chronology of McCarthy's chief legislative aide Roy Cohn's efforts to obtain favorable treatment for a recently drafted friend (and alleged lover).[97] Presented with this damaging material, McCarthy's supporters were forced to acquiesce to a public investigation of his misdeeds: the fabled Army-McCarthy hearings. Transfixed by the drama playing out on their television sets, Americans watched as the Senate's prosecutors cast McCarthy as "cruel," "reckless," and possessing "no decency."[98]

Moderates now had McCarthy on the defensive and saw an opportunity to wound him further. Still, they eschewed collaboration. Thus, when Vermont's Ralph Flanders offered a resolution to revoke McCarthy's committee assignments, he did so without consulting his moderate colleagues—instead opting to work with "people on the fringes of the Eisenhower administration."[99] The proposal met with a predictably lukewarm response. Senators in both parties expressed concern that Flanders's "hot potato" would undermine the chamber's seniority system.[100] Accordingly, Knowland dispatched it to the Rules Committee, chaired by McCarthy ally Indiana's William Jenner, who promptly announced that he had "no plans" to consider it further.[101] Although Flanders would continue to insist that his resolution was "very much alive," he began to consider alternatives, eventually settling on a censure motion "that would not affect [McCarthy's] status or prerogatives."[102] Introducing this new measure on July 20, 1954, Flanders called for the Senate to reprimand McCarthy for "conduct . . . unbecoming a Member of the United States Senate."[103]

Shaping the Endgame

With only days before the Senate was set to adjourn—and several key pieces of Eisenhower's agenda yet to be considered—the measure's fate rested with the majority leader. Unbeknownst to Flanders, Knowland had his own reservations about McCarthy, increasingly convinced that the Wisconsin senator's tendency to "fuzz it up" and be "loose with his figures" was a dangerous liability to the "cause [McCarthy] purport[ed] to be interested in." Though no stranger to the "rough and tumble of partisan battles," he also admitted to being personally "offended" by McCarthy's ad hominem attacks against his fellow senators, which violated the majority leader's sense of decorum. "This was just one of these things that wasn't done."[104] Nevertheless, he remained convinced that McCarthy's accusations of elite perfidy resonated with the public and would bring Republicans the kind of sustained electoral success that had long eluded them.[105] Determined to shear McCarthy's brand of populist conservatism from its unreliable spokesman, Knowland leveraged his party's factional symmetry to formally discipline the senator.

While previous accounts have overlooked the significance of the majority leader's intervention, he made two decisions that proved critical to McCarthy's censure. First, Knowland agreed to permit a "full-dress debate" on the measure, implicitly accepting Flanders's claim that the resolution was "privileged" under Senate rules.[106] His willingness to give the resolution expedited consideration surprised McCarthy's opponents, who had feared he would use "parliamentary maneuvers to sidetrack [it]." Indeed, as majority leader, Knowland had many options at his disposal should he have wished to kill the measure: he could have referred it to the Rules Committee (as he had done with Flanders's first proposal); moved to table it; challenged its privileged status (effectively ensuring that the Senate would adjourn before taking it up); or "divert[ed]" the Senate's attention by allowing a more free-wheeling debate about reforms to the Senate's investigative practices.[107]

Second, Knowland himself moved to create a bipartisan special committee authorized to hold hearings, subpoena witnesses and documents, take testimony, and, if warranted by the evidence, draw up detailed charges against McCarthy.[108] In deciding not to task a standing committee with the investigation, the majority leader ensured that *he* would have the power to select McCarthy's three Republican jurors. Those appointments were critical to determining the outcome and its perceived legitimacy. Were the committee's Republicans to side with the Democrats, who had every incentive to tarnish the GOP's reputation, McCarthy and his defenders would have little basis to suggest that the proceedings were simply a partisan witch hunt.

Betraying no sympathy for the senator, Knowland appointed individuals who, in his view, "would have open and clear minds to examine the facts."[109] His pick for chair, Utah's Albert Watkins, was a devout Mormon and former judge, universally regarded as fair-minded, "thin and ascetic . . . with an unbending devotion to order and propriety."[110] His contemporaries remembered him as "an Old Testament kind of man, a hanging judge, [who] . . . got under McCarthy's skin."[111] To join Watkins,

Knowland tapped Francis Case of South Dakota and Frank Carlson of Kansas. "Mild-mannered, reserved, and conscientious," both were close to Eisenhower, with Carlson having served as an advisor during Ike's 1952 run for the presidency.[112] By disposition, these men were likely to focus on McCarthy's personal failings, rather than the bankruptcy of his ideas.

Blessed with a symmetric factional configuration, the majority leader made these choices without regard to what his Senate colleagues hoped to achieve. Indeed, the archival record provides little evidence that he consulted with either conservatives or moderates, nor is there any indication that either side mobilized to protest the slight. As one Republican senator recalled, Knowland was free to "run a one-man show" when it came to McCarthy's censure and to the Senate's business, more generally: "He made up his own mind, he made his own plans, we had no general party meetings . . . and none of us knew . . . what the program was."[113] Dirksen, in particular, resented Knowland's independence, noting that "he did not keep us informed. . . . We felt . . . that he just wanted to run everything without ever conferring with anybody."[114] But even that frustration was insufficient incentive to persuade either moderates or conservatives to collectively resist the majority leader.

With both factions failing to collaborate, Knowland worked to further insulate the special committee from members' interference, publicly declaring that "the type of the report, the nature of the report, and the finding is a matter that the committee [would] have to determine for itself."[115] Privately, the message to its members was much the same. As Watkins later recalled, Knowland "did not instruct me, even to the slightest degree, to go easy on McCarthy."[116] To insulate McCarthy's jurors from undue pressure or allegations that the deck was stacked against the accused, Knowland worked hard to ensure a "judicial atmosphere" for the proceedings. While insisting that McCarthy have an opportunity to appear before the committee and present a defense, Knowland nevertheless refused to enable the senator's theatrics, declining to "open up [the] hearings to television and similar activities."[117]

Although the majority leader's critics charged that delegating responsibility to a special committee was "mere camouflage for inaction," Watkins and his colleagues soberly executed their assigned task.[118] Believing that the Senate itself was "on trial," the Utah senator declared his hope that the committee would succeed in "maintain[ing] the American sense of fair play."[119] After nearly a month of hearings, the Watkins Committee formally recommended that the Senate censure McCarthy for his "unrighteous use of authority," charging him with two counts of contempt.[120] Debate on these charges opened in November 1954 (safely after the midterms), but the committee had done its work well. While McCarthy would attempt to tar his prosecutors as "handmaidens of the communist party," the committee's dispassionate presentation of the evidence left the outcome in little doubt.[121] As reflected in the debate preceding the vote, Knowland had succeeded in ensuring that Senate Republicans would judge McCarthy for his misconduct and not his beliefs. The final vote to "condemn" him passed, 67–22.[122]

With McCarthy's censure assured, the majority leader cast his personal vote to exonerate him—a move that puzzled many observers, including the president. "What's the guy trying to do?" Eisenhower asked his aides. "He personally picked the committee to draw up the censure charges, he vouched for their honor and integrity, and then he turns around and votes against them."[123] But Knowland had his eyes on the future, including a possible run for the White House. Although, as Ike recognized, he had done as much as anyone to sideline McCarthy, the majority leader could not afford to sever ties with his party's conservative faction altogether.[124] For his part, McCarthy tried to make light of the vote to censure him, quipping that "it wasn't exactly a vote of confidence."[125] In truth, he was increasingly isolated. Though he publicly vowed "to get back to the real work of digging out communism, crime, and corruption," McCarthy's colleagues saw a "changed man."[126] "It was pathetic," one journalist recalled, "to watch him prowling the corridors of the Capitol, button-holing newsmen and offering them stories they refused to file."[127] Long a hard drinker (even by Senate standards), he rapidly declined. He would be dead less than three years later.

Preserving Populist Conservatism

The Senate's formal reprimand of McCarthy marked the end of an era. The anticommunist hysteria that had preoccupied Americans in the early 1950s began to recede. In Washington, career bureaucrats breathed easier, no longer fearful that their names would cross the lips of Congress's professional red-baiters. A similar shift was soon felt outside the nation's capital, as blacklisted authors and screenwriters from New York to Hollywood were again credited for their creative output. Eager to move past the politics of grievance and accusation that had marred his first term in office, the newly reelected Eisenhower took pains to emphasize a progressive, forward-looking agenda for the Republican Party. Quoting the Norwegian playwright Henrik Ibsen, the president declared at the 1956 Republican convention, "I hold that man is in the right who is most clearly in league with the future."[128] By the early 1960s, McCarthy's brand of populist conservatism was decidedly out of fashion, as an array of popular commentators dismissed much right-wing thought as outmoded and dangerous.[129]

And yet the conservative ideology that McCarthy had done so much to popularize would survive, initially nurtured by fringe organizations like the John Birch Society that sprouted up to oppose what they feared to be a growing liberal consensus within the party, and then by Goldwater and his 1964 presidential campaign. Indeed, as the Republican nominee, Goldwater freely borrowed from the political tropes that McCarthy had deployed to such great effect. Laying the groundwork for his run for the White House, Goldwater styled himself as the Wisconsin senator's heir: the defender of those "silent" Americans "who quietly go about the business of paying and praying, working and saving." It was they, he argued, who had been left furthest behind by the country's political class.[130] Indeed, the senator's celebrated book—*Conscience of a Conservative*—observed that the United States was most likely to "succumb to internal weakness rather than fall before a foreign foe."[131]

Goldwater was far from alone in picking up what McCarthy had put down. Future president Ronald Reagan, a popular movie actor in the 1940s who had testified before McCarthy's subcommittee and become increasingly involved in conservative politics, sounded these same themes in a televised address announcing his support for Goldwater's run for the presidency, warning Americans against the dangers of a "little intellectual elite in a far-distant capital" that believed it could "plan our lives for us better than we can plan them ourselves."[132]

To be sure, populist conservatism has had many authors more brazen and celebrated than Knowland. But the majority leader's decision to reprimand McCarthy for his personal misbehavior rather than the ideas he popularized ensured that the Wisconsin senator's heralded successors could use his ideas without being tarred as his acolytes—to create, as Knowland had intended, a McCarthy-style politics divorced from the senator himself.

Much like McCarthy, however, Knowland would soon fade from the political scene. Having decided that his hopes for a presidential run were best served by seeking the governorship of California, he announced in early 1957 that he would not seek a third term in the Senate, stunning his colleagues in the upper chamber.[133] Yet despite the backing of many prominent figures within the GOP—among them Nixon, who persuaded the incumbent governor to seek Knowland's old seat rather than challenge him in the primary—his campaign stumbled. Increasingly out of step with politics in his home state, the former majority leader lost the general election by over a million votes to the state's Democratic attorney general, Edmund G. "Pat" Brown.[134] Dispirited, he left politics to run the family newspaper and publishing business. There, his personal life soon unraveled. Bankrupted by a gambling habit and a ruinous second marriage, he died by suicide in February 1974.

Conclusion

Perhaps it is because Knowland's Senate career ended so abruptly that he plays only bit parts in accounts of the mid-twentieth-century Congress. Or perhaps history has given him the cold shoulder because he failed to reach the White House or to secure a significant legislative accomplishment akin to Taft's labor-management law or Dirksen's civil rights bill. Perhaps, too, aspects of his personality limited his public acclaim. Lacking the charisma of his more celebrated colleagues, Knowland did not cultivate a coterie of journalist-admirers to chronicle his exploits the way Johnson did, nor was he renowned for his wit or sparkling oratory like Dirksen or Goldwater.

In burnishing the legacies of Knowland's contemporaries, however, we have underestimated the majority leader's influence in orchestrating McCarthy's censure and accelerating his demise. As this chapter has shown, Knowland intervened at a delicate moment in the campaign to subdue the Wisconsin senator. Bucking both wings of his party, he made certain that the Senate considered the censure motion and McCarthy's fate on *his* terms. By appointing as jurors individuals he believed would fairly evaluate the charges leveled against McCarthy, the majority leader saw to it that the upper chamber's repudiation of the senator was cabined to his personal excesses. In so doing, he preserved the substance of the politics McCarthy had championed before his fall from grace: a rejection of traditional small-government conservatism in favor of a newly populist approach that embraced social programs but limited their aid to "ordinary" Americans.

Knowland's capacity to wield power in this way was neither the result of pure happenstance nor attributable to exceptional features of his biography. Rather, the majority leader—like House Speakers Rayburn and Pelosi—benefited from a favorable factional configuration. Throughout his Senate career, conservative and moderate Republicans refrained from collaboration, relying instead on the auspices of resourceful individuals, like Taft and Flanders, to do battle with each other. It was this parity in collaborative activity between the two wings of the Republican Party that provided Knowland the opening to move against McCarthy. With his party frozen in equipoise, the majority leader was free to steer the GOP in the direction he thought best.

CHAPTER EIGHT

Learning from Divided Parties

Leadership means asserting your independence. —Nancy Pelosi[1]

For decades, students of Congress have viewed divided parties as a critical constraint on leadership. The general consensus is that the more a party's rank and file agree with one another, the stronger their leaders will be. As member preferences begin to diverge, however, leader power is thought to diminish. Yet as we have seen, party divisions are not inherently limiting. Leaders who govern symmetrically divided parties—that is, parties where both factions are collaborating with equal intensity—are often able to transcend and even draw strength from their warring ranks. It is more often leaders of asymmetrically divided parties—parties with a single, collaboratively ascendant faction—who struggle to impose their will.

In chapter 3, we observed how the same legislative leader navigated two very different factional configurations with varying results. In the battle to pass comprehensive healthcare reform, Speaker Nancy Pelosi was repeatedly hamstrung by moderate Democrats. Far better organized than progressives, their reluctance to embrace many of the Speaker's preferred interventions won the day. A decade later, however, the Speaker would find a changed bargaining environment. With progressives newly committed to robust collaboration, Pelosi was able to compel moderates to look past their misgivings and support her flagship legislative initiative: sweeping climate change policy.

In chapters 4 and 5, we saw firsthand the challenges of governing asymmetrically divided parties. We began with Republican Speaker John

Boehner. Struggling to deter his mobilized right flank from pursuing a legislative strategy he opposed, and lacking comparably organized moderate allies, Boehner found little room to maneuver. Forced to accede to conservative demands, the Speaker hoped in vain that the public fallout from the conservatives' desired government shutdown would undermine their influence within the party. Instead, in the absence of equally robust moderate collaboration, the fight further emboldened conservatives to challenge Boehner's hold on the speakership itself. Three decades earlier, Speaker Tip O'Neill confronted a similar factional configuration in his Democratic Party. With liberals fragmented and conservatives organized and eager to have their say, O'Neill could do little to block passage of Ronald Reagan's budget plan. Burdened by his party's asymmetry, the Speaker was instead compelled to pursue a strategy he and many of his colleagues feared would be a losing one: discredit the president's economic policy on television.

Finally, chapters 6 and 7 showcased the virtues of factional symmetry. Speaker Sam Rayburn had for decades experienced considerable difficulty keeping collaboratively ascendant southern conservatives in line. It was only when liberals began to work together in earnest that Rayburn gained the upper hand, using their organizational might to wrest the Rules Committee from southerners' control. Rayburn's Republican Senate counterpart, Majority Leader William Knowland, similarly benefited from his party's symmetry. Unencumbered by collaborating factions, Knowland was free to decide Senator Joseph McCarthy's fate as he saw fit. Defying the demands of both moderate and conservative Republicans, he chose to reprimand the Wisconsin senator for his personal misbehavior rather than the ideas he popularized. In so doing, the majority leader was instrumental in helping to divorce McCarthy's style of politics from the man himself.

Underscoring the Importance of the Collaborative Dimension of Legislative Politics

Given the historical record, it is worth asking why legislative scholars have consistently misjudged the potential for leaders of divided parties to exercise real power. This book contends that they have done so because of their broader tendency to conceptualize legislative behavior in exclusively ideological terms. For instance, when thinking about inter-party conflict in Congress, "contemporary analysts . . . literally *equate* [it] with party polarization on the ideological continuum. They have adopted methodologies explicitly assuming that partisan patterns in congressional roll-call votes can be reduced down to members' individual policy preferences."[2] Scholars, in other words, begin and end with the proposition that what most matters in Congress is what is inside members' heads.

Applied to the study of leadership, however, thinking in exclusively ideological terms has important limitations. As I have argued, we ought to doubt that congressional institutions, including leadership positions, will be quite as responsive to changes in member preferences as the conventional wisdom implies. It requires no stretch of the imagination to believe that the more members disagree with each other, the more they might *wish* to see power decentralized. Why risk leaders using that power to serve ends they might find objectionable? But altering the distribution of power is more easily said than done. Members must be able to resolve both collective action and coordination challenges. At minimum, they must identify a new level of leader power they collectively prefer, settle on a joint strategy they believe is likely to yield it, and then commit to pursuing that strategy together—all the while cognizant that leaders will do what they can to maintain the status quo. Members must also grapple with the possibility that some within their ranks may see discord as reason to strengthen the prerogatives and autonomy of leadership, in the hopes that insulating those at the top of the party hierarchy will prevent their rivals from infiltrating the party's machinery and using it to further ends they oppose.

Further, privileging members' preferences underestimates the potential of leaders to engage in spirited resistance when members push back against their authority. Not only are leaders likely to loathe seeing their power reduced, but they possess an array of institutional resources to prevent that possibility. Particularly in the contemporary Congress, leaders can leverage their significant informational advantages and procedural prerogatives to quash efforts to undercut their authority. They may well be aided in this cause by influential party stakeholders who have grown accustomed to the status quo and found ways to benefit from it. Whatever these lawmakers' disagreements with leadership, and they may be substantial, those who see themselves as beneficiaries of a particular distribution of authority may prefer the current equilibrium to uncertain alternatives.

Given these dynamics, this book has argued that legislative scholars have by and large overlooked the *collaborative dimension* of legislative politics. Its intellectual point of departure is straightforward. Like other political actors, lawmakers seek out allies with whom they share a broad worldview or, if they are fortunate, similar policy preferences on the issues they care most about. But within every group of like-minded lawmakers — that is, within every faction — members get to choose whether to join forces or go it alone.

The exercise of this choice matters greatly for legislative politics generally and for leader power specifically. At the level of a single faction, lawmakers' decision to work together may yield a variety of assets. At minimum, collaboration generates information about what members of a faction think and can agree on. Over time, and especially as their joint efforts intensify, it can also confer greater credibility when members negotiate with leaders or rivals. Collaboration is understood by others to reflect and reinforce participating members' commitment to one another and to their shared priorities. At the level of the party, these decisions — taken together and played out across time — serve as the foundation for a broader collaborative architecture. At any given time, a faction can be collaborating more than, less than, or on a par with rivals. Thus, as politics evolves, a party's collaborative configuration can change, too, as its constitutive factions elect to increase or diminish their collaborative efforts. What party leaders encounter, then, is a political environment where member preferences are mobilized differentially *and* dynamically.

As we have seen, some configurations are more advantageous to party leaders than others. In one form of party symmetry — situations where a party's rival factions have all chosen to eschew collaboration — leaders can pursue their aims with the knowledge that they are unlikely to encounter much, if any, organized resistance. The logic here is that absent some demonstrated commitment to collective action, no faction is likely to effectively marshal its members to counter a leader intent on getting what that leader wants. In a second form of party symmetry — situations where all factions are collaborating — the mechanism is different, but the result similar. Here, rather than rely on members' disorganization to work their will, leaders can leverage the organizational might of one faction to bully competing factions into submission. The key virtue of this form of symmetry is that leaders can be reasonably certain that whichever faction is most amenable to their preferred course of action will have, or be perceived to have, the collaborative capacity to equal any faction that decides to resist.

Party asymmetry, by contrast, offers leaders far less certainty that they will be able to get their way. Indeed, as we have seen, an organizationally dominant faction hostile to leaders' preferences can be a consistent headache. Without the ballast of an equally capable ally, leaders must depend on the support of factions ill-equipped to do battle against a well-organized foe, or simply go it alone. But even in situations where the leader and ascendant faction align in the short term, asymmetry can yield unstable partnerships in the long term. In time, members may seek to renegotiate the terms of the relationship to gain the upper hand. Alternatively, they may turn against leadership altogether, the better to distinguish themselves from the party's establishment. And in those rare cases where the bond between leader and faction remains strong, leaders may nevertheless see both their reputation and the authority that flows from it diminish, as lawmakers and actors outside the legislature begin to question who is really calling the shots.

None of this is to suggest that legislative scholars should focus on the collaborative dimension alone. As we have seen throughout this book, how lawmakers think about the salient policy and procedural questions of their day shapes the interaction between factional politics and leader power. For instance, the more that the preferences of a faction's membership overlap, the easier it ought to be for them to resolve the collective action and coordination challenges that might otherwise impede their efforts to get what they mutually desire. Factional preference alignment, in this sense, should—all else equal—pose a threat to party leaders. But this possibility is mitigated by a second, competing dynamic. The more lukewarm a faction's collective opposition to a leader's preferred intervention, the easier it ought to be for the leader to push it through without much difficulty.

For these reasons, this book's theoretical approach, coupled with the evidence it marshals in support of its core claims, is intended to serve as a corrective to legislative scholars' overriding focus on preferences as dispositive to legislative outcomes. Its motivating purpose is to bring to the study of legislative politics an insight we have long appreciated in other political contexts—that how like-minded people mobilize to achieve their ends matters as much to their success as what they believe. The balance of this conclusion explores the broader implications of this worldview.

Legislative Politics Is Not Just a Numbers Game

Given how important legislative scholars generally think preferences are to what happens in Congress, it is not surprising that they typically rely on head counts to explain legislative action and inaction. The congressional press corps tends to frame lawmaking in numerical terms, too. Bills are said to fail when a proposal simply didn't have the votes; bills pass when enough members want them to. Treating legislative politics as a numbers game makes obvious sense. In the majoritarian House, bills live or die at the hands of the members who, together, constitute a chamber majority. As one House leader put it, "The only thing that counts is 218 votes . . . nothing else is real."[3] The same goes for the Senate where, in recent decades, a supermajority of members has been required to do most legislating.

But a renewed emphasis on the collaborative dimension of legislative politics makes clear that congressional outcomes cannot necessarily be reduced to a numbers game. Collaborating effectively can make a small faction more powerful than its numbers alone would suggest. The reverse is also true. Minimal or ineffective collaboration can weaken a large faction and undercut its numerical advantage. Throughout this book, we have seen both dynamics at play. In the contemporary House, for instance, conservative Republicans have consistently exercised greater influence over the party's leadership than their moderate colleagues, who boast similar numbers but have failed to replicate the conservatives' collaborative apparatus. Likewise, we saw that liberal Democrats in the postreform Congress were far more numerous than their conservative rivals and yet failed to capitalize on that advantage because their ranks were fractured. Though fewer in number, conservative Democrats in the early 1980s pooled their votes and thus ensured themselves the necessary leverage to bargain directly with the Reagan White House over the president's budget plan.

Thinking about legislative politics along the collaborative dimension also complicates the view that policy and procedural outcomes reflect the preferences of members privileged by virtue of their spatial position. On this account, it is the member whose position relative to others along a unidimensional ideological continuum—the floor median in the majoritarian House and the sixtieth vote (also known as the filibuster pivot) in the supermajoritarian Senate—that matters most to legislative outcomes. The intuition is straightforward. Unless those members are satisfied by a bill on offer, they can doom it to failure by siding with colleagues who oppose it. The challenge, as politics today underscores, is to understand why party leaders sometimes prioritize the wants of lawmakers who do not occupy these pivotal positions.

Attending to collaboration offers some answers. For a faction at the ideological extreme of a party coalition, collaboration presents the chance to control the necessary votes to deny the party its majority. In this way, they, too, can play a decisive role within the party. By the same token, the absence of collaboration can weaken otherwise spatially advantaged members. The less they work together, the more vulnerable they are to threats or promises offered by party leaders.

As with numbers, recent history provides ample evidence that collaboration can magnify the power of ideological extremists within the majority party and undercut that of members who occupy ostensibly pivotal spatial positions. We saw, for instance, that by the mid-2010s, Republican moderates' unwillingness to invest in collaboration eroded what influence they could claim from representing the floor median. This asymmetry in factional collaboration has grown only more pronounced in subsequent years, putting both Republican leaders and moderates in a perennial bind. But the GOP is not uniquely predisposed to favor hardline positions. Recall that House progressives' decision to augment their collaborative capacity over the same period magnified their influence within the Democratic Caucus and helped offset the power of the party's moderates, whose spatial advantage had long been reinforced by their organizational prowess.

How should legislative scholars proceed, then, if counting heads and attending to spatial position are only part of the story? The history detailed in this book suggests that students of Congress would do well to incorporate the collaborative dimension more routinely into accounts of legislative behavior and outcomes. The qualitative, narrative approach used here is one way to do this. But it is surely not the only way to be attentive to the collaborative choices lawmakers make. Indeed, students of Congress are already drawing on data sets that use cosponsorship, "Dear Colleague" letters, and official travel records to assess the consequences of members' efforts to forge relationships with one another.[4] There are many other indicators that could be tapped. As detailed in chapter 2, factional collaboration produces a distinct evidentiary footprint, including records of meetings and confidential exchanges between members, that can help scholars map the collaborative dimension across legislative chamber and historical era.

Representation and the Collaborative Dimension

Attending to patterns of collaboration should also prompt us to think differently about the representational capacity of Congress. Start with the relationship between individual constituents and the politicians elected to represent them in Congress. Democratic theorists generally frame that relationship in ideological terms. Lawmakers, we are taught, represent their constituents best when they hold the same opinions, at least on those issues constituents believe to be most relevant to their district or state.[5] As Hanna Pitkin writes, "The representative . . . must act in their [constituents'] interest, and this means he must not normally come into conflict with their wishes."[6] The greater the degree of overlap in opinion, the stronger the representational connection between constituents and their representatives.

But it is possible to evaluate individual-level representation in collaborative terms as well. Holding constant the degree of overlap in constituent and member opinion, we might say that constituents are better served the more their senator or representative works with similarly situated colleagues to pursue their respective constituents' shared aims. Take, for example, progressive voters in districts represented by members of the Congressional Progressive Caucus. They receive higher-quality representation today than similarly progressive voters in similarly progressive districts received in periods when progressive lawmakers struggled to collectively advocate for left-of-center policy goals. Indeed, thanks in part to contemporary progressive House members' willingness to engage in collective action, progressive issue positions are now better understood, more frequently discussed, and more influential in shaping policy proposals than in decades prior.

Collaboration also mediates the relationship between Congress as a collective body and the electorate at large. Underlying most legislative scholarship is the view that what Congress does should reflect what the public wants. As John Hibbing and Christopher Larimer point out, Congress was "designed to be a permeable institution. If it is doing its job, public opinion should . . . affect the policy actions that Congress takes."[7] On this account, the more the legislative agenda mirrors the public's priorities, the stronger the representational connection between the American people and the legislative branch. Notably, this appears to be how most Americans think representation should work. In a recent poll, 84 percent of respondents agreed that "the goal of Congress should be to make the decisions that a majority of Americans would make."[8]

But just as we think that congressional activity in the aggregate ought to reflect the public's preferences, it is equally possible for members' own patterns of collaboration to reflect how the public is mobilized. That is, when movements coalesce in the electorate, we might expect to observe the formation of related organizations for lawmakers. And there is at least suggestive evidence that Congress works in this very way, both today and in the past. Consider, for example, that in the mid-twentieth century, liberal collaboration in Congress paralleled liberal mobilization in the electorate, ebbing in the early 1950s during the height of McCarthy's Red Scare and peaking in the late 1960s and early 1970s alongside social movements for racial and gender justice and consumer and environmental protection. By the same token, in the present day, the collaborative efforts of right-wing lawmakers have followed closely on the heels of robust organizing by conservative voters at the grass roots. This hypothesized relationship may also work in reverse. The less mobilized a segment of the electorate, the lower the odds that members sympathetic to the views of such voters will choose to augment their collaborative efforts. Thus, for example, the larger-scale demobilization of moderate Republican voters has mirrored the declining organization of the party's centrist flank in Congress.

Materialism may explain this connection, at least in part. Given that groups of mobilized citizens, including activists and donors, can direct tangible rewards toward those factions that share their goals, it stands to reason that the returns to collaboration in Congress might increase as the resources of allied outsiders multiply and efforts to coordinate their distribution improve. In the heyday of 1960s-era liberal collaboration, for instance, an array of sympathetic interest groups, from the NAACP to the AFL-CIO, helped raise money for the Democratic Study Group's campaign fund. This, in turn, created financial incentives for members of the Democrats' left-wing faction to collaborate with their fellows. By the same token, we might point to moderate Republicans' eagerness to avoid attacks from grassroots conservative groups as one possible reason for why they have scaled back their organizational activities in recent years.

Time and the Collaborative Dimension

Historical comparison is endemic to the study of Congress. As with any longstanding institution, it is only natural to ask how the legislature today stacks up to Congresses of yesteryear. New developments in our politics are often accompanied by a scholarly rush to identify possible parallels in congressional history and to explain their lessons for the present. When it comes to studying legislative leaders, students of Congress often rely on measures of ideology to help identify possible comparators. This approach makes sense if one believes that leader power is conditional on a party's ideological composition. By charting large-scale shifts in the distribution of legislative preferences over time using metrics like DW-NOMINATE, we can identify similarly situated leaders on the ideological dimension of legislative politics. Thus, legislative scholars have compared the tenures of mid-twentieth-century Speakers, like Rayburn and John McCormack of Massachusetts, who led ideologically divided parties, as well as those of postreform Speakers like O'Neill and Jim Wright of Texas, who led increasingly ideologically unified ones.

Given that ideological change is often a slow-moving process, it follows that such comparisons have tended to pair leaders with their immediate predecessors or successors. Indeed, attention to the ideological dimension often discourages less historically proximate comparisons. Leaders of the "textbook" Congress, it is suggested, have little in common with their contemporary counterparts, as the distribution of member preferences within the two parties has changed substantially since the days of Rayburn and Lyndon Johnson. Thus, we are left to presume that leaders separated by significant swaths of secular time—Rayburn and Pelosi, for instance—will have little in common by virtue of governing two ideologically distinct incarnations of the same party. As we have seen, Rayburn is thought to be the paragon of an institutionally weak persuader, while Pelosi is understood to embody the lower chamber's contemporary return to czar rule.

But attending instead to the collaborative dimension makes clear that leaders who occupy disparate moments in secular time can still have much in common with each other. Indeed, the often cyclical nature of factional collaboration means that we can liberate ourselves from "simple periodization schemes and modern-traditional dichotomies" to focus instead on "recurrent patterns" in Congress.[9] Revisiting the Rayburn and Pelosi comparison, recall that although Rayburn's Democratic Party was considerably more ideologically heterogenous than Pelosi's according to prevailing measures of ideology, both Speakers reached the apex of their power as House Democrats' factional configuration became increasingly symmetric. The parallels between their late-in-life legislative accomplishments are more than a historical curiosity. Properly understood, they hold at least one key to understanding why these two leaders stand out among their peers when it comes to both longevity and accomplishment.

Grouping leaders along the collaborative dimension also provides a distinct lens through which subsequent studies might profitably view the politics of leadership. On the basis of the Rayburn-Pelosi comparison, we might ask whether other long-serving leaders also benefited from a favorable factional configuration or whether we should instead attribute their durability to other factors. Likewise, when we consider particularly weak leaders, can we reasonably attribute their failings primarily to asymmetry, or were they constrained in other ways? While answering such questions is beyond the scope of this book, it is important to appreciate that we would have been unlikely to ask them absent greater attention to the collaborative choices members make.

In a similar vein, comparing leaders who encountered similar factional configurations but achieved varying results might allow legislative scholars to specify with greater precision how much a given leader's success is owed to structure and how much to agency. Indeed, no less than the study of presidents, the sustained examination of congressional leaders can help us see "how different sets of power arrangements are juxtaposed within government institutions and how institutional actors, by engaging all these different arrangements simultaneously, continually alter the range of political possibilities."[10]

As a first cut, it stands to reason that some leaders, by virtue of their irreducibly personal qualities, might be better able than others to leverage factional symmetry to their advantage or to manage the downsides of factional asymmetry. In this context, for instance, it should strike us as unusual that McCormack is widely understood to be a weak leader, despite inheriting the same symmetric factional configuration that Rayburn in his last years was able to exploit to such great effect. An emphasis on the collaborative dimension should therefore prompt us to ask about those aspects of McCormack's personality or biography that made him particularly ill-equipped to take advantage of his party's symmetry. In this way, the book deepens our understanding of the dialectic at the center of effective leadership. By identifying a new, structural, source of leader power, we can pinpoint with greater accuracy a new source of leader agency.

Reform and the Collaborative Dimension

Finally, thinking about legislative politics and its pathologies in collaborative terms points to new and perhaps more profitable avenues for reform. As American politics has polarized, many of Capitol Hill's most astute observers have expressed concern that Congress is no longer capable of engaging in the kind of bipartisan lawmaking that was once its hallmark. Since the 1980s, they note, the number of moderate legislators has declined significantly, as members strategically retire or lose to more extreme candidates. This trend, while troubling in and of itself, has sown doubt that legislative leaders can still broker sensible solutions to the nation's pressing problems. "Our Madisonian system," Thomas Mann and Norm Ornstein write, "is predicated on the willingness of elected officials representing highly diverse interests to engage in good faith negotiations and compromise." But with both parties "ideologically polarized, tribalized, and strategically partisan," those leaders willing to "set aside politics and enact responsible policies" increasingly find that they lack ready partners among their rank and file.[11]

Anxiety about the consequences of this "hollowing out of the middle" has led many observers to advocate reforms to increase the number of moderates in Congress.[12] The thinking goes that if only more moderate candidates could be persuaded to run for office, and to stay there once elected, the first branch might shed some of its toxicity and dysfunction. But getting a critical mass of moderates, particularly Republican moderates, to run for Congress and win is no easy task. As moderates themselves readily acknowledge, the current legislative environment is not hospitable to members who prize compromise over partisan warfare. Said one retiring member, "Our Venn diagram is two circles [that are] miles apart . . . [most members today] have zero interest in compromising."[13] As a consequence, recruiting moderate candidates to run is a perennial challenge. Few qualified candidates see it in their interest to participate in an institution that offers little reward for "getting things done." The system is now best suited to those who "want to be more performers than producers."[14]

Given moderates' hesitancy to run, reformers argue that something fundamental needs to change about how campaigns and elections are conducted. But many of their proposals are either impractical or unlikely to achieve the desired result—and sometimes both. Start with proposals to create more competitive electoral districts in the House. "If I had a magic wand," one member confided, "I would love to change . . . the redistricting process [because] . . . if the base of my district is so far to the right or to the left it makes it difficult for us to negotiate to the center."[15] While it is understandable why moderate candidates might prefer to run in more competitive districts, it isn't clear they would win. Indeed, political scientists have found that many of the districts whose composition we would expect to favor moderates end up electing more extreme partisans instead.[16]

Reformers have also turned their attention to the rules that govern party primaries. Closed primaries, they argue, discourage moderate candidates from running because only registered party members, who tend to favor ideologically extreme candidates, get a say. But political scientists have so far found little evidence that voters in open primaries are any less partisan than voters in closed ones.[17] Moreover, studies of nonpartisan primaries offer no support for the idea that "taking the primaries away from the party" will induce moderate candidates to run or cause them to win. If anything, nonpartisan primaries seem to attract *more* extreme candidates to run than closed ones.[18]

For others, money is the most proximate reason why moderates are disappearing from legislative politics. Moderate candidates and officeholders, reformers posit, both need more money to win and are simultaneously worse fundraisers than individuals on the ideological extremes. Were campaign finance laws to limit the flow of cash or mandate public funding for congressional elections, moderates might find themselves on more equal footing and run for election (and reelection) at higher rates. Here, however, whatever the merits of the reform, the barriers to change are staggering. While Republicans have long been hostile to reforming the country's campaign finance system, Democrats in recent election cycles have outraised them, considerably slowing momentum for such change on the left. Interest has been further dampened by a conservative Supreme Court, poised to strike down or limit even modest reform proposals. If present trends continue, it is hard to believe that campaign finance reform is on the horizon.

In view of all of this, scholars have begun to look elsewhere for inspiration. Perhaps the most radical idea on offer is to increase the number of political parties with representation in Congress. "We need some new parties," Lee Drutman observes, "to provide a welcoming home to new members of Congress, particularly center-right moderates."[19] As reformers are quick to concede, however, transforming the current two-party system would require substantial changes. For instance, ballots in all fifty states would have to be reformatted to permit fusion voting, and state election laws would need to be changed to allocate seats proportionally. Given that both major parties benefit from the status quo, it is unlikely that either would embrace the changes necessary to allow new party entrants.

What, then, are reformers to do? This book offers a prescription that is both clear-eyed about the challenges of enacting reform and realistic about what is likely to work. Perhaps more important, it puts the power to change how Congress operates back in the hands of moderates themselves. To make the first branch a better place for moderates to work—and to improve the chances that they will "fit" within their party, however awkwardly—they must find ways to collaborate more effectively.[20] Moderates, even with small numbers, should not accept a spot on the sidelines, for, as we have seen, numbers alone do not guarantee lawmakers influence. No less essential, given how unpleasant life in the current Congress has been for moderates (particularly on the Republican side of the aisle), sustained collaboration may help members forge lasting relationships with one another and tie them more tightly to Congress as an institution.

Here, history provides a blueprint for success. For existing organizations like the Republican Governance Group, meetings should be more than just opportunities to "talk . . . [and] complain." They must be structured so as to permit members to collectively "do what they say they're going to do."[21] To this end, members need to decide not only how to make decisions but also what mechanisms they will adopt to enforce them, be that on the front end with membership requirements or on the back end with procedures to expel members who shirk. The importance of this step cannot be overstated: "Going head-to-head" with factional rivals requires both that you "know what you want and are willing to fight for it" and that "no one can think you are going to cave."[22]

But the history chronicled in this book suggests there can be room within a single faction for iterative organizing efforts. Just as the House Freedom Caucus sought to improve upon the perceived deficiencies of the Republican Study Committee, moderates might think about alternatives to existing organizations. Beyond facilitating even more regular engagement, competition can foster institutional experimentation, as lawmakers try out various collaborative strategies with the aim of identifying more effective approaches.

At the same time, moderates must figure out how to insulate themselves from attack should their collective action bear fruit. Here, they might consider two paths forward. Perhaps, like the Freedom Caucus in its early years, they might keep their membership lists secret. If colleagues, activists, and voters hostile to their aims cannot be certain who is to blame for dissent they do not appreciate, moderates may find that they are no more exposed than they were before they began to collaborate. Alternatively, moderates might do more to collectively overhaul how they and their opponents are publicly perceived. Moderate Democrats, for their part, have worked to recast themselves as "normal Democrats" who value "policy... and understand the importance of compromise," styling themselves steady anchors in a sea roiled by progressive waves of greater and greater magnitude.[23] Across the aisle, a handful of moderate Republicans have made similar attempts to rebrand themselves as "members who overwhelmingly want to deliver... conservative policy wins" and their opponents as a "chaos caucus." But without a concerted and coordinated messaging campaign, they are unlikely to undercut the power of those who accuse them of being RINOs—"Republicans in name only."[24]

Moderates need not undertake these tasks alone. Legislative leaders can help facilitate greater collaboration among their rank and file, should they wish to. They might, for instance, simply nudge their colleagues to "get organized," as Minority Leader Bob Michel encouraged moderate Republicans to do in the late 1980s.[25] Or, as Pelosi reminded her party's left wing, success rarely comes from a "one-person show."[26] Leaders can also work to increase the returns to collaboration. These can be largely symbolic gestures, such as meeting with members of a collaborating faction or with their designated leaders, or more tangible ones, such as proactively offering them a shared seat at the negotiating table, as both Rayburn and Kevin McCarthy did (albeit with mixed results).[27]

This book has demonstrated that it is not naïve to expect leaders to promote collaboration in these ways. To the extent that doing so can improve their party's overall symmetry, leaders stand to gain directly from bringing members together. This is particularly true for House Republicans. As our recent politics makes clear, a consistent challenge for Republican Speakers is that they lack a cadre of pragmatic members sufficiently organized so as to counterbalance the influence of those in their conference who believe any deal is a bad one.[28] For Republican leaders to get what they want—be it a positive legislative record or simply job security—they need both wings of their party to compete on a more equal basis than they do at present. But whether Republican Speakers will have the fortitude to help their party's centrists help themselves remains to be seen.

Collaboration and Continuity

Those of us who study the first branch are regularly called on to assess whether Congress today works differently than it did in the past. The tenor of many such assessments is that there is something uniquely wrong with our current legislative politics. While criticisms are legion—lawmakers spend too much time fundraising; they are out of Washington too frequently; they do not intend to make long-term careers as legislators; they care more about grandstanding than legislating—the overriding concern is that lawmakers now routinely harbor such extremist views that the institution cannot operate as designed. For students of Congress, one consequence of this new reality is that earlier eras in congressional history will have little to teach us about our current legislative woes.

By attending to the collaborative dimension of legislative politics, this book has taken another tack. Its emphasis on the enduring logic of collective action is intended to identify meaningful continuities in congressional behavior over time. To the extent that Congress is constituted as a collective body, patterns in how members work (or don't work) together will recur. The collaborative arcs of some factions will inevitably be on the upswing, paralleling the efforts of groups who opted to augment their collaboration in prior eras. Those of others will be on the downswing, mirroring the decline of earlier factions whose members chose to go their separate ways.

These recurrent patterns necessarily shape how Congress works, both then and now. In this study, we have seen how the collaborative choices rank-and-file members make meaningfully determine levels of leader power. But there are surely other ways in which patterns of collaboration matter to legislative politics. The crucial point for readers is this: there remain key commonalities between our legislature today and Congresses of the past that are grounded in the institution's structure as a body where collective action is essential. The more we know about what has stayed the same, the better we can specify what is truly new, for better and worse, about Congress in the present.

Acknowledgments

In the process of writing this book, I have incurred numerous debts and benefited from the generosity of many people. To begin, I am deeply grateful to the lawmakers and staff members who made time to answer my questions candidly and with good humor. I also owe a great deal of thanks to the archivists who scanned records when their libraries were closed because of COVID-19 pandemic restrictions and who subsequently welcomed researchers back into their stacks when operations resumed. I hope this book does their work justice.

Closer to home, I would like to recognize the contributions of my colleagues at the University of Chicago, including John Brehm, Mark Hansen, Eric Oliver, and Patricia Posey, for providing a stimulating and supportive intellectual environment where creativity is valued over convention. I am particularly grateful to Will Howell and Jon Rogowski for their kindness and encouragement. Notwithstanding their shared preference for the executive branch, they were eager interlocutors and careful readers. I benefited greatly from their efforts to help me think more precisely about what the book was really about and for giving me license to make ambitious arguments.

At various stages of writing, I also benefited from generative conversations with colleagues outside Chicago. Special thanks to Jim Curry, John Dearborn, Larry Evans, Jacob Hacker, Bruce Oppenheimer, Paul Pierson, Ellie Powell, Wendy Schiller, Danielle Thomsen, Rob Van Houweling, and Greg Wawro for providing constructive criticism as the project germinated and helpful advice and kind words as the manuscript progressed. I owe an even greater debt to Alan Wiseman for taking the time to travel to Hyde Park for my book conference and for providing exceptional feedback while there. I am likewise grateful to Sara Doskow at the University of Chicago Press for seeing potential in the project early on, soliciting thorough and careful reviews, and offering her own counsel at critical junctures. Special thanks as well to Rosemary Frehe and Caterina MacLean, respectively, for managing the book's acquisition and production, Lori Meek Schuldt for providing excellent copyedits, Derek Gottlieb for compiling a terrific index, and Vikram Ramaswamy for giving the page proofs a thorough read.

As should be apparent, my thinking about Congress has been profoundly shaped by Frances Lee and Eric Schickler. The manuscript is undoubtedly better for their time and input. It was Frances who consistently demanded more of the project—more clarity, rigor, and attention to detail. And when I found myself adrift, I invariably found answers in her work on the limits of ideology and the importance of teamwork in the first branch. Eric, too, pushed for more precision and richer historical analysis throughout the project's maturation. As is his way, these were mostly subtle nudges to refine the book's theory and sharpen its empirical interventions. When trying to get the balance right, I looked to his early work on Congress and subsequent writing on the civil rights movement. In those books I found a model for engaging with the animating ideas of American political development, while also keeping the history grounded and accessible. I am beholden to them both.

Finally, I'd like to thank my family. My husband, Gregory, deserves acclamation beyond what I can provide here. The ideas articulated in these pages are the result of countless (sometimes fraught, occasionally harried) conversations at neighborhood playgrounds, on lakeside runs, and while prepping dinner. This book is as much his as it is mine, and it wouldn't have happened without him. That said, the joint projects I am most proud of are our three children: Zora, Solomon, and Celia, who bring us so much joy. It is to them that this book is dedicated.

I am also incredibly grateful to my parents, Michele and Jeff, who have been doting grandparents and lifesavers throughout. Their commitment to family is unparalleled, and we would be at sea without them. I would also like to thank Ariel, Helen, Ted, Kate, Elise, Sarah, and Franklin for modeling how to get on with getting on. They are a constant reminder that whatever life brings, the real tragedy is leaving without any good stories. Last but not least, I owe a deep debt of gratitude to Ana Elisa, whose love for my children knows no bounds and who has helped me be a better parent and scholar. *Nosotros no podriamos hacerlo sin ti.*

Appendix A
Archival Collections Consulted

Arizona State University, Special Collections, Tempe
  Barry Goldwater Papers

Boston College Burns Library
  Tip O'Neill Papers

Carl Albert Center, University of Oklahoma
  Carl Albert Papers
  Dick Armey Papers

Dirksen Congressional Center, Pekin, IL
  Everett Dirksen Papers

Dwight D. Eisenhower Presidential Library, Abilene, KS
  Stephen Benedict Papers

Gerald Ford Presidential Library, Ann Arbor, MI
  Vernon C. Loen and Charles Leppert Files

LBJ Presidential Library, Austin, TX
  Lyndon Johnson, Senate Papers

Library of Congress Manuscript Division, Washington, DC
  Democratic Study Group Papers
  Robert Taft Papers
  Maurice Rosenblatt Papers
  Nancy Pelosi Papers

Louisiana State University, Special Collections, Baton Rouge
    Gillis Long Papers

Marquette University, Raynor Memorial Library, Milwaukee, WI
    Joseph McCarthy Papers

Ronald Reagan Presidential Library, Simi Valley, CA
    Donald T. Regan Papers

South Dakota State University Archives and Special Collections, Brookings
    Benjamin Reifel Papers
    Thomas A. Daschle Papers

University of California, Berkeley, Bancroft Library
    Earl Warren Oral History Project
    William Knowland Papers

University of Southern Mississippi McCain Library, Hattiesburg
    William Colmer Papers

University of Texas–Austin Briscoe Center for American History
    Ralph Yarborough Papers
    Sam Rayburn Papers

Wisconsin State Historical Society, Madison
    Alexander Wiley Papers

Yale University Special Collections, Sterling Memorial Library, New Haven, CT
    George H. E. Smith Papers

Appendix B

Interview Procedures

I interviewed nineteen former members of Congress and longtime legislative staffers for this book. Several members and staff served in leadership; many members and staff self-associated with a party faction; and several members and staff considered themselves independent of any factional organization (formal or informal). The vast majority of members and staff served only in the House, though a few had experience in the Senate as well. Slightly more than half of those individuals interviewed either identified as Republicans or worked for a Republican lawmaker.

In accordance with the University of Chicago's Institutional Review Board guidelines, all interviewees agreed to participate on the condition that the interview be "not for attribution" or anonymous. The conversations were unstructured, and most lasted for forty to sixty minutes. Depending on the interviewees' relevant experience, questions centered on their perceptions of how members of their own faction interacted, how members of rival factions operated, and how party leaders managed their relationships with factions and addressed interfactional disputes. More detailed policy questions were also asked depending on the interviewees' party affiliation and time in office.

In addition to the interviews conducted specifically for this project, chapters 6 and 7 draw on six interviews originally conducted for my first book, *Building the Bloc: Intraparty Organization and the U.S. Congress* (2017). Because those earlier interviews were completed immediately following some of the legislative battles profiled in chapters 6 and 7, they provide a closer-to-real-time evaluation of the factional politics at play.

Notes

Chapter 1

1. Robert Dahl, *Who Governs? Democracy and Power in an American City* (New Haven, CT: Yale University Press, 1974), 6.
2. Carl Hulse, "The Pelosi Era Comes to a Close, *New York Times*, January 3, 2023.
3. As quoted in Paul Kane, "Pelosi on the Verge of Cementing Legacy as One of the Most Powerful Members of Congress Ever—or Ending Her Career on a Sour Note," *Washington Post*, October 2, 2021.
4. Norm Ornstein, as quoted in Karen Tumulty, "A Troublemaker with a Gavel," *Washington Post*, March 25, 2020. During Pelosi's two terms as Speaker, the House passed, among other Democratic priorities, the Affordable Care Act, the Dodd-Frank Wall Street Reform and Consumer Protection Act, the Lilly Ledbetter Fair Pay Act, the American Recovery and Reinvestment Act, the Student Aid and Fiscal Responsibility Act, the Hate Crimes Prevention Act, the American Clean Energy and Security Act, the Fair Sentencing Act, the Don't Ask, Don't Tell Repeal Act, the American Rescue Plan Act, and the Inflation Reduction Act.
5. Hastert resigned after losing his majority in the 2006 midterms and later went to prison after a federal conviction for child abuse.
6. As quoted in Philip Elliot, "Johnson at Risk of Becoming a SINO: Speaker In Name Only," *Time Magazine*, January 22, 2024.
7. As quoted in Kyle Stewart, Julie Tsirkin, and Ali Vitali, "Another Republican Joins Effort to Oust Johnson, Putting the Speaker in Real Peril," *NBC News*, April 19, 2024, https://www.nbcnews.com/politics/congress/third-republican-oust-mike-johnson-vote-democrats-rcna148582.
8. Barack Obama as quoted in Susan Page, *Madam Speaker: Nancy Pelosi and the Lessons of Power* (New York: Hachette, 2021), 14.
9. Page, *Madam Speaker*, 13–15.

10. E. E. Schattschneider, *The Semisovereign People: A Realist's View of Democracy in America* (New York: Cengage Learning, 1975), 71.

11. To be sure, members may not simply differ in *what* they want but *how* they want to get it. See Hans Noel, "Ideological Factions in the Republican and Democratic Parties," *Annals of the American Academy of Political and Social Science* 667 (2016): 166–88.

12. See appendixes A and B for a list of archives consulted and a description of my interview process.

13. Heather Caygle, Sarah Ferris, and John Bresnahan, "Progressive Caucus Eyes Shakeup to Boost Power Next Congress," *Politico*, October 26, 2020, https://www.politico.com/news/2020/10/26/progressive-caucus-eyes-shakeup-to-congress-432587; Leah Greenberg and Ezra Levin, "House Progressives Are Building Something New, Exciting and Powerful," *Roll Call*, November 20, 2020. See also Ruth Bloch Rubin, "Organizing at the Extreme: Hardline Strategy and Institutional Design," *Congress & the Presidency* 49, no. 1 (2022): 1–30.

14. Matthew Green, *Legislative Hardball: The House Freedom Caucus and the Power of Threat-Making in Congress* (New York: Cambridge Elements, 2019); Danielle M. Thomsen, *Opting Out of Congress: Partisan Polarization and the Decline of Moderate Candidates* (New York: Cambridge University Press, 2017).

15. Elliot, "Johnson at Risk of Becoming a SINO."

16. Sarah Binder and Frances Lee, "Making Deals in Congress," in *Political Negotiation: A Handbook*, ed. Jane Mansbridge and Cathie Jo Martin (Washington, DC: Brookings Institution Press, 2016), 91.

17. Jacob Hacker and Paul Pierson, *Off Center: The Republican Revolution and the Erosion of American Democracy* (New Haven, CT: Yale University Press, 2006).

18. See, for example, Richard H. Pildes, "Romanticizing Democracy, Political Fragmentation and the Decline of American Government," *Yale Law Journal* 124 (2014): 804–52; Nathaniel Persily, "Stronger Parties as a Solution to Polarization," in *Solutions to Political Polarization in America*, ed. Nathaniel Persily (New York: Cambridge University Press, 2015).

19. Nancy Pelosi, "Dear Colleague: On the Power of Democratic Unity," press release, November 16, 2020, https://speakeremeritapelosi.house.gov/newsroom/111620.

20. David W. Rohde and Kenneth A. Shepsle, "Leaders and Followers in the House of Representatives: Reflections on Woodrow Wilson's *Congressional Government*," *Congress and the Presidency* 14 (1987): 122–23; David W. Rohde, *Parties and Leaders in the Postreform House* (Chicago: University of Chicago Press, 1991), 38.

21. Rohde, *Parties and Leaders*, 16.

22. David W. Rohde, "Reflections on the Practice of Theorizing: Conditional Party Government in the Twenty-First Century," *Journal of Politics* 75, no. 4 (August 2013): 849–64. As with CPG in its original flavor, these are critical insights that

help explain trends in leadership power over time, including the centralization of leaders' formal authority since the 1990s. But the revised version of CPG cannot help us make sense of why we observe differences in leadership power and performance within the *same* period. If everyone is subject to the same trends in polarization, polarization itself sheds limited light on why Pelosi outlasted her Republican counterparts in the House, or why there have been fewer disparities in leadership performance in the Senate.

23. C. Lawrence Evans, *The Whips: Building Party Coalitions in Congress* (Ann Arbor: University of Michigan Press, 2018), 68.

24. D. Roderick Kiewiet and Mathew D. McCubbins, *The Logic of Delegation* (Chicago: University of Chicago Press, 1991), 54–55.

25. Barbara Sinclair, *Majority Leadership in the U.S. House* (Baltimore: Johns Hopkins University Press, 1983), 2–3.

26. Gary W. Cox and Mathew D. McCubbins, *Setting the Agenda: Responsible Party Government in the U.S House of Representatives* (New York: Cambridge University Press, 2005), 24, 37–38. The authors argue that leaders' willingness to use their "negative agenda power is *unconditional*, in the sense that its exercise does not vary with the similarity of the party's members' . . . ideas of good public policy."

27. Cox and McCubbins, *Setting the Agenda*, 27. Myriad studies offer empirical support for this proposition. See Barbara Sinclair, "House Special Rules and the Institutional Design Controversy," *Legislative Studies Quarterly* 19, no. 4 (November 1994): 477–94; Stephen Ansolabehere, James M. Snyder, and Charles Stewart, "The Effects of Party and Preferences on Congressional Roll-Call Voting," *Legislative Studies Quarterly* 26, no. 4 (November 2001): 533–72; Bryan Marshall, "Explaining the Role of Restrictive Rules in the Postreform House," *Legislative Studies Quarterly* 27, no. 1 (February 2002): 61–85; Sean Gailmard and Jeffrey A. Jenkins, "Negative Agenda Control in the Senate and House: Fingerprints of Majority Party Power," *Journal of Politics* 69, no. 3 (August 2007): 689–700.

28. This is not to say that leaders will not press wavering or dissident members to join the party in enacting "must-pass" legislation, but these instances are said to be the exception and not the rule. For a thoughtful discussion of must-pass legislation and leader strategy, see Steven Smith, *Party Influence in Congress* (New York: Cambridge University Press, 2007), 137–40.

29. Cox and McCubbins, *Setting the Agenda*, 24.

30. As they explain elsewhere: "Positive agenda control is ever present, but the frequency with which the party uses this power varies with the degree to which the party membership agrees on . . . what should be done." Gary W. Cox and Mathew D. McCubbins, "Agenda Power in the U.S. House of Representatives, 1877–1986," in *Party, Process, and Political Change in Congress: New Perspectives on the History of Congress*, ed. David W. Brady and Mathew D. McCubbins (Stanford, CA: Stanford University Press, 2002), 109.

31. Frances E. Lee, *Insecure Majorities: Congress and the Perpetual Campaign* (Chicago: University of Chicago Press, 2016), 52. Legislative scholars do recognize that the constraining effects of party divisions will depend on more than just the relative ideological cohesion of the party's rank and file. Take, for instance, the size of a party's majority. On the one hand, when the majority is narrow, majority party members may be more willing to grant their leaders sufficient authority to dissuade wayward colleagues from defecting, as every lost vote threatens the party's control of the floor. See John W. Patty, "Equilibrium Party Government," *American Journal of Political Science* 52, no. 3 (July 2008): 636–37. On the other hand, it is precisely when the majority is thin that leaders may be least willing to deploy that authority, as doing so might prompt dissenting members to join forces with the minority party on a more permanent basis. See Eric Schickler and Andrew Rich, "Controlling the Floor: Parties as Procedural Coalitions in the House," *American Journal of Political Science* 41, no. 4 (October 1997): 1340–75.

32. See, for example, Kathleen Thelen, "Historical Institutionalism in Comparative Politics," *Annual Review of Political Science* 2 (1999): 369–404; Jacob Hacker, *The Divided Welfare State: The Battle over Public and Private Social Benefits in the United States* (New York: Cambridge University Press, 2002); Paul Pierson, *Politics in Time: History, Institutions and Social Analysis* (Princeton, NJ: Princeton University Press, 2004).

33. Pierson, *Politics in Time*, 151–52.

34. See, for example, Kathleen Thelen, *How Institutions Evolve: The Political Economy of Skills in Germany, Britain, the United States, and Japan* (New York: Cambridge University Press, 2004), 27; Avinash Dixit, Gene M. Grossman, and Faruk Gul, "The Dynamics of Political Compromise," *Journal of Political Economy* 108, no. 3 (2000): 441–662.

35. Eric Schickler, *Disjointed Pluralism: Institutional Innovation in the U.S. Congress* (Princeton, NJ: Princeton University Press, 2001), 16.

36. Paul Pierson, "Not Just What, but *When*: Timing and Sequence in Political Processes," *Studies in American Political Development* 14, no. 1 (April 2000): 75.

37. James L. Sundquist, *The Decline and Resurgence of Congress* (Washington, DC: Brookings Institution Press, 1981), 438.

38. Paul Pierson, "Increasing Returns, Path Dependence, and the Study of Politics," *American Political Science Review* 94, no. 2 (June 2000): 252.

39. Schickler, *Disjointed Pluralism*, 15.

40. For more on these challenges, see Ruth Bloch Rubin, *Building the Bloc: Intraparty Organization in the U.S. Congress* (New York: Cambridge University Press, 2017), 13–16; James M. Curry, *Legislating in the Dark: Information and Power in the House of Representatives* (Chicago: University of Chicago Press, 2015), 33–36.

41. In the context of legislative-executive relations, Sundquist refers to these as "perplexing subsidiary questions." He writes: "Even if . . . the answer to the question of whether Congress should reassert its power seems generally affirmative,

the initial queries remain. How? In What respects?" Simply achieving "something close to collective resolve" would not be enough to guarantee lawmakers' success. Sundquist, *Decline and Resurgence of Congress*, 7–10.

42. Ruth Bloch Rubin, "Organizing for Insurgency: Intraparty Organization and the Development of the House Insurgency, 1908–1910," *Studies in American Political Development* 27, no. 2 (October 2013): 86–110. Notably, Cannon considered himself to be a leader of a divided party, observing that "there is no coherent Republican majority in the House." In such circumstances, it was incumbent upon the Speaker to "have the courage of [his] convictions." As quoted in Charles Moser, *The Speaker and the House: Coalitions and Power in the United States House of Representatives* (Washington, DC: Free Congress Research and Education Foundation, 1979).

43. As Sinclair observes: "Most political scientists see congressional leaders as agents of their members." Barbara Sinclair, "Transformational Leader or Faithful Agent? Principal-Agent Theory and House Majority Party Leadership," *Legislative Studies Quarterly* 24, no. 3 (August 1999): 421. For a thoughtful critique of principal-agent theory as applied to legislative politics, see C. Lawrence Evans and Walter J. Oleszek, "The Strategic Context of Congressional Party Leadership," *Congress & the Presidency* 26, no. 1 (1999): 1–20.

44. Alternatively, one might describe a party's membership as a collective principal, which is subject to "the very same collective action problems that delegation is intended to overcome—prisoners' dilemmas, lack of coordination, and social choice instability." See Kiewiet and McCubbins, *Logic of Delegation*, 26–27.

45. Terry M. Moe, "The New Economics of Organization," *American Journal of Political Science*, 28, no. 4 (November 1984): 768. Or, as Gailmard writes in the context of bureaucratic oversight, "the multiplicity of principals reduces their collective control over the agent even though they have common interests about the agent's actions." Sean Gailmard, "Multiple Principals and Oversight of Bureaucratic Policy-Making," *Journal of Theoretical Politics* 21, no. 2 (2009): 161–86. Randall Strahan, too, makes a similar point. He argues: "Principal-agent theory supplies some important insights about why legislative leaders *always* enjoy a certain degree of autonomy from their followers. Multiple principals sometimes have difficulty controlling agents because agents can play groups of their principals off against one another, replacing the agent in this setting can be difficult and costly for the principals, and the agent may have a number of important strategic advantages over principals in terms of access to information and control over decision-making procedures." Randall Strahan, *Leading Representatives: The Agency of Leaders in the Politics of the U.S. House* (Baltimore: Johns Hopkins University Press, 2007), 22.

46. Moe, "New Economics of Organization," 769.

47. Commenting on the 1970s decentralizing reforms, one majority party senator acknowledged that "there is this growing feeling, we've got to give a little more power back to the leaders; we are so fractured . . . that nobody can deliver

anything." As quoted in Frank H. Mackaman, *Understanding Congressional Leadership* (Washington, DC: CQ Press, 1981), 19.

48. James M. Curry and Frances E. Lee, *The Limits of Party: Congress and Lawmaking in a Polarized Era* (Chicago: University of Chicago Press, 2020), 187. For an account tracing similar themes in an earlier era, see C. Lawrence Evans and Walter J. Oleszek, *Congress Under Fire: Reform Politics and the Republican Majority* (Boston: Houghton Mifflin, 1997).

49. Steven Smith suggests as much in his account of the response to the 1970s-era procedural reforms that passed the House and Senate. Noting that the changes in procedure made work in committee and on the floor more complex, Smith observes that legislators delegated greater authority to their leadership in the hopes that doing so would alleviate confusion and streamline the lawmaking process. Steven Smith, *Call to Order: Floor Politics in the House and Senate* (Washington, DC: Brookings Institution Press, 1989).

50. Robert V. Remini, *The House: The History of the House of Representatives* (Washington, DC: Smithsonian Books, 2006), 300–302.

51. Matthew N. Green and Douglas B. Harris, *Choosing the Leader: Leadership Elections in the U.S. House of Representatives* (New Haven, CT: Yale University Press, 2019), 28.

52. Green and Harris, *Choosing the Leader*, 28–29. Indeed, as Strahan notes, "the frequency with which presidential ambitions have been visible among speakers, would-be speakers, and former speakers . . . indicates that the office has regularly been sought and held by figures whose political ambitions transcended remaining a leader in the House." Strahan, *Leading Representatives*, 31.

53. As quoted in Jonathan Easley, "Rep. Ryan: Republicans Can't Play the 'Villain' in Obama's 'Morality Play,'" *The Hill*, January 26, 2013.

54. As David Truman writes: "Judging from the behavior of Majority Leaders and the comments of informants, the Floor Leader . . . regards with great jealousy his authority." David B. Truman, *The Congressional Party: A Case Study* (New York: Wiley & Sons, 1959), 105.

55. Strahan, *Leading Representatives*, 34. Different leaders may calculate the odds of a leadership challenge differently and may have a different tolerance for bearing that risk. See Strahan, *Leading Representatives*, 32.

56. Adam D. Sheingate, "Political Entrepreneurship, Institutional Change, and American Political Development," *Studies in American Political Development* 17, no. 2 (October 2003): 188. See also Gregory Wawro, *Legislative Entrepreneurship in the U.S. House of Representatives* (Ann Arbor: University of Michigan Press, 2000); Wendy J. Schiller, "Senators as Political Entrepreneurs: Using Bill Sponsorship to Shape Legislative Agendas," *American Journal of Political Science* 39, no. 1 (February 1995): 186–203; Eric Schickler, *Disjointed Pluralism*.

57. Strahan, *Leading Representatives*, 37.

58. Schickler, *Disjointed Pluralism*, 13.

59. Matthew N. Green, "Institutional Change, Party Discipline, and the House Democratic Caucus, 1911–19," *Legislative Studies Quarterly* 27, no. 4 (November 2002): 601–33; Kathryn Pearson, *Party Discipline in the U.S. House of Representatives* (Ann Arbor: University of Michigan Press, 2015); David C. King and Richard J. Zeckhouser, "Congressional Vote Options," *Legislative Studies Quarterly* 28, no. 3 (August 2003): 387–411; Keith Krehbiel, Adam Meirowitz, and Alan E. Wiseman, "A Theory of Competitive Partisan Lawmaking," *Political Science Research and Methods* 3, no. 3 (2015): 423–48.

60. Christopher J. Deering and Steven S. Smith, "Majority Party Leadership and the New House Subcommittee System," in Mackaman, *Understanding Congressional Leadership*, 290.

61. Curry, *Legislating in the Dark*, 32–36.

62. Scott R. Meinke, *Leadership Organizations in the House of Representatives: Party Participation and Partisan Politics* (Ann Arbor: University of Michigan Press, 2016).

63. For example, in the early twentieth century, Senate Republican leader Nelson Aldrich called on Republican president William H. Taft to pressure progressive members of the party to back tariff legislation they opposed. In the midcentury, members of the House Democratic leadership used former Speaker John Nance Garner, Roosevelt's first vice president, as an intermediary to share the names of wavering Democrats with the White House to shore up support for the New Deal. In later decades, Lyndon Johnson made a variety of calls at the behest of Democratic leaders in the House and Senate to ensure passage of Democratic legislation through Congress. In more recent years, Republican Speakers directed officials in the Trump administration to help persuade uncommitted members to support the party's healthcare and tax reform drives.

64. Bloch Rubin, *Building the Bloc*, 13–19; Nils Ringe, Jennifer Nicoll Victor and Christopher J. Carman, *Bridging the Information Gap: Legislative Member Organizations as Social Networks in the United States and European Union* (Ann Arbor: University of Michigan Press, 2013). For a fuller discussion of how this choice plays out in the modern Congress, see Andrew J. Clarke, "Party Sub-Brands and American Party Factions," *American Journal of Political Science* 64, no. 3 (July 2020): 452–70; Green, *Legislative Hardball*.

65. For a thoughtful discussion of congressional opportunity structures and how legislative entrepreneurs navigate them, see Adam Sheingate, "Structure and Opportunity: Committee Jurisdiction and Issue Attention in Congress," *American Journal of Political Science* 50, no. 4 (October 2006): 844–59.

66. Strahan, *Leading Representatives*, 29.

67. See Schickler, *Disjointed Pluralism*, 5 (describing members' institutional, partisan, and policy interests). See also Matthew N. Green, *The Speaker of the House: A Study of Leadership* (New Haven, CT: Yale University Press, 2010); Burdett A. Loomis, "Congressional Careers and Party Leadership in the Contemporary

House of Representatives," *American Journal of Political Science* 28, no. 1 (February 1984): 180–202; Ronald M. Peters Jr., *The American Speakership*, 2nd ed. (Baltimore: Johns Hopkins University Press, 1997), 299.

68. Frances E. Lee, *Beyond Ideology: Politics, Principles, and Partisanship in the U.S. Senate* (Chicago: University of Chicago Press, 2009), 27.

69. Lee, *Beyond Ideology*, 46. As Margaret Levi has argued, it is important not to assume the conclusion by reflexively treating evidence of behavior as a "revealed preference." Margaret Levi, "A Model, a Method and a Map: Rational Choice in Comparative and Historical Analysis," in *Comparative Politics: Rationality, Culture, and Society*, ed. Mark Irving Lichbach and Alan S. Zuckerman (New York: Cambridge University Press, 2009), 24.

70. Thank you to Alan Wiseman for this formulation. Rohde makes a similar distinction, noting that legislators have both personal preferences ("what he or she would choose if no other influences were present") and operative preferences ("the preferences that actually govern the voting choice, when all other forces pressuring the member ... are taken into account"). Rohde, *Parties and Leaders*, 41.

71. As Lee argues, "parties do more than reflect the underlying policy disagreements that exist in American government.... Parties also systematically institutionalize, exploit, and deepen those divisions." Lee, *Beyond Ideology*, 5. See also S. Smith, *Party Influence in Congress*; John Gerring, *Party Ideologies in America, 1828–1996* (New York: Cambridge University Press, 1998).

72. But as Lee argues, scholars today invariably "describe individual legislators' policy orientations" (their preferences) "without any acknowledged role for groups or factions in constructing or bundling together the combinations of issues that are thought of as 'liberal' or 'conservative.'" See Lee, *Beyond Ideology*, 33.

73. Bloch Rubin, *Building the Bloc*, 16. Legislators must make similar compromises when they work together in partisan teams. As Cox and McCubbins observe, "Team production ... means confronting and overcoming a variety of collective action and coordination problems. For example, all members would like to spend more money in their own districts than might be optimal from their party's perspective; all members would like to have free access to floor time, but the result could be that nothing can get done reliably." Cox and McCubbins, *Setting the Agenda*, 22.

74. Bloch Rubin, *Building the Bloc*, 14.

75. David R. Mayhew, *Congress: The Electoral Connection* (New Haven, CT: Yale University Press, 1974).

76. Mancur Olson, *The Logic of Collective Action: Public Goods and Theory* (Cambridge, MA: Harvard University Press, 1965), 2. For a more detailed description of these collective action problems, see Bloch Rubin, *Building the Bloc*, 10–11.

77. Former Freedom Caucus member Mick Mulvaney put it this way: "I learned ... years ago that people lie about how they are going to vote. And you cannot go into this kind of fight [against leadership] with people you do not trust. We

walked onto the floor two years ago with signed pledges — handwritten promises — from more than enough people to deny [John] Boehner his job. But when it came time to vote, almost half of those people changed their minds. [Our] coup was bound to fail." As quoted in Kaveh Waddell, "GOP Congressman: 'Coup' against Boehner was 'Bound to Fail,'" *Atlantic*, January 6, 2015.

78. Interview with member of Congress, March 2023. All interviews were conducted in confidentiality, and the names of interviewees are withheld by mutual agreement. See appendix B for further details about interview procedures.

79. Interview with former staffer, November 2022.

80. For more on how institutional and electoral factors shape members' propensity to collaborate, see Bloch Rubin, *Building the Bloc*, 16–19.

81. Clarke, "Party Sub-Brands," 452–70. This dynamic can sometimes work in reverse, as the higher profile that collaborating members garner may be something that publicity-averse lawmakers wish to avoid.

82. Bloch Rubin, *Building the Bloc*, 13–16.

83. Bloch Rubin, "Organizing at the Extreme," 1–30.

84. It is certainly conceivable that when all factions are collaborating, they will be more likely to collectively resist an offending leader. But if congressional history is any guide, these kinds of alliances are unlikely.

85. Strahan, *Leading Representatives*, 39.

86. As quoted in Bloch Rubin, *Building the Bloc*, 187.

87. Bloch Rubin, *Building the Bloc*, 13–16.

88. Richard Hall and Alan V. Deardorff, "Lobbying as Legislative Subsidy," *American Political Science Review* 100, no. 1 (February 2006): 69–84. To the extent that warring factions in a symmetric configuration seek to invest in ever-more-elaborate institutional machinery in an effort to gain an edge over their rivals, the bigger the potential grant to leaders.

89. This logic also applies to symmetric configurations where a party's factions have chosen to collaborate less extensively. Although in these situations the potential subsidy a leader can hope to collect is likely to be smaller, even modest resources can generate efficiency gains. For instance, in a situation where each faction gets together regularly, a leader seeking to gauge support within the party can consult with members in their respective blocs rather than on an individual basis. Similar gains arise when each faction has empowered a spokesperson to communicate pertinent information on behalf of their members.

90. As Moe observes in the context of the federal bureaucracy, political rivals will "impose constraints on one another in a competitive effort to see to is that their own interests are protected from the intrusions of politician-opponents. . . . The net result is that . . . this can only tend to strengthen the foundations of bureaucratic autonomy." A similar logic applies to rival factions competing to limit the influence of their adversaries. The net effect of these machinations is to strengthen leadership autonomy. See Moe, "New Economics of Organization," 769.

91. Collaboration can immunize members from leader pressure in two ways. First, by working together, members of factions can generate resources of their own to offset whatever leaders might threaten to withhold or promise to supply in return for good behavior. Alternatively, when members join forces, it may become harder for leaders to identify the correct individuals to punish or reward—or to justify singling out some members rather than others—which may incline a leader to discipline or buy off everyone in the faction, notwithstanding the inefficiency of the strategy.

92. For example, after initially backing a proposal for a bipartisan commission to investigate the January 6, 2021, Capitol insurrection, Minority Leader Kevin McCarthy withdrew his support under pressure from members of the House Freedom Caucus. Democrats, for their part, expressed little shock at McCarthy's reversal. As Speaker Pelosi put it, the Republican leader's unwillingness to buck his party's right flank was "disappointing but not surprising." As quoted in. Rebecca Shabad, Sahil Kapur, and Farrett Haake, "McCarthy Opposes Bipartisan Commission to Investigate Jan. 6 Capitol Attack," *NBC News*, May 18, 2021, https://www.nbcnews.com/politics/congress/mccarthy-opposes-bipartisan-commission-investigate-jan-6-capitol-attack-n1267743.

93. For more on how factions develop branding strategies, see Clarke, "Party Sub-Brands," 452–70.

94. See, for example, Schickler and Rich, "Controlling the Floor"; Diana Evans, *Greasing the Wheels: Using Pork Barrel Projects to Build Majority Coalitions in Congress* (New York: Cambridge University Press, 2004), 178.

95. Barbara Sinclair, *Legislators, Leaders, and Lawmaking* (Baltimore: Johns Hopkins University Press, 1998), 248.

96. See, for example, Keith Krehbiel, *Pivotal Politics: A Theory of U.S. Lawmaking* (Chicago: University of Chicago Press, 1998), 165–72.

97. To be sure, some of these concerns are of considerable interest to legislative scholars who might not self-identify as "doing APD." For instance, there are prominent scholars in both intellectual traditions that are committed to understanding how context constrains the agency of individual actors. See, for example, work by Adam Sheingate on endogenous institutional change and legislative entrepreneurs and Alan Wiseman's account of leadership performance as determined by variation in selection mechanisms and institutional opportunities. Adam Sheingate, "Rethinking Rules: Creativity and Constraint in the House of Representatives," in *Explaining Institutional Change: Ambiguity, Agency, and Power*, ed. James Mahoney and Kathleen Thelen (New York: Cambridge University Press, 2010), 168–203; Alan Wiseman, "Filters and Pegs in Holes: How Selection Mechanisms and Institutional Positions Shape (Perceptions of) Political Leadership," in *Leadership in American Politics*, ed. Jeffery A. Jenkins and Craig Volden (Lawrence: University of Kansas Press, 2017), 267–88.

98. This is also how some congressional historians describe eras in congressional history. As Julian Zelizer explains, "historical periods in America's Congress are

best defined by the changing nature of the legislative process itself. The periods of congressional history gain their flavor from the formal and informal 'rules of the game,' the process and the structures through which all participants operate and all decisions are made." Julian E. Zelizer, *The American Congress: The Building of Democracy* (Boston: Houghton Mifflin, 2004), xvi–xvii.

99. Stephen Skowronek, *The Politics Presidents Make: Leadership from John Adams to Bill Clinton* (Cambridge, MA: Harvard University Press, 1997), 29–30.

100. Skowronek, *Politics Presidents Make*, 30.

101. Randall Ripley's account of leadership patterns in the House provides another method of keeping political time. He describes four "periods" of leadership: "leadership by the Speaker, leadership by the Majority Leader, leadership by a collegial group, and leadership by the President." As is true of factional configurations, these periods cut across historical eras—so, for instance, between 1861 and 1899, the House alternated between periods where the Speaker was the principal leader making decisions about legislative strategy and tactics for the majority party and periods where "an important committee chairman . . . made the bulk of the strategic and tactical decisions affecting legislation in the House." Randall B. Ripley, *Party Leaders in the House of Representatives* (Washington, DC: Brookings Institution Press, 1967), 82–87.

102. Ripley, *Party Leaders in the House*, 29.

103. Eric Schickler, *Racial Realignment: The Transformation of American Liberalism, 1932–1965* (Princeton, NJ: Princeton University Press, 2016), 14; Karen Orren and Stephen Skowronek, *The Search for American Political Development* (Cambridge: Cambridge University Press, 2004), 117.

104. Schickler, *Racial Realignment*, 14–16.

105. As quoted in John Lawrence, *Arc of Power: Inside Nancy Pelosi's Speakership, 2005–2010* (Lawrence: University Press of Kansas, 2023), 176–77.

106. Theda Skocpol and Caroline Tervo, *Upending American Politics: Polarizing Parties, Ideological Elites, and Citizen Activists from the Tea Party to the Anti-Trump Resistance* (New York: Oxford University Press, 2020).

107. John Boehner, *On the House: A Washington Memoir* (New York: St. Martin's Press, 2021), 172.

108. Michael Bowen, *The Roots of Modern Conservatism: Dewey, Taft, and the Battle for the Soul of the Republican Party* (Chapel Hill: University of North Carolina Press, 2011), 197–98.

Chapter 2

1. See Robert Dahl, "The Concept of Power," *Behavioral Science* 2 (1957): 201–15.

2. Curry, *Legislating in the Dark*, 34–35.

3. William G. Howell, *Thinking about the Presidency: The Primacy of Power* (Princeton, NJ: Princeton University Press, 2015), 13.

4. See, for example, Keith Krehbiel, "Where's the Party?" *British Journal of Political Science* 23, no. 2 (April 1993): 235–66.

5. An exemplary account is offered by Curry in *Legislating in the Dark*.

6. As Nolan McCarty observes, notwithstanding the fact that they are not "pure measures of legislator ideology," vote-based estimates of member preferences like DW-NOMINATE have some important advantages that help explain their popularity in the discipline. They help reveal, among other things, how "choices across different issues" are linked and facilitate comparisons among individual legislators and across time. See Nolan McCarty, "In Defense of DW-NOMINATE," *Studies in American Political Development* 30 (October 2016): 172–84. Although vote-based metrics remain ubiquitous, new measures have cropped up to estimate lawmakers' ideal points using other sources of data, including campaign finance records. These measures make it possible to compare the ideology of officeholders in a variety of institutional settings, as well as that of candidates. However, because fundraising (like voting) is not walled off from leadership influence, it, too, risks aggregating the inputs that reflect members' true wants and those that are induced by leaders.

7. See, for example, Gary W. Cox and Mathew D. McCubbins, *Legislative Leviathan: Party Government in the House* (Berkeley: University of California Press, 1993); Sinclair, *Legislators, Leaders, and Lawmaking*. In the context of the presidency, Neustadt characterizes the distinction in these terms: "Formal powers . . . [are] synonymous with legal or customary 'authority' and power, always in the singular, no quotation marks, [is] . . synonymous with personal influence." Richard E. Neustadt, *Presidential Power and the Modern Presidents: The Politics of Leadership from Roosevelt to Reagan* (New York: Free Press, 1990), 7.

8. Strahan, *Leading Representatives*, 5.

9. Where archival records remain unprocessed or embargoed and in-depth interviews with lawmakers and their staff in short supply, I rely on other evidentiary sources, including newspaper and magazine articles, as well as the *Congressional Record*.

10. Early legislative scholars appreciated the virtues of assessing leader power through archival holdings. The earliest study of the speakership, for example, observed that "the reason why there has hitherto been no study of the Speaker, founded on investigation, is the . . . records of his activity are buried in the interminable reports of debates, or are diffused among letters and reminiscences." See Mary Parker Follett, *The Speaker of the House of Representatives* (New York: Longmans, Green, 1896), xii.

11. David Mayhew, *Partisan Balance: Why Political Parties Don't Kill the U.S. Constitutional System* (Princeton, NJ: Princeton University Press, 2011), 39.

12. Harold D. Lasswell, "Faction," in *Encyclopedia of the Social Sciences* (New York: Macmillan, 1931), 49.

13. David Mayhew, *Placing Parties in American Politics* (Princeton, NJ: Princeton University Press, 1986), 79.

14. Daniel DiSalvo, *Engines of Change: Party Factions in American Politics, 1868–2010* (New York: Oxford University Press, 2012), 5.

15. See, for example, DiSalvo, *Engines of Change*; Gisela Sin, *Separation of Powers and Legislative Organization: The President, the Senate, and Political Parties in the Making of House Rules* (New York: Cambridge University Press, 2014).

Chapter 3

1. Lee Glendinning, "Barack Obama Declares 'Change Has Come to America,'" *Guardian*, November 5, 2008, https://www.theguardian.com/world/2008/nov/05/barack-obama-victory-speech-chicago.

2. As quoted in Lawrence, *Arc of Power*, 30.

3. Interview with staffer, November 2021.

4. Interview with member of Congress, September 2011.

5. Mike Ross as quoted in "Conservative Democrats Seek Larger Role," *ABC News*, November 15, 2006, https://www.nbcnews.com/id/wbna15736316.

6. John Nichols, "Building a Progressive Caucus," *Nation*, July 5, 1999, 17.

7. David Dayen, "The Progressive Caucus Wields Power," *American Prospect*, October 1, 2021; Nichols, "Building a Progressive Caucus," 20.

8. As quoted in Ronald M. Peters Jr. and Cindy Simon Rosenthal, *Speaker Nancy Pelosi and the New American Politics* (New York: Oxford University Press, 2010), 185.

9. John Lawrence, "Pelosi's Power," interview by Jim Gilmore, Michael Kirk, and Mike Wiser, *Frontline*, PBS, March 22, 2022, https://www.pbs.org/wgbh/frontline/interview/john-lawrence/.

10. Interview with staffer, March 2023.

11. As quoted in Jean Parvin Bordewich, "Nancy Pelosi's Big Stick," *Washington Monthly*, August 27, 2023.

12. See, for example, Page, *Madam Speaker*.

13. As David Axelrod noted, "It's harder . . . than it was even 12 years ago to pass a major piece of legislation . . . because you have a 50/50 Senate and an almost 50/50 House." David Axelrod, "Pelosi's Power," interview with Michael Kirk, *Frontline*, PBS, March 22, 2022, https://www.pbs.org/wgbh/frontline/interview/david-axelrod-2/.

14. Interview with staffer, November 2019.

15. David Obey as quoted in Harold Meyerson, "How Nancy Pelosi Took Control," *American Prospect*, May 12, 2004. Pelosi, however, characterized her approach to bargaining differently: "Where we cannot find that common ground, we must stand our ground." As quoted in Nancy Pelosi, *The Art of Power* (New York: Simon & Schuster, 2024), 43.

16. Interview with member of Congress, November 2023. Judy Lemons, Pelosi's first chief of staff, described the Speaker's policy acumen in these terms: "[She would tell members]: Don't you see? If we take this path, it's going to lead us to this spot and this spot and this spot.... Don't you get it?" Judy Lemons, "Pelosi's Power," interview with Mike Kirk, *Frontline*, PBS, March 22, 2022, https://www.pbs.org/wgbh/frontline/interview/judy-lemons/.

17. James Sundquist as quoted in G. Calvin Mackenzie and Robert Weisbrot, *The Liberal Hour: Washington and the Politics of Change in the 1960s* (New York: Penguin, 2008), 59.

18. Julian E. Zelizer, "When Liberals Were Organized," *American Prospect*, January 22, 2015.

19. John Breaux as quoted in Margot Hornblower and T. R. Reid, "After Two Decades, the 'Boll Weevils' Are Back, and Whistling Dixie," *Washington Post*, April 26, 1981.

20. As quoted in Richard L. Lyons, "Conservative House Democrats Seeking Larger Role in Party," *Washington Post*, November 20, 1980, A3.

21. Glenn English as quoted in Denise Gamino, "Boll Weevils Losing Clout in Congress, But Can Occasionally Muster Influence," *Oklahoman* (Oklahoma City), June 26, 1983.

22. Wes Watkins as quoted in Gamino, "Boll Weevils Losing Clout in Congress"; G. V. Montgomery and Charles Stenholm as quoted in Steven V. Roberts, "Congress: The Eclipse of the Boll Weevils," *New York Times*, March 26, 1983.

23. As quoted in Nichols, "Building a Progressive Caucus," *Nation*, July 5, 1999, 21.

24. Zelizer, "When Liberals Were Organized."

25. Interview with member of Congress, November 2023.

26. Interview with staffer, September 2011.

27. Interview with member of Congress, November 2011; Bloch Rubin, *Building the Bloc*, 198–200.

28. Interview with Blue Dog staffer, October 2011.

29. Interview with member of Congress, November 2011.

30. Bloch Rubin, *Building the Bloc*, 206.

31. Blue Dog aide as quoted in Erin P. Billings, "Blue Dogs Marking Decade in the Middle," *Roll Call*, March 4, 2005.

32. Charles Stenholm as quoted in Meyerson, "How Nancy Pelosi Took Control."

33. As quoted in Meyerson, "How Nancy Pelosi Took Control."

34. As quoted in Meyerson, "How Nancy Pelosi Took Control."

35. Interview with Blue Dog staffer, August 2011.

36. As quoted in Lawrence, *Arc of Power*, 29.

37. Barack Obama, "Remarks of President Barack Obama—As Prepared for Delivery, Address to Joint Session of Congress," White House Office of the Press

Secretary, February 24, 2009, https://obamawhitehouse.archives.gov/the-press-office/remarks-president-barack-obama-address-joint-session-congress.

38. As quoted in Lawrence, *Arc of Power*, 176–77. While campaigning, Obama argued that "energy we have to deal with today. Health care is priority No. 2."

39. As quoted in Lawrence, *Arc of Power*, 179–81.

40. Jennifer Bendery, "Liberals Try to Influence Healthcare Debate," *Roll Call*, April 2, 2009.

41. Interview with staffer, September 2023.

42. Interview with member of Congress, June 2023; interview with member of Congress, November 2023.

43. Interview with staffer, August 2011.

44. Interview with staffer, September 2011.

45. Nancy Pelosi, "Capitol Hill News Conference on McDermott-Conyers Bill," aired September 23, 1993, on C-SPAN.

46. Health Policy Team, memorandum to President-elect Barack Obama, December 10, 2008 (on file with author).

47. Lawrence, *Arc of Power*, 180; Steven T. Dennis and Tory Newmyer, "Chairmen Insist on Public Plan for Health Care Bill," *Roll Call*, June 9, 2009.

48. Blue Dog Coalition to Nancy Pelosi and Steny Hoyer, July 9, 2009 (letter on file with author).

49. As quoted in Steven T. Dennis and Tory Newmyer, "Blue Dogs' Objections Could Delay Release of the Healthcare Bill," *Roll Call*, July 9, 2009.

50. Interview with staffer, November 2011.

51. As quoted in Lawrence, *Arc of Power*, 185.

52. As quoted in Alex Wayne and Jonathan Allen, "Blue Dogs Bare Teeth at Health Bill Markup," *CQ*, July 17, 2009.

53. As quoted in Ronald Brownstein, "Why the New Democratic Majority Could Work Better Than the Last," *Atlantic*, January 3, 2019.

54. As quoted in Dennis and Newmyer, "Blue Dogs' Objections Could Delay Release of the Healthcare Bill."

55. As quoted in Suzy Khimm, "Scenes from the Progressive Revolt," *New Republic*, July 30, 2009.

56. As quoted in Noam N. Levey and James Oliphant, "Liberal Democrats Threaten to Reject House Healthcare Deal," *Los Angeles Times*, July 31, 2009.

57. As quoted in Joan McCarter, "The Netroots and the House Progressives: Toward More Progressive Policy," *Daily Kos*, June 28, 2009, https://www.dailykos.com/stories/2009/6/28/747842/-.

58. As quoted Glenn Thrush, "Pelosi: Insurers Are 'Immoral' Villains," *Politico*, July 7, 2009, https://www.politico.com/story/2009/07/pelosi-insurers-are-immoral-villains-025651.

59. Interview with member of Congress, November 2011.

60. As quoted in Lawrence, *Arc of Power*, 207.
61. Interview with staffer, October 2011.
62. As quoted in David M. Herszenhorn and Jackie Calmes, "Abortion Was at Heart of Wrangling," *New York Times*, November 2, 2009.
63. As quoted in Lawrence, *Arc of Power*, 207.
64. As quoted in Robert Pear and David M. Herszenhorn, "House Democrats End Impasse on Health Bill," *New York Times*, July 30, 2009, A1. Also confirmed in interview with member of Congress, June 2023.
65. Molly Ball, *Pelosi* (New York: Picador, 2020), 192.
66. Ball, *Pelosi*, 193.
67. Lawrence, *Arc of Power*, 267.
68. Sam Brodey, "How Keith Ellison Made the Congressional Progressive Caucus into a Political Force That Matters," *MinnPost*, July 21, 2015, https://www.minnpost.com/dc-dispatches/2015/07/how-keith-ellison-made-congressional-progressive-caucus-political-force-matter/.
69. Interview with staffer, June 2023.
70. Interview with member of Congress, November 2023.
71. CPC member as quoted in Ryan Grim, "Congressional Progressives Are Revamping Their Caucus with an Eye Toward 2021," *Intercept*, October 20, 2020, https://theintercept.com/2020/10/26/congressional-progressives-are-revamping-their-caucus-with-an-eye-toward-2021/.
72. Grim, "Congressional Progressives Are Revamping Their Caucus."
73. CPC member as quoted in Grim, "Congressional Progressives Are Revamping Their Caucus."
74. As quoted in Robert P. Baird, "Inside the Democrats' Battle to Build Back Better," *New Yorker*, November 8, 2021.
75. Interview with staffer, May 2023.
76. Elaine Godfrey, "House Progressives Celebrate a 'New Kind of Centrism,'" *Atlantic*, November 13, 2018.
77. As quoted in Rachel Bade, "Leaders of House Liberal Caucus Consider New Membership Rules," *Washington Post*, February 25, 2019.
78. Rachel Bade, "We Will Only Get Stronger: Inside a Liberal Leader's Balancing Act on Pushing the House to the Left," *Washington Post*, February 25, 2019.
79. Interview with member of Congress, November 2023.
80. Caygle, Ferris, and Bresnahan, "Progressive Caucus Eyes Shakeup."
81. Baird, "Inside the Democrats' Battle to Build Back Better."
82. As quoted in Anthony Adragna and Zack Colman, "'The Existential Threat of Our Time': Pelosi Elevates Climate Change on Day One," *Politico*, January 3, 2019, https://www.politico.com/story/2019/01/03/nancy-pelosi-climate-change-congress-1059148.
83. Interview with staffer, October 2023.
84. As quoted in Lawrence, *Arc of Power*, 167.

85. As quoted in Sahil Kapur, "Ocasio-Cortez Breaks with Pelosi in Key Early Vote for Democrats," *Boston Globe*, January 2, 2019.

86. "FAQs on PAYGO," House Committee on the Budget, July 13, 2020, https://democrats-budget.house.gov/publications/report/faqs-paygo.

87. Nancy Pelosi, "Floor Speech on Pay-As-You-Go Legislation," press release, July 22, 2009, https://pelosi.house.gov/news/press-releases/pelosi-floor-speech-on-pay-as-you-go-legislation.

88. Interview with staffer, September 2023.

89. As quoted in Rachel Frazin, "Pelosi Touts Climate and Social Spending Bill in Glasgow," *The Hill*, November 9, 2021.

90. Blue Dog Coalition Leadership to Chairman John Yarmuth [cc Speaker Nancy Pelosi], January 4, 2021, Committee for a Responsible Federal Budget, https://www.crfb.org/sites/default/files/210104%20PAYGO%20Rules%20Package%20letter.pdf.

91. Interview with staffer, September 2023.

92. Pramila Jayapal as quoted in Baird, "Inside the Democrats' Battle to Build Back Better."

93. Interview with staffer, September 2023; Lindsey McPherson, "How 'Build Back Better' Started, and How It's Going: A Timeline," *Roll Call*, July 21, 2022.

94. Interview with member of Congress, May 2023.

95. Interview with staffer, June 2023.

96. As quoted in Jonathan Cohn, "How They Did It (Part Five)," *New Republic*, May 19, 2010.

97. Julia Rock and Ryan Grim, "Bernie Sanders to House Progressives: Hold Strong or the Senate Will Tank Biden's Agenda," *American Prospect*, September 28, 2021.

98. As quoted in Emily Cochrane, Jim Tankersley, and Jonathan Weisman, "Biden Signs On to a Bipartisan Infrastructure Compromise, but Says It Must Be Accompanied by a Larger Package," *New York Times*, June 25, 2021.

99. As quoted in Emily Williams, "Moderate House Dems to Pelosi: 'There Will Be No Budget Resolution Until Infrastructure Bill Is Signed," *Fortune*, August 13, 2021.

100. Baird, "Inside the Democrats' Battle to Build Back Better."

101. As quoted in Sarah Ferris, "The 'Velvet Hammer' Leads Resurgent Blue Dogs," *Politico*, May 7, 2019, https://www.politico.com/story/2019/05/07/stephanie-murphy-democrats-blue-dogs-moderates-1305398.

102. As quoted in Lawrence, *Arc of Power*, 207.

103. As quoted in Jonathan Martin and Jonathan Weisman, "Biden Throws In with Left, Leaving His Agenda in Doubt," *New York Times*, October 2, 2021.

104. Interview with staffer, April 2023.

105. Interview with member of Congress, November 2023.

106. Interview with committee staffer, May 2023.

107. Pramila Jayapal, Katie Porter, and Ilhan Omar, "Why We're Willing to Put Our Votes on the Line for the Build Back Better Act," CNN, September 27, 2021, https://www.cnn.com/2021/09/27/opinions/biden-spending-bill-infrastructure-vote-jayapal-porter-omar/index.html.

108. Sarah Ferris, "The Real Power in the New Congress Isn't Where Matt Gaetz Thinks It Is," *Politico Magazine*, January 13, 2023, https://www.politico.com/news/magazine/2023/01/13/josh-gottheimer-congress-power-player-00074987.

109. The moderates issued a formal statement recording their pledge: "We commit to voting for the [climate bill] in its current form . . . as expeditiously as we receive fiscal information from the Congressional Budget Office—but in no event later than the week of November 15th—consistent with the toplines for revenues and investments." As quoted in Barbara Sprunt, Caitlyn Kim, and Deepa Shivaram, "Biden Says Final Passage of $1 Trillion Infrastructure Plan Is a Big Step Forward," NPR, November 6, 2021, https://www.npr.org/2021/11/05/1050012853/the-house-has-passed-the-1-trillion-infrastructure-plan-sending-it-to-bidens-des.

110. Emily Cochrane and Jonathan Weisman, "House Narrowly Passes Biden's Social Safety Net and Climate Bill," *New York Times*, November 19, 2021.

111. As quoted in Hope Yen, "Sen. Joe Manchin Says No to $2T Bill: 'I Can't Vote for It,'" *PBS NewsHour Weekend*, December 19, 2021, https://www.pbs.org/newshour/politics/sen-joe-manchin-says-no-to-2t-bill-i-cant-vote-for-it.

112. As quoted in Emily Cochrane, "House Passes Sweeping Climate, Tax, and Health Care Package," *New York Times*, August 12, 2022.

Chapter 4

1. As quoted in Jeff Zeleny, "G.O.P. Captures House, but Not Senate," *New York Times*, November 3, 2010, A1.

2. Skocpol and Tervo, *Upending American Politics*.

3. As quoted in "Dick Armey: The TT Interview," *Texas Tribune*, August 31, 2010, https://www.texastribune.org/2010/08/31/an-interview-with-former-us-rep-dick-armey/; Lisa Mascaro, "End of an Era? Tea Party Class of House Republicans Fades," *AP News*, June 3, 2018, https://apnews.com/article/64b634a91a2d4933b8bca4c95baa1309.

4. For a detailed history of moderate Republicans' organizational decline, see Geoffrey Kabaservice, *Rule and Ruin: The Downfall of Moderation and Destruction of the Republican Party, from Eisenhower to the Tea Party* (New York: Oxford University Press, 2012), 363.

5. Interview with member of Congress, April 2023.

6. Interview with member of Congress, April 2023. In 2020, the Tuesday Group renamed itself the Republican Governance Group.

7. Interview with member of Congress, October 2022 and April 2023. Most lawmakers interviewed described the Republican conference's right flank as an

association of "hardcore conservatives." In making this designation, they emphasized that Republicans as a group identify as conservative but that members of the "crazy caucus" or "chaos caucus" (as Boehner called his adversaries) favored policies and tactics outside the norm ("they were always wanting to fight something") or were unusually inflexible in making trade-offs between competing conservative principles and priorities ("they hated compromise, even when we [Republicans] wanted the deal").

8. Interview with member of Congress, November 2022.

9. Devin Nunes as quoted in Ryan Lizza, "A House Divided," *New Yorker*, December 6, 2015.

10. Boehner, *On the House*, 170.

11. Donald Critchlow, *The Conservative Ascendancy: How the GOP Right Made Political History* (Cambridge, MA: Harvard University Press, 2007); Bowen, *Roots of Modern Conservatism*.

12. Kabaservice, *Rule and Ruin*, xviii.

13. Kabaservice, *Rule and Ruin*, xix.

14. John Boehner, "Panic Rooms, Birth Certificates, and the Birth of GOP Paranoia," *Politico*, April 2, 2021, https://www.politico.com/news/magazine/2021/04/02/john-boehner-book-memoir-excerpt-478506; interview with member of Congress, May 2023.

15. See, for example, Green, *Legislative Hardball*.

16. Interview with member of Congress, November 2022.

17. Bloch Rubin, *Building the Bloc*, 261–94. See also Zachary A. McGee, "Keeping Your Friends Close: How the House Freedom Caucus Organized for Survival," (PhD diss., University of Texas–Austin, 2017).

18. In 2011, conservative Republicans persuaded their colleagues to back a plan called Cut, Cap, and Balance, which required that any dollar increase in the debt ceiling be matched by an equal cut in federal spending, a cap on future spending, and a constitutional amendment obliging Congress to balance the federal budget. Although the bill passed the House, Boehner openly mocked the plan (nicknaming it "Snap, Crackle, and Pop" after the cartoon mascots for Rice Krispies cereal) and, predicting its quick demise in the Democratic-controlled Senate, suggested it was a "half-assed" strategy. On a party conference call in August 2013, Boehner announced his "intent . . . to move quickly on a short-term continuing resolution that keeps the government running and maintains current sequester spending levels." As quoted in Caren Bohan and Rachelle Younglai, "Boehner Warns Against Shutting U.S. Government over 'Obamacare,'" Reuters, August 22, 2013.

19. Tom Cole as quoted in Lizza, "House Divided."

20. Boehner as quoted in Tim Alberta, "John Boehner Unchained," *Politico Magazine*, November/December 2017, https://www.politico.com/magazine/story/2017/10/29/john-boehner-trump-house-republican-party-retirement-profile-feature-215741/.

21. Tom Cole as quoted in Lizza, "House Divided."

22. The letter closed with the following reference to James Madison's Federalist paper No. 58: "James Madison wrote in Federalist No. 58 that the 'power over the purse may, in fact, be regarded as the most complete and effectual weapon . . . for obtaining a redress of every grievance. . . .' We look forward to collaborating to defund one of the largest grievances in our time and to restore patient-centered healthcare in America." Mark Meadows et al. to John Boehner and Eric Cantor, August 21, 2013, https://www.hcpress.com/img/Meadows-Letter-1.jpg.

23. As quoted in Glenn Thrush, "The Prisoner of Capitol Hill: Can John Boehner Save House Republicans from Themselves?" *Politico Magazine*, January/February 2015, https://www.politico.com/magazine/story/2015/01/john-boehner-profile-113874/; interview with member of Congress, April 2023.

24. Interview with member of Congress, April 2023.

25. R. Caldwell Butler, "New Approach to Solving Problems," January 1975, pp. 1–2, folder 2, box 2, Benjamin Reifel Papers, South Dakota State University (hereafter cited as Reifel Papers). Growing collaboration between moderate Republicans in Congress paralleled the institutionalization of moderate Republicanism at the grassroots level, with the creation in 1962 of the Ripon Society and Bow Group.

26. "House Wednesday Group: A Brief History," p. 7, folder 2, box 2, Reifel Papers.

27. Henry Z. Scheele, "Prelude to the Presidency: An Examination of the Gerald R. Ford-Charles A. Halleck House Minority Leadership Contest," *Presidential Studies Quarterly* 25, no. 4 (1995): 767–85. Two Wednesday Group members spearheaded Ford's campaign against Halleck; several other members campaigned publicly on his behalf. Although the Wednesday Group succeeded in elevating Ford, the group's favored candidates for conference chair and party whip lost to more conservative candidates, in no small part because moderates did not back their nominees as a bloc.

28. For instance, Ford would use several of the Wednesday Group's model bills ("lead legislation" in the group's parlance) and studies on childcare and day care centers authored in the late 1960s as the basis for the 1976 Child and Dependent Care Credit, which was one of the first federal programs to provide childcare assistance to American families in need. The group also played an important role in executive efforts to reform the selective service system. Its 1967 report "How to End the Draft: The Case for an All-Volunteer Army" provided the blueprint for the Nixon administration (and later, the Ford administration) to transition from a military draft to an all-volunteer army. Robert K. Griffith, "About Face? The U.S. Army and the Draft," *Armed Forces & Society* 12, no. 1 (Fall 1985): 108–33. See also Annelise Anderson et al., "Ending the Draft: The Creation of the All-Volunteer Force," Nixon Legacy Forum Transcript, January 19, 2012, Richard Nixon Presidential Library, https://www.nixonfoundation.org/wp-content/uploads/2012/01/Nixon-Legacy-Forum-Nixon-Ends-the-Draft.pdf.

29. Bill Frenzel, "Where Are We Going," September 8, 1972, p. 12, folder 2, box 2, Reifel Papers.

30. Butler, "New Approach to Solving Problems," p. 1. Some moderate lawmakers left the GOP altogether. Rep. John Anderson of Illinois, for example, was so incensed by Reagan and the New Right that he declared himself an independent in 1980—taking with him "most of the liberal wing of the Republican party." As quoted in Kabaservice, *Rule and Ruin*, 362.

31. Butler, "New Approach to Solving Problems," p. 1; Bill Frenzel, "Where Are We Going," September 8, 1972, p. 12, folder 2, box 2, Reifel Papers. Franzel later expressed regret that "if you're a moderate Republican, you get the worst of both worlds, because you get punished both for being socially liberal and for being fiscally conservative. You're doubly handicapped." As quoted in Kabaservice, *Rule and Ruin*, 367.

32. Many of these members called themselves "Gypsy Moths" (in reference to the Boll Weevils across the aisle) and were regularly frustrated by Reagan's tendency to take their votes for granted, while he "lavished attention and favors on conservative southern Democrats." As quoted in Eric Pianin, "We Will Be the Center of Power," *Washington Post*, January 17, 1995, A4.

33. As quoted in "Stressing the Force of Ideas: Description of the Group," 1988, p. 3, folder 2, box 2, Reifel Papers. By the 1980s, Wednesday Group members would include Representatives Dick Cheney of Wyoming, Lynn Martin of Illinois, and Mickey Edwards of Oklahoma. By the group's own estimation, it represented "a balance of . . . liberals, conservatives, and moderates."

34. As quoted in Jesse Zwick, "Tuesday Mourning," *New Republic*, January 28, 2011. Notably, Michel was not supportive of intraparty organizations more generally. The minority leader expressed concern that such groups were "diffusing, denigrating, and even in some cases destroying the legitimate functions of the House, its leadership and its committees." As quoted in John de Ferrari, "Congress' Own Special-Interest Groups," *Nation's Business*, August 1983, 39–40.

35. Pianin, "We Will Be the Center of Power." Johnson and Gunderson were joined by New Jersey's Marge Roukema and Dick Zimmer, New York's Sherwood Boehlert, and Michigan's Fred Upton.

36. Edwin J. Feulner Jr. *Conservatives Stalk the House: The Republican Study Committee, 1970–1982* (Ottawa, IL: Green Hill Publishers, 1983), 1.

37. Feulner, *Conservatives Stalk the House*, 39; William F. Buckley Jr., "Say It Isn't So, Mr. President," *New York Times*, August 1, 1971, SM8.

38. As quoted in Willard Edwards, "Nixon Wins Over Conservatives," *Chicago Tribune*, June 14, 1969, N10.

39. Lou Cannon, "Conservatives Show Dismay on President," *Washington Post*, January 26, 1974.

40. As quoted in Tim Alberta, "The Cabal That Quietly Took Over the House," *Atlantic*, May 24, 2013.

41. H. R. Haldeman, *The Haldeman Diaries: Inside the Nixon White House* (New York: G. P. Putnam's 1994), 286.

42. Edward Derwinski, as quoted in Feulner, *Conservatives Stalk the House*, 65.
43. As quoted in Alberta, "Cabal That Quietly Took Over."
44. Mary Russell, "Fighting Conservative Chic," *Washington Post*, March 17, 1976, A4.
45. As quoted in Feulner, *Conservatives Stalk the House*, 202.
46. As quoted in Kabaservice, *Rule and Ruin*, 173.
47. As quoted in Feulner, *Conservatives Stalk the House*, 202.
48. Henry Hyde, as quoted in "Republicans Elect Gingrich New Speaker of U.S. House," *Atlanta Daily World*, December 8, 1994, 1.
49. Bloch Rubin, *Building the Bloc*, 278–79.
50. Jerry Gray, "'Bad Boys' among House Republicans Make a Point," *New York Times*, March 22, 1997, 12.
51. As quoted in Dan Balz, "Moderates Seeking 'Meaningful Role' in Party," *Washington Post*, November 24, 1996, A10.
52. As quoted in Scott S. Greenberger, "On Tuesday It's Pizza for Some Republicans," *New York Times Magazine*, June 11, 1995, 8–9; Sherwood Boehlert as quoted in John E. Yang and Helen Dewar, "Finding Strength in the Middle: Once Marginalized, Republican Moderates Now Play Pivotal Role," *Washington Post*, October 23, 1995, A6.
53. As quoted in Balz, "Moderates Seeking 'Meaningful Role' in Party." Gingrich was an outlier in his approach to moderate Republicans. While many on his leadership team disdained the party's more liberal members, the Speaker maintained an open door. As one moderate described it, "Newt says that if you don't tell me what you're worried about, then it's your problem. He's essentially inviting people to talk to him." As quoted in Barbara Sinclair, "Leading the Revolution: Innovation and Continuity in Congressional Party Leadership," in *The Republican Takeover of Congress*, ed. Dean McSweeney and John E. Owens (New York: St. Martin's Press, 1998), 90.
54. Dan Burton, CAT founding member, as quoted in Greenberger, "On Tuesday It's Pizza for Some Republicans."
55. As quoted in Katharine Q. Seelye, "A Time to Negotiate, A Time for Courtship: Gingrich Continues to Reach Out to GOP Conservatives," *New York Times*, April 11, 1997, A1.
56. Interview with member of Congress, May 2023.
57. As quoted in Alberta, "John Boehner Unchained."
58. Guy Gugliotta and Juliet Eilperin, "Gingrich Steps Down in Face of Rebellion," *Washington Post*, November 7, 1998, A1.
59. As quoted in Carl Hulse, "G.O.P. Agenda in House Has Moderates Unhappy," *New York Times*, July 8, 2006, A11. The Iraq War only deepened the divide; roughly half of the Tuesday Group's membership favored withdrawal from the Middle East, "even if it meant the war was judged a loss" and told the president as much. Others continued to publicly back the conflict and did not take part in

meetings between the group and the White House. See Carl Husle and Jeff Zeleny, "G.O.P. Moderates Warn Bush Iraq Must Show Gains," *New York Times*, May 10, 2007, A1.

60. As quoted in Raymond Hernandez, "Democrats' Rise Has Pluses, Say G.O.P. Centrists," *New York Times*, April 7, 2007.

61. Charlie Dent as quoted in Zwick, "Tuesday Mourning."

62. John Bresnahan, "House GOP Dazed after Bailout Failure," *Politico*, October 1, 2008, https://www.politico.com/story/2008/10/house-gop-dazed-after-bailout-failure-014156.

63. As quoted in Bernie Becker, "Leading the G.O.P. Vanguard against the Bailout," *New York Times*, September 26, 2008.

64. Hensarling as quoted in Richard E. Cohen, "House Conservatives Push on Policy," *Politico*, February 3, 2011, https://www.politico.com/story/2011/02/house-conservatives-push-on-policy-048738.

65. Jim Vandehei and Richard E. Cohen, "Boehner's Boys: The New Power Club," *Politico*, November 4, 2010, https://www.politico.com/story/2010/11/boehners-boys-the-new-power-club-044682.

66. Tom Price as quoted in Alberta, "Cabal that Quietly Took Over."

67. Adam Brandon, spokesperson for FreedomWorks, as quoted in Chris Good, "GOP Reads the Tea Leaves," *Atlantic*, April 15, 2009.

68. Paul Teller, RSC aide, as quoted in Lydia DePillis, "Meet the New GOP Centrists," *New Republic*, January 12, 2010.

69. Steven LaTourette, Tuesday Group member, as quoted in Ben Pershing, "Moderate Republicans Crash the House's Tea Party," *Washington Post*, January 17, 2011.

70. As quoted in Vandehei and Cohen, "Boehner's Boys."

71. As quoted in "Boehner Elected House Speaker, Succeeding Pelosi," *ABC-13 Eyewitness News*, KTRK-TV Houston, January 5, 2011, https://abc13.com/archive/7880185/.

72. As he told the press, "We've got a lot of divergent opinions in the caucus and the key to any leadership job is to . . . listen, learn, [and then] help." Jake Tapper, "Boehner Learned Hard Lesson in Failed House Coup," *CNN Politics*, October 2, 2013, https://www.cnn.com/2013/10/01/politics/boehner-shutdown/index.html.

73. As quoted in Kathleen Hennessy and Lisa Mascaro, "Boehner Loses Some Ground as House Leader," *Los Angeles Times*, December 23, 2011.

74. As quoted in Thrush, "Prisoner of Capitol Hill."

75. Bob Cusack, "Lawmakers Who Signed 'Cut' Pledge Will Decide Fate of Boehner Bill," *The Hill*, July 28, 2011.

76. Ball, *Pelosi*, 214. One moderate member recalled, "There was no endgame [with Cut, Cap, and Balance]. We'd just shut the place down. Harry Reid had no reason to give us anything." Interview with member of Congress, April 2023.

77. Interview with member of Congress, March 2023.

78. Interview with member of Congress, March 2023.

79. Boehner recalled, "I began to talk to the president about the need to deal with our budget problem. And numerous times during the winter and spring of 2011, I suggested . . . that we had to get serious about this. And so [after we] played golf . . . I suggested to the president, 'Why don't we have a conversation?' And he agreed." As quoted (and verified with White House staff) in an interview with Jim Gilmore and Mike Wiser, in John Boehner, "Cliffhanger," interview by Jim Gilmore and Mike Wiser, *Frontline*, PBS, January 23, 2013, https://www.pbs.org/wgbh/pages/frontline/government-elections-politics/cliffhanger/the-frontline-interview-john-boehner/.

80. Boehner, "Cliffhanger."

81. Interview with member of Congress, April 2023; Boehner quoted in Jake Sherman and John Bresnahan, "Boehner Quiets Rebellion on Right," *Politico*, July 28, 2011, https://www.politico.com/story/2011/07/boehner-quiets-rebellion-on-right-060022.

82. As quoted in Sherman and Bresnahan, "Boehner Quiets Rebellion." See also Elizabeth Titus, "RSC Chair: Boehner Doesn't Have the Votes," *On Congress Blog, Politico*, July 26, 2011, https://www.politico.com/blogs/on-congress/2011/07/rsc-chair-boehner-doesnt-have-the-votes-037784.

83. As quoted in Molly K. Hooper and Russell Berman, "In Sales Pitch, Boehner Assures House GOP That Debt Deal is 'All Spending Cuts,'" *The Hill*, August 1, 2011.

84. As quoted in "Nancy Pelosi 'Absolutely' Voting Yes on Debt Ceiling Deal Despite Drawbacks," *ABC News*, August 1, 2011, https://abcnews.go.com/Politics/nancy-pelosi-absolutely-vote-debt-ceiling-deal-drawbacks/story?id=14205456.

85. Interview with member of Congress, April 2023.

86. As quoted in Thrush, "Prisoner of Capitol Hill."

87. As quoted in Ball, *Pelosi*, 222.

88. As quoted in Robert Costa, "An RSC Divided," *New Republic*, August 4, 2011.

89. Costa, "RSC Divided."

90. Interview with member of Congress, March 2023.

91. As quoted in Ben Pershing, "Legacies Intertwined," *Atlantic*, November 14, 2014.

92. Interview with member of Congress, April 2023.

93. Interview with member of Congress, April 2023. Moderate Republicans were also appalled by their conservative colleagues' tactics. As one member observed, "All of this knife fighting, it crippled Boehner. I'm not sure he can even manage this group [of conservatives]. If they did this [mutiny] on the floor, imagine what's coming next." As quoted in Robert Costa, "Boehner the Survivor," *National Review*, January 4, 2013.

94. As quoted in Jonathan Strong, "The Tuesday Group Still Lives," *National Review*, June 20, 2013.

95. As quoted in Alberta, "John Boehner Unchained." The first target of the "terrorists" was Boehner's job. Twelve members of the RSC "signed their name in blood" to vote against Boehner in the opening of the new Congress in January 2013.

96. Jonathan Strong, "The Jedi Council's Debt-Ceiling Plan," *National Review*, August 23, 2013, https://www.nationalreview.com/2013/08/jedi-councils-debt-ceiling-plan-jonathan-strong/.

97. As quoted in Anna Palmer and Jake Sherman, "Ryan Gives Advice on Battling Obama," *Politico*, January 17, 2013, https://www.politico.com/story/2013/01/paul-ryan-gives-gop-leaders-advice-on-battling-obama-086348.

98. Interview with member of Congress, March 2023. See also Strong, "Tuesday Group Still Lives."

99. As quoted in Kim Dixon, "House Republicans Search for Unity, Strategy on Fiscal Battles Ahead," Reuters, January 16, 2013, https://www.reuters.com/article/world/us-politics/house-republicans-search-for-unity-strategy-on-fiscal-battles-ahead-idUSBRE90F1NB/.

100. As quoted in Jake Sherman, "House GOPers Urge Defunding," *Politico*, August 28, 2013, https://www.politico.com/story/2013/08/80-house-gopers-urge-boehner-to-defund-obamacare-095806.

101. Interview with member of Congress, March 2023.

102. Interview with member of Congress, April 2023.

103. As quoted in Alberta, "John Boehner Unchained."

104. As quoted in Alex Altman, "Cruz Control," *Time Magazine*, August 19, 2013.

105. Interview with member of Congress, April 2023.

106. As quoted in Alberta, "John Boehner Unchained." Corroborated in interview with member of Congress, April 2023.

107. As quoted in Ed O'Keefe, "Boehner Appearing on Leno: GOP Is to Blame for Shutdown," *Washington Post*, January 24, 2014.

108. Sean Sullivan and Ed O'Keefe, "Peter King, House Contrarian," *Washington Post*, September 30, 2013.

109. Interview with member of Congress, April 2023.

110. As quoted in Ashley Parker, "A G.O.P. Moderate in the Middle . . . of a Jam," *New York Times*, October 7. 2013.

111. Interview with member of Congress, April 2023.

112. As quoted in Sahil Kapur, "Cantor to GOP: Hang Tight, Dems Will Cave in Shutdown Fight," *Talking Points Memo*, October 3, 2013, https://talkingpointsmemo.com/livewire/cantor-to-gop-hang-tight-dems-will-cave-in-shutdown-fight.

113. For instance, Dent, alongside Wisconsin Democrat Ron King, drafted a six-month spending bill that included a repeal of a medical device tax unpopular with both Republicans and some Democrats. By his own admission, this was a deal

the two representatives crafted on their own auspices; Dent was not negotiating on behalf of the Tuesday Group, which he co-chaired.

114. As quoted in Thrush, "Prisoner of Capitol Hill."

115. As quoted in Tim Alberta, *American Carnage: On the Front Lines of the Republican Civil War and the Rise of President Trump* (New York: Harper, 2019), 192.

116. Mick Mulvaney, as quoted in Lizza, "House Divided."

117. Interview with member of Congress, April 2023.

118. As quoted in Jennifer Steinhauer, "John Boehner, House Speaker, Will Resign from Congress," *New York Times*, September 25, 2015.

119. As quoted in Alberta, *American Carnage*, 256.

120. As quoted in Eliana Johnson, "Ryan Aims for Party Unity in Bid to Avoid 2012 Repeat," *National Review*, December 14, 2015.

121. As quoted in David Weigel, Mike DeBonis, and Kelsey Snell, "Will Obamacare Repeal Break the Freedom Caucus? It Depends on Trump," *Washington Post*, March 11, 2017.

122. Lindsey McPherson, "Freedom Caucus Chairman Predicts Tax Bill Will Pass," *Roll Call*, November 13, 2017.

123. As quoted in Naomi Jagoda, "House GOP Not Sold on Ryan's Tax Reform Plan," *The Hill*, May 16, 2017.

124. As quoted in Susan Davis, "House Conservatives Say They Will Challenge Speaker Ryan on Any Broad Immigration Plan," *All Things Considered*, NPR, February 14, 2018, https://www.npr.org/2018/02/14/585841218/house-conservatives-say-they-will-challenge-speaker-ryan-on-any-broad-immigratio.

125. As quoted in Sheryl Gay Stolberg and Thomas Kaplan, "Ryan Found Himself on the Margins as GOP Embraces Trump," *New York Times*, April 11, 2018.

126. Sarah Binder, "McCarthy Paid a Steep Price for his Speakership—Now What?" Brookings Institution, January 10, 2023, https://www.brookings.edu/articles/mccarthy-paid-a-steep-price-for-his-speakership-now-what/.

127. As quoted in Jonathan Blitzer, "What Kevin McCarthy Will Do to Gain Power," *New Yorker*, December 19, 2022.

128. As quoted in Jonathan Blitzer, "The Risky Gamble of Kevin McCarthy's Debt-Ceiling Strategy," *New Yorker*, April 28, 2023. Corroborated in interview with member of Congress, April 2023.

129. As quoted in Jonathan Blitzer, "How Kevin McCarthy Defied the Freedom Caucus and Averted a Shutdown," *New Yorker*, October 1, 2023.

130. As quoted in Catie Edmondson, "McCarthy Is Ousted as Speaker, Leaving the House in Chaos," *New York Times*, October 3, 2023.

131. As quoted in Jeff Stein and Jacob Bogage, "As House GOP Flails, Government Shutdown Fears Reemerge," *Washington Post*, October 5, 2023.

132. Sarah Ferris and Olivia Beavers, "Inside the bipartisan deal that might have saved Kevin McCarthy," *Politico*, October 6, 2023, https://www.politico.com/news/2023/10/06/bipartisan-attempt-to-save-mccarthy-speaker-00120438.

133. As quoted in Chris Lehmann, "How the Freedom Caucus Bomb Throwers Guarantee Bloated Spending Bills," *Nation*, August 5, 2024, https://www.thenation.com/article/politics/congress-mike-johnson-budget/.

Chapter 5

1. As quoted in John A. Farrell, *Tip O'Neill and the Democratic Century* (Boston: Little, Brown, 2001), 546.
2. Farrell, *Tip O'Neill*, 544.
3. As quoted in Jonathan Bartho, "Reagan's Southern Comfort: The 'Boll Weevil' Democrats in the 'Reagan Revolution' of 1981, *Journal of Policy History* 32 (2020): 218.
4. As quoted in John A. Lawrence, *The Class of '74: Congress after Watergate and the Roots of Partisanship* (Baltimore: Johns Hopkins University Press, 2018), 5.
5. As quoted in Rohde, *Parties and Leaders*, 47.
6. See Rohde, *Parties and Leaders*, 48–49.
7. Abner Mikva to DSG Members, 13 May 1977, folder 5, box 18, part 2, Democratic Study Group Papers, Library of Congress Manuscript Division (hereafter cited as DSG Papers, LOCMD); Richard Conlon, "Statement of Staff Director Democratic Study Group," June 1, 1977, folder 10, box 19, part 2, DSG Papers, LOCMD.
8. Chris Matthews, *Tip and the Gipper: When Politics Worked* (New York: Simon & Schuster, 2013), 51.
9. "I'm a liberal and a progressive liberal. There are people who talk about saving the whales, and clean water, and things of that nature. . . . I believe in the economy of the area. I believe that there should be jobs out there; that people should be able to take care of their family." As quoted in interview by Larry King, *CNN Weekend News with Larry King*, aired August 6, 1986, on CNN.
10. In his memoirs, O'Neill recalled describing Reagan as "Herbert Hoover with a smile . . . a cheerleader for selfishness," whose economic program "had no compassion." As quoted in Thomas P. O'Neill, *Man of the House* (New York: St. Martin's, 1987), 416.
11. As quoted in Tony Kornheiser, "Tip O'Neill's Toughest Inning: The Sermon on the Mound," *Washington Post*, May 31, 1981.
12. As quoted in Farrell, *Tip O'Neill*, 167.
13. "Oral History Transcript, Thomas P. O'Neill, Jr., Interview 1 (I), 1/28/1976, by Michael Gillette," p. 21, LBJ Library Oral Histories, LBJ Presidential Library, https://www.discoverlbj.org/item/oh-oneillt-19760128-1-77-18.
14. Farrell, *Tip O'Neill*, 235.
15. Tip O'Neill to Dart Thaiman, February 5, 1973, folder 13, box 364, Tip O'Neill Papers, Boston College Burns Library (hereafter cited as BCBL).
16. Peters, *The American Speakership*, 212.

17. Peters, *American Speakership*, 218–19.

18. Joseph Cooper and David W. Brady, "Institutional Context and Leadership Style: The House from Cannon to Rayburn," *American Political Science Review* 75, no. 2 (June 1981): 424.

19. As quoted in Sinclair, *Majority Leadership*, 89; Farrell, *Tip O'Neill*, 434.

20. Rohde, *Parties and Leaders*, 37–39.

21. See Lawrence C. Dodd and Bruce I. Oppenheimer, "Consolidating Power in the House," in *Congress Reconsidered*, 4th ed., ed. Lawrence C. Dodd and Bruce I. Oppenheimer (Washington, DC: CQ Press, 1989), 52. As the authors note, the Speaker also benefited from "increases in the financial and staff resources of the party whip office and in the number of whips appointed by the party leadership" (52).

22. Steven S. Smith, "O'Neill's Legacy for the House," *Brookings Review* 5, no. 1 (Winter 1987): 29.

23. Schickler, *Disjointed Pluralism*, 238.

24. Roger H. Davidson, "The New Centralization on Capitol Hill," *Review of Politics* 50, no. 3 (Summer 1988): 357.

25. Samuel Kernell, *Going Public: New Strategies of Presidential Leadership* (Washington, DC: CQ Press, 1997).

26. Farrell, *Tip O'Neill*, 544.

27. As quoted in Kornheiser, "Tip O'Neill's Toughest Inning."

28. As quoted in Sinclair, *Majority Leadership*, 89–90.

29. For those skeptical that such an alliance would ever have been possible with a Republican in the White House, it is worth remembering that liberal Republicans in the Senate attempted, with the aid of Democratic leaders, to restore just under $1 billion of federal spending slated to be cut in the administration's budget plan. Ultimately, that cross-party alliance was defeated by another, when conservative southern and western Democrats joined the Republican majority in backing Reagan's original proposal. See David Rogers, "Reagan's Budget Gets Senate Boost," April 1, 1981, *Boston Globe*, in folder 2, box 26, subseries 6, O'Neill Papers, BCBL.

30. Smith, "O'Neill's Legacy," 31. As Schickler observes, "roll call data suggests that the majority party remained extremely divided into the late 1970s." Schickler, *Disjointed Pluralism*, 233.

31. Dodd and Oppenheimer, "Consolidating Power in the House," 42.

32. As quoted in Bartho, "Reagan's Southern Comfort," 219.

33. As quoted in Hornblower and Reid, "After Two Decades, the 'Boll Weevils' Are Back."

34. Roger Porter to Donald Regan, December 11, 1985, folder "Budget," box I, Donald T. Regan Papers, Ronald Reagan Presidential Library.

35. As quoted in Hornblower and Reid, "After Two Decades, the 'Boll Weevils' Are Back."

36. As quoted in Kabaservice, *Rule and Ruin*, 365–66.

37. Sinclair, *Majority Leadership*, 236.
38. As quoted in Farrell, *Tip O'Neill*, 550–57.
39. See Rohde, *Parties and Leaders*, 66.
40. Schickler, *Disjointed Pluralism*, 231; Lawrence, *Class of '74*, 96.
41. Schickler, *Disjointed Pluralism*, 233.
42. Nelson W. Polsby, *How Congress Evolves: Social Bases of Institutional Change* (New York: Oxford University Press, 2004), 70; Schickler, *Disjointed Pluralism*, 228–29.
43. As quoted in Karl Gerard Brandt, *Ronald Reagan and the House Democrats: Gridlock, Partisanship and the Fiscal Crisis* (Columbia: University of Missouri Press, 2009), 137.
44. See Schickler, *Racial Realignment*.
45. As quoted in Lawrence, *Class of '74*, 280.
46. To be sure, legal change was not the only important factor driving the resurgence of the Republican Party in the South. As Polsby highlights, northerners in the immediate post–World War II period (both retirees and white-collar workers) began for the first time to migrate to warmer climes, spurred in many ways by the technological innovation of air-conditioning. These internal migrants brought with them their allegiance to the GOP. See Polsby, *How Congress Evolves*, 81–85.
47. Scholars have suggested that these two developments are linked through "sometimes tacit, sometimes overt collusion." To the extent that minority-majority districts concentrate Democratic voters, Republicans outside those districts are able to run in more favorable jurisdictions. Charles Cameron, David Epstein, and Sharyn O'Halloran, "Do Majority-Minority Districts Maximize Substantive Black Representation in Congress?" *American Political Science Review* 90, no. 4 (December 1996): 794–812.
48. On the origins of the Southern Delegations, see Bloch Rubin, *Building the Bloc*, 141–45.
49. In 1972 "an ad hoc group of moderate to conservative Democratic members" attempted to organize along the lines of the DSG. The ten-member group that formed, known as the Democratic Research Organization, soon fizzled, leaving little trace of its influence or activities. See Michael J. Malbin, "Where There's a Cause There's a Caucus on Capitol Hill," *Congress Report*, in folder 10, box 19, part 2, DSG Papers, LOCMD; Tom Loeffler, March 24, 1976, "Schedule Proposal: Congressional Leaders of the Democratic Research Organization," box 30, Vernon C. Loen and Charles Leppert Files, Gerald Ford Presidential Library.
50. See Farrell, *Tip O'Neill*, 467.
51. Peters, *American Speakership*, 219.
52. Rohde, *Parties and Leaders*, 47.
53. As quoted in Lawrence, *Class of '74*, 281.
54. Steven V. Roberts, "The Importance of Being a Boll Weevil: At the Start, Their Goal Was Attention," *New York Times*, June 14, 1981, E4.

55. "Interview with Richard Conlon, Staff Director, Democratic Study Group," July 5, 1974, folder 12, box 2, part 2, DSG Papers, LOCMD.

56. Democratic Study Group, DSG Activity Report (undated), folder 11, box 56, part 1, DSG Papers, LOCMD.

57. Frank Thompson to DSG Members, January 25, 1967, "Democratic Caucus," folder 3, box 48, part 1, DSG Papers, LOCMD; Jonathan B. Bingham to Members of the DSG Task Force on Congressional Reform, October 20, 1971, folder 6, box 68, part 1, DSG Papers, LOCMD.

58. As quoted in Zelizer, "When Liberals Were Organized."

59. Zelizer, "When Liberals Were Organized." To be sure, the DSG's permissive membership rules and the absence of an ideological litmus test meant that some members did not share the group's liberal mission. Dodd and Oppenheimer estimate the number of liberals in the House by the late 1970s to be closer to 135. See Lawrence C. Dodd and Bruce I. Oppenheimer, "The House in Transition," in *Congress Reconsidered*, 6th ed., ed. Lawrence C. Dodd and Bruce I. Oppenheimer (New York: Praeger, 1977), 34–35.

60. Rohde, *Parties and Leaders*, 49. As one younger liberal described this earlier generation of liberal Democrats, "[They] grew up in the Depression. [Their] politics have always been straight New Deal. In 1981, the New Deal doesn't carry a lot of water." Les Aspin, "Constituent Newsletter: Battle of the Reagan Budget Leaves Dems Reeling," May 6, 1981, folder 13, box 25, subseries 6, O'Neill Papers, BCBL.

61. As quoted in John Jacobs, *A Rage for Justice: The Passion and Politics of Phillip Burton* (Berkeley: University of California Press, 1995), 258. The liberal newcomers soon came to "irritate" their more senior colleagues, who found their approach (if not their goals) off-putting. As one senior member groused, "They act as if they invented social activism." As quoted in Sanford J. Ungar, "Bleak House," *Atlantic*, July 1977, in folder 4, box 32, part 2, DSG Papers, LOCMD.

62. As quoted in Lawrence, *Class of '74*, 5, 82–83.

63. "Constitution and By-Laws of the United Democrats of Congress," October 1973," folder 19, box 364, O'Neill Papers, BCBL.

64. As quoted in Marjorie Hunter, "Capitol Hill Clubs Have Many Rolls," December 26, 1975, *New York Times*, 33.

65. By then a senior statesman, Richard Bolling described his fellow liberals as possessing "particularized unity" but lacking the "generalized unity . . . [to do] something concrete." As quoted in David Rogers, "House Panel Rejects Reagan Budget," April 8, 1981, *Boston Globe*, in folder 2, box 26, subseries 6, O'Neill Papers, BCBL. Abner Mikva, the departing chair of the DSG, offered a similarly grim picture: "The liberals are restless and frustrated." Mikva estimated that only about half the DSG members were "committed" to working together to advance a common agenda. As quoted in Gerald Rosen, "Will the Liberals Buck Carter?" *Dunn's Review*, August 1977, in folder 4, box 32, part 2, DSG Papers, LOCMD.

66. Zelizer, "When Liberals Were Organized."

67. Richard E. Cohen, "Gillis Long Presses House Democrats to Establish a New Party Identity," *National Journal*, December 4, 1982, folder 13, box 30, Gillis Long Papers, Louisiana State University, Special Collections (hereafter cited as LSUSC).

68. Richard E. Conlon, "Statement of Staff Director Democratic Study Group," June 1, 1977, folder 10, box 19, part 2, DSG Papers, LOCMD.

69. As quoted in Hornblower and Reid, "After Two Decades, the 'Boll Weevils' Are Back."

70. As quoted in Bartho, "Reagan's Southern Comfort," 217. Other CDF members expressed resentment at "the arrogant, liberal leadership [that] has tried to run roughshod over the conservative wing of the Democratic Party." As quoted in "Southern Democrats Seek Stronger House Influence," November 14, 1980, folder 16, box 59, Long Papers, LSUSC.

71. Art Pine, "Whistling Dixie on Tax Bill: Can GOP Rise Again?" *Washington Post*, June 21, 1981, G1. According to Sonny Montgomery, the CDF looked to replicate the DSG's success in the 1960s. "The liberals had the DSG. The blacks have the Black Caucus. Maybe if we organize, the leadership will listen to us. . . . They're not listening to us now." As quoted in Richard Lyons, "House Dixie Bloc Losing Clout," *Washington Post*, 1977, in folder 4, box 32, part 2, DSG Papers, LOCMD.

72. Pine, "Whistling Dixie on Tax Bill."

73. Lyons, "Conservative House Democrats Seeking Larger Role"; Peters, *American Speakership*, 233.

74. Lyons, "Conservative House Democrats Seeking Larger Role."

75. As quoted in Martin F. Nolan, "The Reagan Honeymoon," March 19, 1981, *Boston Globe*, folder 1, box 26, subseries 6, O'Neill Papers, BCBL.

76. Max Friedersdorf as quoted in Stephen Knott and Russell L. Riley, *Ronald Reagan Oral History Project: Final Edited Transcript; Interview with Max Friedersdorf, October 24–25, 2002* (Charlottesville: University of Virginia Miller Center, 2020), 57, https://s3.amazonaws.com/web.poh.transcripts/Friedersdorf_Max.Rearchived.pdf.

77 Hedrick Smith, "Republican Moderates Won't Be Pushovers," *New York Times*, September 20, 1981, E1.

78. Karl Gerard Brandt, "Deficit Politics and Democratic Unity: The Saga of Tip O'Neill, Jim Wright, and the Conservative Democrats in the House of Representatives During the Reagan Era" (PhD diss., Louisiana State University, 2003), 16–17. The collaborative imbalance between the two Democratic factions was so pronounced that party strategists increasingly worried about the influence of "liberals and moderates being replaced by radical conservatives." If liberals continued to flounder, "even with a nominal Democratic majority," the House would "be skewed to the right of the people." William Connell to Democratic Leadership, "A Defensive Strategy for Democrats," [undated, 1981], folder 9, box 25, subseries 6, O'Neill Papers, BCBL.

79. As quoted in Lyons, "House Dixie Bloc Losing Clout."

80. John D. Shales and Eric M. Licht, *Movers and Shakers: Congressional Leaders in the 1980s* (Washington, DC: Free Congress Research and Education Foundation, 1985), 16. For their part, members of the CDF described the group as "the most important bloc in the next four years . . . [able] to control the House." Their strategy: fierce unity. "You can't be timid in this thing. No bedwetters allowed." As quoted in "Southern Democrats Seek Stronger House Influence."

81. Peters, *American Speakership*, 234. Tip O'Neill, "Budget Notes," January 19, 1979, folder 7, box 25, subseries 6, O'Neill Papers, BCBL; Tip O'Neill, "Statement by the Speaker," May 13, 1981, folder 7, box 25, subseries 6, O'Neill Papers, BCBL.

82. Fred Barnes, "Support for Economic Plan Sought," March 5, 1981, *Baltimore Sun*, in folder 1, box 26, subseries 6, O'Neill Papers, BCBL.

83. Max Friedersdorf as quoted in Knott and Riley, *Interview with Max Friedersdorf*, 54.

84. As quoted in Matthews, *Tip and the Gipper*, 124.

85. Farrell, *Tip O'Neill*, 554; Sinclair, *Majority Leadership*, 192. Even ignorant of Gramm's maneuvering, O'Neill and his staff expressed concern that "if we are not careful . . . conservative Democrats will give the Republicans a majority." Jack Lew to Tip O'Neill, March 18, 1981, "Subject: Notes from the first Budget Committee Caucus," folder 9, box 202, O'Neill Papers, BCBL.

86. Martin Tolchin, "The Troubles of Tip O'Neill," *New York Times*, August 16, 1981, SM8.

87. As quoted in Farrell, *Tip O'Neill*, 556. Still other liberals complained that "the Speaker [did not] accomplish anything. . . . They [the CDF] sandbagged him the first chance they got, because there's no satisfying guys like Gramm and Stump." As quoted in Gerald Rosen, "The Men Reagan Must Woo," *Dun's Review*, June 1981, in folder 16, box 59, Long Papers, LSUSC.

88. As quoted in Sinclair, *Majority Leadership*, 196.

89. As quoted in Benjamin Waterhouse, *Lobbying America: The Politics of Business from Nixon to NAFTA*, (Princeton, NJ: Princeton University Press, 2014), 214. See also Bill Brodhead to CDF, "Lobby Alert," May 6, 1981, folder 13, box 25, subseries 6, O'Neill Papers, BCBL.

90. As quoted in Farrell, *Tip O'Neill*, 555. Many liberals were outraged by O'Neill's concession. In newsletters to constituents, they acknowledged Reagan's popularity but insisted that Democratic leaders could have done more to fight the administration and discipline his Democratic allies. "The Democrats ought to remember that Reagan is riding the crest of a wave of public outrage. We should be up there on that crest too, instead of looking back over our shoulders at a wave about to crash down on us. . . . But Democrats continue to flounder . . . [the party] needs some new leadership and needs it badly." Les Aspin, "Constituent Newsletter: Battle of the Reagan Budget Leaves Dems Reeling," May 6, 1981, folder 13, box 25, subseries 6, O'Neill Papers, BCBL.

91. Max Friedersdorf as quoted in Knott and Riley, *Interview with Max Friedersdorf*, 58.

92. As quoted in Sinclair, *Majority Leadership*, 200. Liberals felt similarly about Republicans, insisting that Democrats on the Rules Committee structure the budget vote "to make Republicans walk the hot coals." Gillis Long, "Statement for Democratic Caucus," May 18, 1981, folder 12, box 59, Long Papers, LSUSC.

93. Max Friedersdorf as quoted in Knott and Riley, *Interview with Max Friedersdorf*, 58.

94. Francis X. Clines, "O'Neill Ready to Rejoin Battle Over the Budget," *New York Times*, July 1, 1981, A16. A cadre of liberals attempted to threaten the CDF with sanctions in the Democratic Caucus, but their effort was so disorganized they failed to gain even majority support among their fellow liberals. See Gillis Long to Democratic Caucus, July 15, 1981, folder 7, box 59, Long Papers, LSUSC.

95. As quoted in Farrell, *Tip O'Neill*, 559. According to one Republican on the Budget Committee, the chair had thrown everything at conservatives to make a deal, presumably with O'Neill's backing. "I don't know how much blessing he has from Tip but I assume he's been given a lot of room to compromise." Dennis Farney, "House Budget Panel Chief Seen Retreating Toward Bigger Cuts Urged by President," March 27, 1981, *Wall Street Journal*, in folder 1, box 26, subseries 6, O'Neill Papers, BCBL.

96. As quoted in Cathie J. Martin, *Shifting the Burden: The Struggle Over Growth and Corporate Taxation* (Chicago: University of Chicago Press, 1991), 124.

97. Caroline Atkinson and Lou Cannon, "White House Quickly Squelches GOP Talk of Tax Compromise," *Washington Post*, July 10, 1981, A1; Peters, *American Speakership*, 236.

98. As quoted in Martin, *Shifting the Burden*, 133.

99. As quoted in Tolchin, "Troubles of Tip O'Neill"

100. As quoted in Farrell, *Tip O'Neill*, 561.

101. Gillis Long, "The House Budget 'How' May Be More Important Than the 'What,'" House Democratic Caucus 1981–1984, folder 13, box 30, Long Papers, LSUSC.

102. As quoted in Peters, *American Speakership*, 237.

103. As quoted in Margot Hornblower, "O'Neill Thinks Democrats' Timing on Budget May Be Off," April 8, 1981, *Washington Post*, in folder 2, box 26, subseries 6, O'Neill Papers, BCBL. Throughout the budget fight, O'Neill worried to his aides that a public relations battle would do more harm than good. "I can't stand up to him [Reagan], because he will go on television, and he will overwhelm us," Steve Roberts recalled the Speaker telling confidantes. As quoted in "Celebrating the Life of Tip O'Neill," December 9, 2012, Kennedy Library Forum, John F. Kennedy Presidential Library, https://www.jfklibrary.org/events-and-awards/kennedy-library-forums/past-forums/transcripts/celebrating-the-life-of-tip-oneill.

104. As quoted in Farrell, *Tip O'Neill*, 557.

105. O'Neill would make a similar case in party publications that were circulated in conjunction with his television appearances. See, for example, "Promoting Economic Growth and Opportunity: A Statement of Democratic Principles and Goals," folder 10, box 25, subseries 6, O'Neill Papers, BCBL.

106. As quoted in O'Neill, *Man of the House*, 425–26. In a memo circulated among O'Neill's staff, the Speaker's mission was straightforward: "We must remind the nation that the Democratic Party stands for something, and that the Democrats are not just the party with a heart, but a party which is the firm friend and defender of the working tax-paying family." William Connell, "A Defensive Strategy for Democrats," folder 9, box 25, subseries 6, O'Neill Papers, BCBL, 14.

107. Steven V. Roberts, "O'Neill TV Appearances a Major Shift in Strategy," *New York Times*, June 9, 1981, B11.

108. As quoted in Farrell, *Tip O'Neill*, 568. Matthews would later observe that "Tip always knew the qualities Reagan brought to the stage, and he had to take him on. He didn't want to do it.... TV wasn't for him. He preferred hanging around with you guys, talking in the back room, telling you not to write this stuff. But he had to go on the tube, and he had to take on this guy who was perfect; it was his home turf, his home court. And he did it." As quoted in "Celebrating the Life of Tip O'Neill." Members of the press also characterized O'Neill as habitually "wary of television cameras." Thomas Edsall, "Senate Is 96–0 against Cuts in Social Security," folder 7, box 25, subseries 6, O'Neill Papers, BCBL.

109. Matthews, *Tip and the Gipper*, 141.

110. Matthews, *Tip and the Gipper*, 162.

111. Smith, "O'Neill's Legacy for the House," 30.

112. Julia Malone, "O'Neill's Political Skills Face Their Biggest Test," *Christian Science Monitor*, May 11, 1982.

113. As quoted in Farrell, *Tip O'Neill*, 567.

114. S. Roberts, "O'Neill TV Appearances a Major Shift in Strategy." Records from O'Neill's staff document the shift in strategy. During the spring of 1981, the Speaker's media plans focused on press releases to be issued alongside statements by members of the Budget Committee. By the summer, the Speaker's media plans involved regular appearances on the Sunday morning shows and taped interviews for circulation to network news. See Kirk O'Donnell, "Media Plans," March 5–July 11, 1981, folder 13, box 25, subseries 6, O'Neill Papers, BCBL.

115. Kornheiser, "Tip O'Neill's Toughest Inning." As one journalist close to O'Neill later recalled, "Tip hardly looks like a typical anchor, but television made him the most well-known, if not the most powerful Speaker in history." As quoted in Cokie Roberts, "Leadership and the Media in the 101st Congress," in *Leading Congress: New Styles, New Strategies*, ed. John J. Kornacki (Washington, DC: CQ Press, 1990), 88.

116. Margot Hornblower, "'Horatio' at the Bridge," *Washington Post*, October 10, 1982, A1.

117. Matthews, *Tip and the Gipper*, 162.
118. See Farrell, *Tip O'Neill*, 569–70.
119. Mickey Edwards as quoted in Walter J. Oleszek, ed., *The Cannon Centenary Conference: The Changing Nature of the Speakership* (Washington, DC: Government Printing Office, 2004), 30, https://tile.loc.gov/storage-services/master/gdc/gdcebookspublic/20/23/70/95/69/2023709569/2023709569.pdf.
120. As quoted in Oleszek, *Cannon Centenary Conference*, 21.
121. Walter J. Oleszek, *Congressional Procedures and the Policy Process*, 4th ed. (Washington, DC: CQ Press, 1996), 34.
122. As quoted in Oleszek, *Congressional Procedures*, 34–35.
123. Peters, *American Speakership*, 243.
124. Rohde, *Parties and Leaders*, 80.
125. Peters, *American Speakership*, 212.
126. Dodd and Oppenheimer, "Consolidating Power in the House," 54.
127. Steven V. Roberts, "Assessing the Record-Setting Speaker O'Neill," *New York Times*, January 12, 1986, 34.

Chapter 6

1. Ira Katznelson, *Fear Itself: The New Deal and the Origins of Our Time* (New York: Liveright, 2013), 23.
2. Richard Bolling, *Power in the House: A History of the Leadership of the House of Representatives* (Boston: Dutton Press, 1968), 195.
3. Ira Katznelson, Kim Geiger, and Daniel Kryder, "Limiting Liberalism: The Southern Veto in Congress, 1933–1950," *Political Science Quarterly* 108, no. 2 (Summer 1993): 283–306.
4. John C. Stennis, "Campaign Speech," 1960, folder "Alternative 1960 Campaign Speech," box 12, series 50, Stennis Papers, Mississippi State University Special Collections Library.
5. Eric Schickler and Kathryn Pearson, "Agenda Control, Majority Party Power, and the House Committee on Rules, 1937–52," *Legislative Studies Quarterly* 34, no. 4 (November 2009): 458; Helen Fuller, *Year of Trial: Kennedy's Crucial Decisions* (New York: Harcourt, Brace & World, 1962).
6. Schickler, *Disjointed Pluralism*; Charles O. Jones, "Joseph G. Cannon and Howard W. Smith: An Essay on the Limits of Leadership in the House of Representatives." *Journal of Politics* 30, no. 3 (August 1968): 617–46; William R. MacKaye, *A New Coalition Takes Control: The House Rules Committee Fight of 1961* (New York: McGraw Hill, 1963).
7. As quoted in D. B. Hardeman and Donald C. Bacon, *Rayburn: A Biography* (Chicago: Madison Books, 1987), 448.
8. Jeffery A. Jenkins and Nathan W. Monroe, "Negative Agenda Control and the Conservative Coalition in the U.S. House." *Journal of Politics* 76, no. 4 (October

2014): 1116–27; Julian Zelizer, *On Capitol Hill: The Struggle to Reform Congress and its Consequences, 1948–2000* (New York: Cambridge University Press, 2004).

9. Kenneth Shepsle, "The Changing Textbook Congress," in *Can the Government Govern?* ed. John H. Chubb and Paul Peterson (Washington, DC: Brookings Institution Press, 1989), 238–66; Cooper and Brady, "Institutional Context and Leadership Style," 420.

10. Rohde, *Parties and Leaders*, 36. Rohde, "Reflections on the Practice of Theorizing," 849–64.

11. Rohde, *Parties and Leaders*, 5.

12. Cooper and Brady, "Institutional Context and Leadership Style," 423. Randall Ripley is a notable exception to this characterization of Rayburn's speakership, perhaps because of his proximity to it. He writes: "His method of operation was consistently highly centralized. . . . His preference was for close-lipped, tightly run individual control of his party, a preference clearly expressed in his opposition to the creation of party policy committees in 1946. He consulted with other leading Democrats, but on his own terms. . . . Party policy and many party decisions were made by him alone and communicated to his fellow Democrats at what he considered the proper moment." Ripley, *Party Leaders in the House*, 92.

13. As quoted in Hardeman and Bacon, *Rayburn*, 346–47.

14. As quoted in Hardeman and Bacon, *Rayburn*, 346–47.

15. Roberts, "Assessing the Record-Setting Speaker O'Neill."

16. "Colmer Appoints Eleven Man Committee: Southern Delegations Press Release," February 21, 1948, folder 4, box 464, William Colmer Papers, University of Southern Mississippi McCain Library (hereafter USMML). See also Bloch Rubin, *Building the Bloc*, 141–45.

17. As quoted in Charles Clapp, *The Congressman: His Work as He Sees It* (Washington, DC: Brookings Institution Press, 1963), 325.

18. Bloch Rubin, *Building the Bloc*, 230–44.

19. Richard Bolling, *House Out of Order* (New York: E. F. Dutton, 1966), 56.

20. The notion that leaders in Congress might co-opt the collaborative arrangements of a vulnerable or amenable faction has much in common with how we tend to think about institutional capacity more generally. Scholars have long recognized that politicians often choose to buy capacity rather than make it themselves. The legislative subsidy theory of lobbying is a case in point. On this account, legislators are said to treat lobbyists as "service bureaus," charged with digesting information and serving it up "in a politically user-friendly form" so as "to promote the policy goals that their group and the legislator share." Members of Congress could surely do much of this labor themselves, but by contracting it out, they can put their limited time and resources to better use. Hall and Deardorff, "Lobbying as Legislative Subsidy," 72–76. See also Richard Hall and Frank W. Wayman, "Buying Time: Moneyed Interests and the Mobilization of Bias in Congressional Committees," *American Political Science Review* 84, no. 3 (September 1990): 797–820.

21. As quoted in Kenneth Kofmehl, "The Institutionalization of a Voting Bloc," *Western Political Quarterly* 17, no. 2 (June 1964): 271.

22. See, for example, Polsby, *How Congress Evolves*.

23. Zelizer, *On Capitol Hill*, 56–58.

24. George B. Galloway, *History of the United States House of Representatives* (New York: Crowell 1976), 143.

25. John F. Kennedy, "The President's News Conference, January 25, 1961," American Presidency Project, accessed September 23, 2024, https://www.presidency.ucsb.edu/documents/the-presidents-news-conference-196.

26. Tellingly, Ripley notes that "[Rayburn] worked closely with President Roosevelt, Truman, and Kennedy to pass administration bills, but it was he who determined the strategy to pursue and the tactics to use in the House." Ripley, *Party Leaders in the House*, 92.

27. Schickler and Pearson, "Agenda Control, Majority Party Power," 458.

28. Eric Schickler, Kathryn Pearson, and Brian Feinstein, "Congressional Parties and Civil Rights Politics from 1933 to 1972," *Journal of Politics* 72, no. 3 (July 2010): 672–89.

29. William Colmer to C.F. Peay, 1 March 1948, and William Colmer to J. C. Grubbs, 6 March 1948, both in folder 6, box 464, Colmer Papers, USMML.

30. As quoted in Hardeman and Bacon, *Rayburn*, 288. Publicly, Rayburn took pains to distinguish his approach to leadership from that of "czarist" Speakers Thomas Reed, Joseph Cannon, and John Garner. But behind closed doors, he did not equivocate: "If you shilly-shally and are afraid to say, 'No,' you'll get into trouble." Hardeman and Bacon, *Rayburn*, 346–47.

31. In his 1948 primary campaign, for instance, Rayburn reiterated his opposition to civil rights, telling voters that like most southerners, "I voted against everything that look[s] like an attack on our segregation laws." At the same time, the Speaker was one of the few southern lawmakers in Washington to socialize with the city's wealthy Black elites. He also repeatedly urged the Texas state legislature to abolish the poll tax on the ground that voting was a right all people were entitled to. As quoted in Hardeman and Bacon, *Rayburn*, 332.

32. As quoted in Hardeman and Bacon, *Rayburn*, 7.

33. Sam Rayburn to Jere Cooper, November 15, 1948, folder "1948 Congressman Committee Assignments," box 3R341, Sam Rayburn Papers, University of Texas–Austin Briscoe Center for American History (hereafter cited as BCAH).

34. Sam Rayburn to John Dingell, November 15, 1948, folder "1948 Congressman Committee Assignments," box 3R341, Rayburn Papers, BCAH.

35. Wright Patman to Sam Rayburn, November 17, 1948, folder "1948 Congressman Committee Assignments," box 3R341, Rayburn Papers, BCAH.

36. Wilbur Mills to Sam Rayburn, November 16, 1948, folder "1948 Congressman Committee Assignments," box 3R341, Rayburn Papers, BCAH.

37. Jere Cooper to Sam Rayburn, November 19, 1948, folder "1948 Congressman Committee Assignments," box 3R341, Rayburn Papers, BCAH. Second in command on the House Ways and Means Committee, Cooper would be elected chair of the Democratic Caucus four years later.

38. A. J. Sabath to Sam Rayburn, November 11, 1948, folder "1948 Congressman Committee Assignments," box 3R341, Rayburn Papers, BCAH.

39. Sam Rayburn to Jere Cooper, November 22, 1948, folder "1948 Congressman Committee Assignments," box 3R341, Rayburn Papers, BCAH; Sam Rayburn to John McCormack, December 9, 1948, folder "McCormack, John W.," box 3U110, Sam Rayburn Papers, BCAH. For a detailed history of McCormack's complicated relationship with southern segregationists, see Garrison Nelson, *John William McCormack: A Political Biography* (New York: Bloomsbury Academic, 2017), 360–413.

40. Nelson, *John William McCormack*, 362.

41. As quoted in James A. Robinson, *The House Rules Committee* (Indianapolis: Bobbs-Merrill, 1963), 67.

42. Glendon Schubert, "The Politics of Legislative Procedure: The Twenty-One Day Rule," *Political Science* 5 (1953): 16–29.

43. William S. White, "Sam Rayburn, the Untalkative Speaker," *New York Times*, February 27, 1949, 10.

44. 81 Cong. Rec. 95 (1949), 10. As David Truman writes, "In the [Democratic] caucus," the rule "had the strong support of Representative Rayburn who, when the resolution was offered on the floor of the House, . . . effectively guided it to adoption." Truman, *Congressional Party*, 18.

45. William S. White, "House Gives Speaker Large Grant of Power," *New York Times*, January 9, 1949, 1.

46. As Chet Hollifield, one of the leaders of the DSG, later recalled, "Altogether, during the 81st Congress, eight measures were brought to the floor and passed by resort to the 21-Day rule, and its existence forced the Rules Committee to act in other cases." 86 Cong. Rec. 106 (1960), 19393.

47. As quoted in Hardeman and Bacon, *Rayburn*, 343–44. President Truman celebrated passage of the twenty-one-day rule by toasting the Speaker that same afternoon in Rayburn's hideaway office.

48. 82 Cong. Rec. 97 (1951), 17. See also Hardeman and Bacon, *Rayburn*, 344; Bolling, *Power in the House*, 179–80; Schubert, "Twenty-One Day Rule," 26–27.

49. In 1956, for example, Rayburn worked with Martin to report out the Eisenhower administration's pending civil rights bill and pass it through the House, only to see it die in the Senate. Such was Rayburn's friendship with Martin that Martin allowed Rayburn to keep the suite of offices traditionally occupied by the Speaker even after Rayburn lost his majority in 1954.

50. When Smith cited a fire on his farm as reason for why he could not convene a meeting of the Rules Committee, Rayburn famously remarked, "I knew Howard

Smith would do most anything to block a civil rights bill, but I never knew he would resort to arson." As quoted in Robert Bendiner, *Obstacle Course on Capitol Hill* (New York: McGraw-Hill 1964), 23.

51. As quoted in Mark F. Ferber, "The Democratic Study Group: A Study of Intra-Party Organization in the House of Representatives" (PhD diss., University of California, 1964), 173.

52. "DSG Informational Handout," 1963, folder 2, box 1, part 2, DSG Papers, LOCMD.

53. Bloch Rubin, *Building the Bloc*, 230–36.

54. Clem Miller to undisclosed recipients, 15 April 1960, folder 11, box 56, part 1, DSG Papers, LOCMD. According to the Speaker's liberal protégé Richard Bolling, "The Democratic Study Group came into being really with Rayburn's concurrence and approval." As quoted in "Oral History Transcript, Richard Bolling and Jim Grant Bolling, Interview 1 (I), 2/27/69, by Paige Mulhollan," LBJ Library Oral Histories, LBJ Presidential Library, https://www.discoverlbj.org/item/oh-bollingr-19690227-1-74-179.

55. Clem Miller to undisclosed recipients, 15 April 1960.

56. "Confidential Draft: A Proposed Plan for Effective Coordination of the Liberal Democratic Bloc in the House," November 8, 1957, folder 8, box 57, part 1, DSG Papers, LOCMD. See also Fuller, *Year of Trial*, 81; Bloch Rubin, *Building the Bloc*, 233–36.

57. Lee Metcalf, as quoted in "What They're Saying about the Democratic Study Group," 1960, folder 11, box 56, part 1, DSG Papers, LOCMD; Edward P. Morgan, March 22, 1960, News American Broadcasting Network, folder 11, box 56, part 1, DSG Papers, LOCMD.

58. Metcalf, as quoted in "What They're Saying about the Democratic Study Group"; Sam Rayburn to John McCormack, August 22, 1957, folder "McCormack, John W.," box 3U110, Sam Rayburn Papers, BCAH. As one of Rayburn's aides, John Holton, recalled, "[He] felt like in order for President Kennedy to have any chance of getting legislation that he knew that he was going to propose considered by the House, we had to get some way to get through the Rules Committee." As quoted in "Oral History Transcript, John Holton, Interview 1 (I), 6/19/1975, by Michael L. Gillette," LBJ Library Oral Histories, LBJ Presidential Library, https://www.discoverlbj.org/item/oh-holtonj-19750619-1-14-33.

59. As quoted in Anthony Champagne, *Congressman Sam Rayburn* (New Brunswick, NJ: Rutgers University Press, 1984), 150.

60. William G. Phillips, "Confidential Draft: The Democratic Study Group in Midstream," 1961, folder 11, box 59, part 1, DSG Papers, LOCMD.

61. 86 Cong. Rec. 106 (1960), 17929; Willard Shelton, "It's Your Washington," July 2, 1960, folder 11, box 56, part 1, DSG Papers, LOCMD.

62. Lee Metcalf, as quoted in "What They're Saying About the Democratic Study Group." See also "Oral History Transcript: John Holton."

63. According to the DSG's records, "The DSG held its first formal meeting in preparation for the new Congress on Friday, December 30 [1960]. It considered reports on various alternative approaches to the problem of the Rules Committee. Most of the members favored the purge of Colmer as being most certain, since it could be accomplished within the Democratic caucus, and as offering a beneficial spur to intraparty discipline by punishing a defector. But no decision was made... since the Study Group wanted to work with him [the Speaker] if at all possible." DSG *Congressional Report*, vol. 10, no. 1, March 4, 1961, folder 2, box 1, part 2, DSG Papers, LOCMD.

64. McCormack continued to defend Colmer but did not attempt to persuade Rayburn to remove someone else from the committee. John McCormack to Sam Rayburn, September 12, 1960, folder "McCormack, John W.," box 3U110, Sam Rayburn Papers, BCAH.

65. Alfred Steinberg, *Sam Rayburn: A Biography* (New York: Hawthorn Books, 1975), 335.

66. Rayburn's papers offer little certainty as to why he favored purging Colmer from the Rules Committee in 1948 but not in 1961. What is clear is that he believed moderate southerners, whose votes he would need to effectuate any possible reform, would have trouble justifying Colmer's purge when the Democratic Caucus had chosen not to discipline Representative Adam Clayton Powell for backing Eisenhower's presidential bid in 1956 on the grounds that Ike was more favorably disposed to civil rights.

67. As quoted in Steinberg, *Sam Rayburn*, 336. See also Carl Albert and Danney Goble, *Little Giant: The Life and Times of Speaker Carl Albert* (Norman: University of Oklahoma Press, 1999), 240; Richard Lyons, "Rayburn Announces Plan to Add 3 Members to Rules Committee," *Washington Post*, January 12, 1961, A1.

68. Fuller, *Year of Trial*, 83. Lyons, "Rayburn Announces Plan to Add 3 Members."

69. Paul Duke, "Kennedy Is Expected to Support Liberal Drive to Curb House Rules Committee," *Wall Street Journal*, August 30, 1960, in folder 11, box 56, part 1, DSG Papers, LOCMD. According to the DSG, "conditions finally seemed ripe for breaking the coalition's stranglehold on the Rules Committee... Rayburn knew that now his responsibility was not merely to the majority of the Democratic membership, but also to deliver a program for a Democratic Administration." DSG *Congressional Report*, March 4, 1961.

70. As quoted in Hardeman and Bacon, *Rayburn*, 451.

71. As quoted in Albert and Goble, *Little Giant*, 240. For examples of the leaked story, see "Democratic Liberal Blocs Map Legislative Strategy," *Hartford Courant*, January 3, 1961, 1; Laurence Burd, "Fight Looms over House Rules Committee," *Chicago Daily Tribune*, January 3, 1961, 3.

72. As Albert explained to anxious southerners, "No attempt is being made to 'pack' the committee, only to make it more representative of the general

membership.... I assure you that if additional members are added to the committee, they will not be extremists.... The effort of the leadership is only to make the Rules Committee function as it was designed to function—as a clearing house of legislation, reflecting in miniature the view of the majority." Carl Albert to W. T. Tipton, January 27, 1961, folder 75, box 53, Carl Albert Papers, Carl Albert Center, University of Oklahoma Special Collections (hereafter cited as Albert Papers).

73. Harold Davis, "Vinson Plays Leading Role in Rules Committee Hassle," *Atlanta Journal*, January 15, 1961, 23. See also "Oral History Transcript, D. B. Hardeman, Interview 3 (III), 4/22/1969, by T. H. Baker," LBJ Library Oral Histories, LBJ Presidential Library, https://www.discoverlbj.org/item/oh-hardemand-19690422-3-89-4. Many moderate southerners warned Rayburn and his leadership team that a "knock-down and drag-out fight over the size of the Rules Committee" would hasten "disintegration of Democratic unity." Rayburn, however, dismissed their concerns. L. H. Fountain to Carl Albert, December 26, 1962, folder 77, box 53, Albert Papers.

74. According to the DSG, a cadre of Republicans were willing to back Rayburn for two reasons. For conservatives, "the Rules Committee is supposed to be ... responsive to the majority leadership." These members "wanted Rayburn to be firmly saddled with this responsibility so that the Democrats could 'no longer make excuses' for their failures." Moderates, by contrast, "believe that the image of their party in coalition with southern Democrats is political suicide. They want a strong positive emphasis on civil rights, which they regard as the acid test of the genuineness of conservatives' concern with individual liberty." DSG *Congressional Report*, March 4, 1961.

75. As quoted in Steinberg, *Sam Rayburn*, 336. According to Rayburn's staff, the Speaker told McCormack and Albert, "If they start messing in our party affairs, we can do the same on Republican nominations to committees—and we have a majority." As quoted in Hardeman and Bacon, *Rayburn*, 455.

76. DSG *Congressional Report*, March 4, 1961.

77. As DSG whip, Thompson kept a detailed card file on every member of the House. These files "contained the Representative's name and Congressional district, his wife's name, his college, his profession, his family relations ... and any other information that might prove useful.... The cards would tell, when the time came, who best could influence each and every member of the House of Representatives on how to cast his vote." Justifying the time spent compiling these files, Thompson said, "Everyone around here is reachable. All you have to do is find out how." See David MacNeil, *Forge of Democracy: The House of Representatives* (New York: David McKay, 1963), 416.

78. As quoted in Hardeman and Bacon, *Rayburn*, 457.

79. According to the DSG's whipping operation, "The White House loomed powerfully in the minds of members who had any doubts as to how they would vote. It was a hovering deterrent to those leaning to the Halleck-Smith position." See DSG *Congressional Report*, March 4, 1961.

80. Fuller, *Year of Trial*, 86. First-time Representatives John Flynt and G. Elliot Hagan of Georgia and North Carolina's Horace Kornegay voted against Rayburn on the floor and received committee assignments they did not prefer from the Committee on Committees. By contrast, Joseph Addabbo of New York, Richard Ichord of Missouri, Ralph Harding of Idaho, and Julia Hansen of Washington voted with the Speaker and received their first choices. See John D. Morris, "Rules Dissidents Charge Reprisal: Some Southern Democrats Who Fought Rayburn Plan Rebuffed on House Posts," *New York Times*, February 2, 1961, 15; Philip Warden, "Both Parties Punish 'Wrong' Vote on Rules," *Chicago Daily Tribune*, February 2, 1961, 6.

81. "House Liberals Gain in Rules Unit Fight as Rayburn Spurns Conservatives' Offer," *Wall Street Journal*, January 10, 1961, 6.

82. "House Liberals Gain in Rules Unit Fight."

83. As quoted in Hardeman and Bacon, *Rayburn*, 454. According to news reports, "Rayburn would settle for nothing less than a written guarantee that all Administration bills would be cleared by the Rules Committee at his request." John D. Morris, "Rayburn Rejects All Compromises on Rules Battle," *New York Times*, January 29, 1961, 1.

84. DSG *Congressional Report*, March 4, 1961.

85. See, for example, "Rules Group Change to be Sought Today: Rayburn Plans Attack on Conservatives," *Chicago Daily Tribune*, January 18, 1961, 7.

86. DSG *Congressional Report*, March 4, 1961.

87. As was true for the Democratic Caucus, the Republican Conference's voice vote "does not bind members and a number of Republicans are known to be ready to vote for the Rules Committee enlargement.... A group of Republicans ... have said that they expect that 30 to 35 GOP members will support Rayburn." Rodney Crowther, "Rules Unit Plan Opposed by GOP," *Baltimore Sun*, January 24, 1961, 1.

88. One journalist for *Time* observed Halleck "grab" Republican Glen Cunningham on the House floor and "literally sh[ake] him as he spat out arguments against 'packing' the Rules Committee." MacNeil, *Forge of Democracy*, 433.

89. As quoted in Hardeman and Bacon, *Rayburn*, 458.

90. Hardeman and Bacon, *Rayburn*, 459. Hardeman recalls in his diary that Rayburn vowed "I'll have those who vote against me come to my office, and there'll be more ass-kicking than they ever dreamed possible. We'll use discharge petitions and Calendar Wednesday and whatever else we can find to get bills to the floor, and we'll just stay here until we get a vote on Kennedy's program."

91. Fuller, *Year of Trial*, 86.

92. As quoted in Hardeman and Bacon, *Rayburn*, 458.

93. John Averill, "Rules Vote Victory for Kennedy: Smile Marks Victory," *Los Angeles Times*, February 1, 1961, 1.

94. 87 Cong. Rec. 107 (1961), 1573.

95. 87 Cong. Rec. 107 (1961), 1576.

96. 87 Cong. Rec. 107 (1961), 1579.

97. 87 Cong. Rec. 107 (1961).

98. MacNeil, *Forge of Democracy*, 446. John D. Morris, "Rayburn Victory: Speaker Leads Fight to Curb the Power of Conservatives," *New York Times*, February 1, 1961, 1.

99. The three representatives who voted for Rayburn's expansion plan on the second go-round were Clarence Cannon (D-MO), George Fallon (D-MD), and Fred Marshall (D-MN).

100. 87 Cong. Rec. 107 (1961), 1589–90.

101. Richard Lyons, "Rayburn Wins Fight on Rules by 217–212," *Washington Post*, February 1, 1961, A1.

102. Hardeman and Bacon, *Rayburn*, 465.

103. At Halleck's suggestion, the Republican Committee on Committees selected a "moderate conservative" to the third seat. "Democratic Appointees Give Liberals Control of House Rules Group," *Wall Street Journal*, February 2, 1961, 10.

104. Immediately following Rayburn's victory, the DSG sent the following missive to its members: "Now that the Rules Committee change has been made we must turn to the work which lies ahead . . . which must be solved through cooperative effort. . . . We desire most earnestly to support our great and beloved Speaker." Chet Hollifield to DSG Members, February 8, 1961, folder 73b, box 48, Albert Papers.

105. Senator Karl Mundt (R-SD), as quoted in Fuller, *Year of Trial*, 95–96.

106. MacKaye, *New Coalition Takes Control*, 29–30.

107. Liberal opposition to the bill was led by Representative James Delaney of New York, a Catholic, who believed that denying funds to religious institutions was discriminatory.

108. Jenkins and Monroe, "Negative Agenda Control and the Conservative Coalition," 1125–26. Indeed, Albert observed two years later that "while it did not solve all problems, it worked" to ensure "majority rule" such that "the Democratic Party controls Congress." Carl Albert to Democratic Caucus, January 8, 1963, folder 35, box 3, Albert Papers.

109. Senator Karl Mundt (R-SD), as quoted in Fuller, *Year of Trial*, 95–96.

110. As quoted in Hardeman and Bacon, *Rayburn*, 451. The Speaker would not have long to enjoy his regained power, however, nor would he live to see Kennedy implement his New Frontier. In November 1961, Rayburn died at his home in Bonham, Texas; his funeral remains the largest gathering of Congress outside the Capitol, with 128 sitting members of Congress and countless former lawmakers having attended the service in Fannin County.

111. Jones, "Joseph G. Cannon and Howard W. Smith," 646.

112. Kofmehl, "Institutionalization of a Voting Bloc," 266.

113. Clem Miller to DSG, April 15, 1960, folder 11, box 56, part I, DSG Papers, LOCMD.

Chapter 7

1. Kim Phillips-Fein, *Invisible Hands: The Businessmen's Crusade Against the New Deal* (New York: W. W. Norton, 2010), 21.

2. As quoted in Richard N. Smith, *Thomas Dewey and His Times* (New York: Simon & Schuster, 1982), 361; Bowen, *Roots of Modern Conservatism*, 21–23.

3. Smith, *Thomas Dewey and His Times*, 576–77.

4. Clarence Kelland to Republican Women's Organization, "Speech on Behalf of Congressional Republicans," September 22, 1942, folder "Republican Campaign Committee," box 812, Robert Taft Papers, LOCMD. See also James T. Patterson, *Mr. Republican: A Biography of Robert A. Taft* (Boston: Houghton Mifflin, 1972), 191–94.

5. Arthur Herman, *Joseph McCarthy: Reexamining the Life and Legacy of America's Most Hated Senator* (New York: Free Press, 1999), 16, 322–23.

6. As quoted in Robert Griffith, *The Politics of Fear: Joseph R. McCarthy and the Senate* (Lexington: University Press of Kentucky, 1970), 103.

7. Margaret Chase Smith, *Declaration of Conscience* (New York: Doubleday, 1972).

8. William F. Knowland to Ed Edwin, "Oral History for the Eisenhower Administration Project," June 20, 1967, Oral History Research Office, Columbia University (hereafter cited as Knowland Oral History 1967), 163.

9. Rick Perlstein, for instance, describes Taft's heir as "unlovable." Rick Perlstein, *Before the Storm: Barry Goldwater and the Unmaking of the American Consensus* (New York: Bold Type Books, 2001), 10. Robert Caro paints a similar picture in his biography of Lyndon Johnson, portraying the senator as "ponderous" and "importunate." Robert A. Caro, *Master of the Senate: The Years of Lyndon Johnson* (New York: Alfred A. Knopf, 2002). The congressional journalist (and Johnson biographer) William S. White may be partially responsible for how Knowland is remembered. In his oral history for Johnson's presidential library, White recalled, "He was very inflexible and not one-tenth as bright as Johnson. . . . [Johnson] really just sort of overwhelmed Knowland with his brilliance as a leader." William S. White, "Interview III," July 21, 1978, Oral History Collection, LBJ Presidential Library (hereafter cited as LBJPL), 18, http://www.lbjlibrary.net/assets/documents/archives/oral_histories/white_w/white3.pdf.

10. Dominic Sandbrook, *Mad as Hell: The Crisis of the 1970s and the Rise of the Populist Right* (New York: Knopf, 2011).

11. Theda Skocpol and Vanessa Williamson, *The Tea Party and the Remaking of American Conservatism* (New York: Oxford University Press, 2016), 65, 68–69; Ashley Jardina, *White Identity Politics* (New York: Cambridge University Press, 2019); Christopher S. Parker and Matt A. Barreto, *Change They Can't Believe In: The Tea Party and Reactionary Politics in America* (Princeton, NJ: Princeton University Press, 2015).

12. See, for example, Julian Zelizer, "Rethinking the History of American Conservatism," *Reviews in American History* 38, no. 2 (2010): 367–92; Kim Phillips-Fein, "Conservatism: A State of the Field," *Journal of American History* 98, no. 3 (November 2011): 723–43. For a more popular reflection, see Rick Perlstein, "I Thought I Understood the American Right: Trump Proved Me Wrong," *New York Times Magazine*, April 11, 2017.

13. See, for example, Lilliana Mason, Julie Wronski, and John V. Kane, "Activating Animus: The Uniquely Social Roots of Trump Support," *American Political Science Review* 115, no. 4 (November 2021): 1508–16; Brian F. Schaffner, Matthew MacWilliams, and Tatishe Nteta, "Understanding White Polarization in the 2016 Vote for President: The Sobering Role of Racism and Sexism," *Political Science Quarterly* 133, no. 1 (Spring 2018): 9–34; John Sides, Michael Tesler, and Lynn Vavreck, *Identity Crisis: The 2016 Presidential Campaign and the Battle for the Meaning of America* (Princeton, NJ: Princeton University Press, 2018); Justin Gest, Tyler Reny, and Jeremy Mayer, "Roots of the Radical Right: Nostalgic Deprivation in the United States and Britain," *Comparative Political Studies* 51, no. 13 (2017): 1694–1719.

14. See, for example, Rogers Smith and Desmond King, "White Protectionism in America," *Perspectives on Politics* 19, no. 2 (2021): 460–78; Gwendoline Alphonso, "One People, under One God, Saluting One American Flag: Trump, the Republican Party, and the Construction of American Nationalism," in *American Political Development and the Trump Presidency*, ed. Zachary Callen and Phillip Rocco (Philadelphia: University of Pennsylvania Press, 2020).

15. For important contributions, see Critchlow, *Conservative Ascendancy*; Phillips-Fein, *Invisible Hands*; Lisa McGirr, *Suburban Warriors: The Origins of the New American Right* (Princeton, NJ: Princeton University Press, 2001); Edward H. Miller, *A Conspiratorial Life: Robert Welch, the John Birch Society, and the Revolution of American Conservatism* (Chicago: University of Chicago Press, 2022).

16. See, for example, Julian Zelizer, *Burning Down the House: Newt Gingrich, The Fall of a Speaker, and the Rise of the New Republican Party* (New York: Penguin Press, 2020).

17. As quoted in Rowland Evans and Robert Novak, *Lyndon B. Johnson: The Exercise of Power* (New York: New American Library, 1966), 82. Neither Johnson's nor Knowland's papers give any indication that Knowland was aware of Johnson's proposal or that the two discussed a select committee before one was formed.

18. Caro, *Master of the Senate*, 554. For his part, the majority leader recalled that he and Johnson "discussed the names" they were considering with each other and sought to reach accord on their respective appointments. William F. Knowland, "Interview I," March 23, 1970, Oral Histories Collection (hereafter cited as Knowland Oral History 1970), LBJPL, https://www.discoverlbj.org/item/oh-knowlandw-19700323-1-00-05.

19. As quoted in Gayle B. Montgomery and James W. Johnson, *One Step from the White House: The Rise and Fall of Senator William F. Knowland* (Berkeley: University of California Press, 1998), 182.

20. Montgomery and Johnson, *One Step from the White House*, 188–201.

21. Ralph Flanders, February 4, 1967, "Oral History for the Eisenhower Administration Project," Oral History Research Office, Columbia University, 50.

22. As Knowland recalled, there were "a lot of Democrats . . . who also believed that there had been a much wider [communist] infiltration that had yet been exposed." Knowland Oral History 1967, 162–63.

23. Maurice Rosenblatt, "Flanders Censure Motion of McCarthy," July 22, 1954, and "Memorandum," July 24, 1954, both in folder "NCEC McCarthy Clearinghouse Censure Resolution Correspondence and Memoranda Mar-July 1954," box 18, Maurice Rosenblatt Papers, LOCMD.

24. Memorandum to Don Montgomery and John Edelman, July 26, 1954, folder "NCEC McCarthy Clearinghouse Censure Resolution Correspondence and Memoranda," box 18, Rosenblatt Papers, LOCMD; W. H. Lawrence, "Senate Enmeshed in M'Carthy Curbs," *New York Times*, January 7, 1954.

25. 83 Cong. Rec. S660 (daily ed. July 30, 1954), 12738.

26. "Confidential Memorandum on Possibility of Senate Floor Action on McCarthy during Remaining Weeks of 83rd Congress," July 1954, folder 14, box 18, Rosenblatt Papers, LOCMD.

27. Memorandum to Don Montgomery and John Edelman, July 26, 1954, folder "NCEC McCarthy Clearinghouse Censure Resolution Correspondence and Memoranda," box 18, Rosenblatt Papers, LOCMD.

28. David Lawrence, "Flanders Is Hurting the Republican Party, Says Lawrence," *Louisville Courier*, June 23, 1954.

29. 83 Cong. Rec. S660 (daily ed. July 30, 1954), 12733.

30. Knowland Oral History 1967, 165.

31. Barry Goldwater, "Untitled Reminiscences," folder 12, box 15, Barry M. Goldwater Papers, Arizona State University, Tempe, AZ.

32. Schickler, *Racial Realignment*.

33. Phillips-Fein, *Invisible Hands*, 6.

34. Phillips-Fein, *Invisible Hands*, 20.

35. Bowen, *Roots of Modern Conservatism*, 17.

36. Samuel Zipp, *The Idealist: Wendell Willkie's Wartime Quest to Build One World* (Cambridge, MA: Belknap Press of Harvard University Press, 2020), 10–11. His links to the Republican Party thin, the former utility executive later accepted Roosevelt's invitation to undertake wartime missions on behalf of the administration.

37. James T. Sparrow, *Warfare State: World War II Americans and the Age of Big Government* (New York: Oxford University Press, 2011), 4–6. See also Elliot A. Rosen, *The Republican Party in the Age of Roosevelt: Sources of Anti-Government*

Conservatism in the United States (Charlottesville: University of Virginia Press, 2014).

38. Bowen, *Roots of Modern Conservatism*, 69, 15–23.

39. William S. White, *The Taft Story* (New York: Harper & Brothers, 1954), 20.

40. As quoted in Anthony Badger, "Republican Rule in the 80th Congress," in McSweeney and Owens, *Republican Takeover of Congress*, 169.

41. William F. Crandell, "A Party Divided against Itself: Anticommunism and the Transformation of the Republican Right, 1945–1956" (PhD diss., Ohio State University, 1983), 145–46.

42. White, *Taft Story*, 57.

43. As quoted in Badger, "Republican Rule in the 80th Congress," 171–73.

44. Badger, "Republican Rule in the 80th Congress," 171–73.

45. George Smith, "Memorandum: Suggestions for Coordinating and Strengthening the Minority in Congress," 1944, folder 335, box 12, George H. E. Smith Papers, Yale Special Collections, Sterling Memorial Library.

46. Wayne Morse, "Will We Have Industrial War or Peace with the Taft-Hartley Law?" *Cornell Law Review* 33 (1948): 539.

47. White, *Taft Story*, 57. Buoyed by widespread public unhappiness with the Truman administration, Republicans picked up twelve Senate seats and, for the first time in fifteen years, seized control of the House with a fifty-five-vote majority. Intent on sweeping out as many of FDR's reforms as possible, one Republican House member greeted his colleagues by handing each of them a broom with a note reading, "Here's yours. Let's do the job." White, *Taft Story*, 34.

48. As quoted in Bowen, *Roots of Modern Conservatism*, 76.

49. Griffith, *Politics of Fear*, 14.

50. Griffith, *Politics of Fear*, 20 and 53. As Senator Burnet Maybank told the Senate's leadership regarding McCarthy's ouster from his committee, "He's a troublemaker, that's why I don't want him."

51. Herman, *Joseph McCarthy*, 16.

52. "'Communists in Government Service,' McCarthy Says," February 9, 1950, United States Senate (website), https://www.senate.gov/about/powers-procedures/investigations/mccarthy-hearings/communists-in-government-service.htm. Not only did McCarthy's disdain for elites permeate his rhetoric, but he used it to justify his tactics, later telling supporters in Ripon, Wisconsin, "I don't care what [liberal critics] have to say. I don't care how much they scream and squeal . . . this task is not going to become a dainty task. Lumberjack tactics are the only kind of tactics that crowd understands." Transcript of McCarthy Radio Address, "Veterans' Chow," February 23, 1952, Joseph R. McCarthy Papers Sound Recordings collection, Raynor Memorial Library, Marquette University.

53. Larry Tye, *Demagogue: The Life and Long Shadow of Senator Joe McCarthy* (New York: Houghton Mifflin Harcourt, 2020), 22–64.

54. Montgomery and Johnson, *One Step from the White House*, 7–19.

55. Knowland Oral History 1967, 1–3.

56. William F. Knowland, October 21, 1969, "Earl Warren's Campaigns: California Republican Politics in the 1930s," Earl Warren Oral History Project, University of California, Berkeley Bancroft Library.

57. Knowland Oral History 1967, 3.

58. Montgomery and Johnson, *One Step from the White House*, 61–62.

59. William White described Knowland as "having one foot in the center of the Republican Party and the other in its Right Wing." William White, "The Ten Who Will Run Congress," 1955, folder "Leadership Clippings," box 363, Lyndon Johnson, Senate Papers, LBJPL.

60. As quoted in Montgomery and Johnson, *One Step from the White House*, 28. See also William F. Knowland, August 2, 1973, "Earl Warren's Campaigns: California Legislatures of 1935 and 1937," Earl Warren Oral History Project 1977.

61. See "FEPC Act," in *CQ Almanac 1950*, 6th ed. (Washington, DC: Congressional Quarterly, 1951), 375–83. On conservative opposition to FEPC legislation, see Anthony Chen, *The Fifth Freedom: Jobs, Politics, and Civil Rights in the United States, 1941–1972* (Princeton, NJ: Princeton University Press, 2009), 32–87. Taft is reputed to have said, "It is just as difficult to prevent discrimination against Negroes as it is to prevent discrimination against Republicans. We know the latter is impossible."

62. For his part, Taft blamed the eastern Republican establishment he so detested for this inchoate rebellion against his leadership. See White, *Taft Story*, 84–85.

63. S. Doc. No. 105-5, at 32 (1997). This document is titled *A History of the United States Senate Republican Policy Committee, 1947–1997*.

64. Patterson, *Mr. Republican*, 427–29.

65. White, *Taft Story*, 255. Later, Knowland managed to stay out of the fight between Taft and Eisenhower for the 1952 GOP presidential nomination by supporting Warren as a potential compromise candidate. Knowland Oral History 1967, 3–4.

66. Montgomery and Johnson, *One Step from the White House*, 81. Knowland's insistence on robust American support for Taiwan (then called Formosa) earned him the nickname "the senator from Formosa."

67. Knowland Oral History 1967, 160.

68. 81 Cong. Rec. S96 (daily ed. January 5, 1950), 79.

69. 81 Cong. Rec. S96 (daily ed. April 5, 1950), 4804–05. In attacking the conduct of Truman's State Department, Knowland would "paraphrase" Winston Churchill's famous quote about the Royal Air Force: "Never have so few contributed so much to destroy the liberty of so many."

70. As quoted in Patterson, *Mr. Republican*, 446.

71. As quoted in Richard H. Rovere, "What's Happened to Taft?" *Harper's Magazine*, April 1952, 38–44.

72. Old guard Senators Owen Brewster (R-ME) and Karl Mundt (R-SD) provided a legal argument in favor of McCarthy's claim that Congress had a right

to view State Department personnel files to identify suspected communists. And fellow conservative Homer Ferguson (R-MI) gave McCarthy a crash course in the internal workings of executive agencies (like the State Department) in the hopes that his junior colleague would sound more credible if questioned by Senate skeptics. See Griffith, *Politics of Fear*, 58–59.

73. Bowen, *Roots of Modern Conservatism*, 93; Griffith, *Politics of Fear*, 62–65.

74. One observer likened Taft's attitude toward McCarthy to an addiction: "He knows it's bad stuff ... but every so often he falls off the wagon." As quoted in Griffith, *Politics of Fear*, 198. The Senate leader apparently told those moderate Republicans quietly urging that the party take a harder line against McCarthy: "I am not going to be forced into a position publicly critical of McCarthy." As quoted in John B. Oakes, "An Inquiry into McCarthy's Status," April 12, 1953, *New York Times Magazine*, 9.

75. As Knowland described the situation, "There was great concern ... on the part of a lot of Senators, both Democrats and Republicans, who had a more moderate viewpoint than McCarthy did, that there had been an infiltration that had taken place in government.... There were [moderate Republicans] ... not only in Massachusetts but other states of the Union, who also believed that there had been a much wider infiltration than had yet been exposed ... and they were the ones who helped vote Eisenhower into office." Knowland Oral History 1967, 152, 162–63.

76. As quoted in Patricia Ward Wallace, *The Politics of Conscience: A Biography of Margaret Chase Smith* (Westport, CT: Praeger, 1995), 101. Chase Smith explained that McCarthy's famous declaration—"I hold in my hand a photostatic copy"— had the "ring of authenticity" (101). She would later recall in her autobiography, "To me, in 1950, the communist threat ... was real." Chase Smith, *Declaration of Conscience*, 421.

77. Bowen, *The Roots of Modern Conservatism*, 111.

78. Wallace, *Politics of Conscience*, 102.

79. The signatories to Chase Smith's "Declaration of Conscience" were Senators George Aiken of Vermont, Robert Hendrickson of New Jersey, Irving Ives of New York, Morse, Edward Thye of Minnesota, and Charles Tobey of New Hampshire. Tobey would later attempt to deny his support, insisting, "I have not disavowed Senator McCarthy." See Wallace, *Politics of Conscience*, 109. See also Griffith, *Politics of Fear*, 104.

80. H. Alexander Smith to John Hawkins, "Reminiscences," November 1962, Oral History Research Office, Columbia University, 202. As New Jersey Senator Alexander Smith later recounted, "I was very careful to have no connection with the McCarthy controversy.... I tried to take no part ... because I felt that we had plenty of problems in our own state and we didn't need to bring that particular problem in" (288).

81. Wallace, *Politics of Conscience*, 109.

82. While McCarthy's champions believed he could win over conservatives in both parties (particularly in the South, where many felt increasingly abandoned

by the Democratic Party), there is little evidence that the senator exercised such outsize influence in congressional races. Indeed, McCarthy's critics were keen to point that out: "The greatest myth which the Wisconsin Senator has propagated, along with the myth that he exposes communists, is the myth that he possesses the political death-ray." Maurice Rosenblatt to Ralph Flanders, "Memorandum," July 24, 1954, folder 14, box 18, Rosenblatt Papers, LOCMD. See also Adam Berinsky and Gabriel Lenz, "Red Scare? Revisiting Joe McCarthy's Influence on 1950s Elections," *Public Opinion Quarterly* 78, no. 2 (2014): 369–91.

83. Rosenblatt to Flanders, "Memorandum." See also Griffith, *Politics of Fear*, 122–23.

84. As quoted in Griffith, *Politics of Fear*, 191; W. H. Lawrence, "Eisenhower to Back M'Carthy If Named, but Assails Tactics," *New York Times*, August 23, 1952. To be sure, throughout his campaign for the presidency, Ike showed restraint in his public criticism of McCarthy. In one stump speech he would give in Milwaukee in October 1952, a frustrated Eisenhower initially drafted text forcefully defending Marshall and condemning McCarthy. But at the urging of Republican officials, including Knowland, Ike agreed to cut the language from the address. As Knowland later recalled, "[I said] General, just don't do it in Wisconsin in McCarthy's backyard." Eisenhower, "Communism and Freedom: Sixth Draft," October 1952, folder "10-3-52 Milwaukee, Wisconsin (1)," box 4, Stephen Benedict Papers, Dwight D. Eisenhower Presidential Library, Abilene, Kansas; and Knowland Oral History 1967, 168.

85. Caught between his Old Guard allies, who were willing to pursue their anticommunist crusade regardless of its toll on the party, and the moderates, who increasingly viewed McCarthyism as a greater threat than the presence of communists in the government, Taft refereed the first of many fights between Eisenhower and McCarthy. That fight concerned the new president's nomination of Charles Bohlen to serve as the US ambassador to the Soviet Union. Bohlen had served as a translator at the 1945 Yalta Conference, the storied meeting between FDR, British prime minister Winston Churchill, and Soviet dictator Joseph Stalin that had subsequently become a shorthand for McCarthyite allegations that Roosevelt and the Democrats had "sold out" the people of Eastern Europe by acquiescing to Soviet domination. When reports surfaced that Bohlen had several close friends who were gay, McCarthy demanded access to Bohlen's FBI file. But Taft—himself a prominent Yalta critic—refused to support McCarthy's request and proposed instead that he (along with Alabama Democrat John Sparkman) would inspect the file and report back to the Senate. After concluding "that Mr. Bohlen was a completely good security risk in every respect," Taft ensured Bohlen's confirmation. See White, *Taft Story*, 230–31, 236–239; Montgomery and Johnson, *One Step from the White House*, 127; William Bragg Ewald, *Who Killed Joe McCarthy?* (New York: Simon and Schuster, 1984), 58–59; 83 Cong. Rec. S99 (daily ed. March 25, 1953), 2279.

86. Taft gave a press conference in June 1953, during which he announced that he had a serious health condition that would require him to be absent from the

Senate and that Knowland would take his place until his return. In a reflection of Taft's continuing hold over his party brethren, Mr. Republican underscored that Knowland was *his* choice: "I appointed him." The party formally ratified that choice two months later, when Knowland was elected majority leader only days after Taft's death. Nevertheless, reflecting Knowland's position at some remove from the McCarthy faction, seven senators—all committed members of the Old Guard (including McCarthy)—chose to abstain rather than cast their vote for Taft's chosen successor. See White, *Taft Story*, 258–59; Montgomery and Johnson, *One Step from the White House*, 134.

87. Knowland was described by contemporaries as having an "awesome exterior and a booming voice." A hard worker, he made up in effort and conviction what he lacked in charisma. No pushover himself, Arizona Senator Barry Goldwater observed that Knowland "was more inclined to tell people what they should do than he was to persuade them to follow a particular course." A columnist for the *Los Angeles Times* concurred: "The fires of moral conviction burn so fiercely within that fullback chest and behind the dead-serious face that the question least likely to bother Bill Knowland is 'What will people say?'" As quoted in Montgomery and Johnson, *One Step from the White House*, 143, 137, 177.

88. With the deaths of Taft and Tobey leaving the GOP one vote short of a majority for the remainder of 1953, Knowland would have to court the support of Morse, now formally an independent (albeit one who voted for Knowland as majority leader), and rely on the tie-breaking vote of Vice President Richard Nixon. Knowland later speculated that the reason the Democrats did not seize the majority in their own right was that "the Republicans had actually won the majority in the Senate in the preceding election. Eisenhower had just gone in, and they felt that while they could do it and had the power to do it, it might put them in a disadvantaged position." Replacements for Tobey and Taft took their seats on January 6, 1954. Knowland Oral History 1970, 6.

89. As quoted in Montgomery and Johnson, *One Step From the White House*, 136, 150. Eisenhower would later compare Knowland unfavorably to Taft: "Knowland means to be helpful and loyal, but he is cumbersome. He does not have the sharp mind and great experience that Taft did. Consequently, he does not command the respect in the Senate that Senator Taft enjoyed." Not surprisingly, Eisenhower and Knowland disagreed most when it came to the country's Asia policy. Knowland, for example, advocated a naval blockade of China, which the new Eisenhower administration strongly opposed. See Andrew Tully, "Knowland's Record Against Ike," *Washington Daily News*, May 7, 1953.

90. Griffith, *Politics of Fear*, 208–10.

91. In response, State Department librarians organized book burnings. Voice of America programs were eliminated, and hundreds of staff across the agency's information arm were purged. See Ewald, *Who Killed Joe McCarthy?*, 61–62.

92. Griffith, *Politics of Fear*, 211–20.

93. As quoted in W. Lawrence, "Senate Enmeshed in M'Carthy Curbs."

94. Griffith, *Politics of Fear*, 222 24.

95. Shelby Scates, *Maurice Rosenblatt and the Fall of Joseph McCarthy* (Seattle: University of Washington Press, 2006), 88. Rosenblatt's "McCarthy Clearing House," the investigative arm of his political action committee, would employ a motley crew of aides, including the dean of the National Cathedral and an administrative assistant to Democratic senator Lister Hill of Alabama (89). One of the Clearing House's important initial triumphs was the discovery that an aide to McCarthy had been critical of mainline Protestant denominations for alleged laxity on communism. That discovery ultimately forced McCarthy to shelve a planned investigation into subversion within the CIA and alienated some of McCarthy's southern Democratic allies with ties to high-ranking clergy. See Griffith, *Politics of Fear*, 229–35.

96. W. Lawrence, "Senate Enmeshed in M'Carthy Curbs."

97. In the winter of 1954, McCarthy set his sights on the commissioning as a US Army major (and subsequent discharge) of a New York dentist and a member of the American Labor Party. When McCarthy sought to have a brigadier general testify before the subcommittee, the secretary of the army personally ordered the general not to appear. In a measure of his ambition, McCarthy told the secretary, "Just go ahead and try it. . . . I am going to kick the brains out of anyone who protects Communists! . . . You just go ahead. I will guarantee you that you will live to regret it." As quoted in Griffith, *Politics of Fear*, 246–47. For his part, Knowland was irate—not because the administration had released the information but because the president's staff had failed to notify him in advance. Given their difficult working relationship with the majority leader, Eisenhower's aides expressed concern that Knowland and his leadership team would seek to keep the report confidential. Montgomery and Johnson, *One Step from the White House*, 151–52.

98. Donald A. Ritchie and Elizabeth Bolling, eds., *Executive Sessions of the Senate Permanent Subcommittee on Investigations of the Committee on Government Operations* [McCarthy Hearings 1953–54] (Washington, DC: General Printing Office, 2003), 107–84.

99. Knowland Oral History 1967, 157–58.

100. Griffith, *Politics of Fear*, 277; Knowland Oral History 1967, 157–58. Democrats had a more prosaic reason for opposing some kind of sanction: they hoped to use McCarthy as a wedge issue in the 1954 midterms. See, for example, Arthur V. Watkins, *Enough Rope: The Inside Story of the Censure of Joe McCarthy by His Colleagues* (Englewood Cliffs, NJ: Prentice Hall; Salt Lake City: University of Utah Press, 1969), 32; Roscoe Drummond, "What the Democratic Strategy Will Be," *New York Herald Tribune*, June 28, 1954.

101. Don Irwin, "2 Anti-McCarthy Rules Referred to Jenner Unit," *New York Herald Tribune*, June 24, 1954; Griffith, *Politics of Fear*, 278–84. There is no evidence that Knowland was unhappy with Jenner's decision. Indeed, he later declared that

he would have moved to table the resolution were it to have reached the floor. "Knowland Fights Curb on M'Carthy," *New York Times*, July 15, 1954, 9.

102. "Confidential Memorandum on Possibility of Senate Floor Action on McCarthy during Remaining Weeks of 83rd Congress," June 21, 1954, folder 14, box 18, Rosenblatt Papers, LOCMD.

103. Griffith, *Politics of Fear*, 285; 83 Cong. Rec. S (daily ed. July 20, 1954), 10993.

104. Knowland Oral History 1967, 161–62, 166.

105. Indeed, as part of their effort to dampen Republicans' electoral appeal and claim some populist rhetoric for themselves, congressional Democrats cast Eisenhower and the Senate GOP as a "millionaires' corporation" eager to exploit the "little fellow." As quoted in Montgomery and Johnson, *One Step from the White House*, 151.

106. 83 Cong. Rec. S100 (daily ed. July 30, 1954), 12690.

107. Memorandum, undated, folder "NCEC McCarthy Clearinghouse Censure Resolution Miscellany 1953–1954," box 19, Rosenblatt Papers, LOCMD. Indeed, given that the Senate was scheduled to adjourn at the end of July, Eisenhower's concerns about enacting his legislative program could have provided Knowland the necessary cover to delay the censure motion, perhaps indefinitely. And the majority leader had many dilatory tactics he could have drawn on had he wished to block consideration of Flanders's proposal. Among the many option, Knowland could have gaveled the Senate into recess at the end of every day until the Senate adjourned as scheduled, or he could have proposed a substitute for Flanders's resolution, which would have to be considered before the motion it was drafted to replace. See Arthur Krock, "M'Carthy Showdown Unlikely This Session," *New York Times*, June 27, 1954; Drew Person, "Flanders Not to Have Aid of Ike," *Washington Post*, June 18, 1954; Don Irwin, "Knowland Sets Full Debate on McCarthy Today: McCarthy May Shun 'Censure,' Democrats Won't Take Party Stand," *New York Herald Tribune*, July 30, 1954.

108. Murrey Marder, "6-Man Committee Set Up to Weigh Censure Charges against Senator," *Washington Post*, August 3, 1954, 1. Formally, Knowland's motion provided for a referral to a "select committee to be composed of 3 Republicans and 3 Democrats," who would be "instructed to act and to report to the Senate as expeditiously as equity and justice will permit." 83 Cong. Rec. S100 (daily ed. August 2, 1954), 12943. New York's Ives then proposed an amendment (which Knowland accepted) to ensure that the committee would report back "prior to the adjournment sine die of the Senate in the 2d session of the 83d Congress." 83 Cong. Rec. S100 (daily ed. August 2, 1954), 12966. The motion passed, 75–12. 83 Cong. Rec. S100 (daily ed. August 2, 1954), 12989. Preferring that the censure motion be debated and voted on by the full Senate, many of McCarthy's harshest critics, including Flanders, Arkansas Democrat William Fulbright, New York Democrat Herbert Lehman, and Oklahoma Democrat Mike Monroney, voted against Knowland's proposal to form a special committee. McCarthy himself voted "present."

109. Knowland Oral History 1967, 159. Knowland later recalled that he and Johnson worked to obtain a "moderate-type of a committee . . . not one that would prejudge the case one way or the other." Knowland Oral History 1970, 22. The three Republicans would be joined by Johnson's picks: Colorado's Edwin Johnson, Mississippi's John Stennis, and North Carolina's Sam Ervin. Stennis had served as a state prosecutor and Ervin as a justice on the North Carolina Supreme Court. Murrey Marder, "Nixon Voices His Confidence in Impartiality of 'Moderates,'" *Washington Post*, August 6, 1954, 1.

110. Griffith, *Politics of Fear*, 295.

111. "Arthur V. Watkins Dies at 86; Led McCarthy Censure Inquiry," *New York Times*, September 2, 1973, 30. As quoted in Scates, *Maurice Rosenblatt and the Fall of Joseph McCarthy*, 108.

112. Marder, "Nixon Voices His Confidence." Case was described in the *New York Times* as a "a highly independent man in action, though seemingly timid and colorless in speech," and lacking association with his pro-McCarthy South Dakota colleague, Karl Mundt. William S. White, "'Grand Jury' on McCarthy has Senate's Full Support," *New York Times*, August 6, 1954, 6. Confidential whip counts prepared by the McCarthy Clearing House before the Watkins Committee was created suggest that both Carlson and Case supported the Flanders resolution. Whip Count, July 1954, folder 14, box 18, Rosenblatt Papers, LOCMD.

113. As quoted in Jean E. Torcum, "Leadership: The Role and Style of Senator Everett Dirksen," in *To Be a Congressman: The Promise and the Power*, ed. Sven Groennings and Jonathan P. Hawley (Washington, DC: Acropolis Books, 1973), 191–92.

114. As quoted in Torcum, "Leadership," 197.

115. Marder, "Nixon Voices His Confidence."

116. Watkins, *Enough Rope*, 33.

117. 83 Cong. Rec. S100 (daily ed. August 2, 1954), 12946; 83 Cong. Rec. S100 (daily ed. July 31, 1954), 12906.

118. "Pettifoggery," *Washington Post*, August 3, 1954, 10.

119. As quoted in Tye, *Demagogue*, 450.

120. As quoted in Richard M. Friend, *Men Against McCarthy* (New York: Columbia University Press, 1976), 300.

121. As quoted in Watkins, *Enough Rope*, 147.

122. Watkins, *Enough Rope*, 150.

123. As quoted in Robert H. Ferrell, *The Diary of James C. Hagerty: Eisenhower in Mid-Course, 1954–1955* (Bloomington: Indiana University Press, 1983), 119–20.

124. Eisenhower's staff posited that Knowland's vote against censure was "pay-off . . . for the right-wing support of his foreign policy statements . . . particularly the diplomatic break with Russia and blockade of China." As quoted in Ferrell, *Diary of James C. Hagerty*, 120.

125. As quoted in Griffith, *Politics of Fear*, 315; Knowland Oral History 1967, 164.
126. Knowland Oral History 1967, 164.
127. As quoted in Tye, *Demagogue*, 459.
128. Dwight D. Eisenhower, *Waging Peace, 1956–1961* (Garden City, NY: Doubleday, 1965), 13.
129. Richard Hofstadter, for one, described McCarthy's politics of grievance in deliberately "pejorative" terms, characterizing the senator's purportedly populist rhetoric as "the animosities and passions of a small minority." See Richard Hofstadter, "The Paranoid Style in American Politics," *Harper's Magazine*, November 1964, 77.
130. Perlstein, *Before the Storm*, 138. Hofstadter famously observed that Goldwater's right-wing politics mirrored those of McCarthy. Like his senior colleague, Goldwater combined a sense of "sustained conspiracy" that socialism and communism were imminent threats with the belief that "top government officialdom ha[d] been so infiltrated by Communist agents" that the American state was no longer working in the interests of "loyal Americans." Hofstadter, "Paranoid Style."
131. Barry Goldwater, *Conscience of a Conservative* (Shepherdsville, KY: Victor Publishing, 1960), 22.
132. Ronald Reagan, "Address on Behalf of American Senator Barry Goldwater 'A Time for Choosing,'" October 27, 1964," American Presidency Project, accessed August 25, 2024, https://www.presidency.ucsb.edu/documents/address-behalf-senator-barry-goldwater-time-for-choosing.
133. Montgomery and Johnson, *One Step from the White House*, 230.
134. Associated Press, "William F. Knowland Is Apparent Suicide: Former GOP Senator was 65," February 24, 1974, *New York Times*, 1.

Chapter 8

1. As quoted in Thrush, "Prisoner of Capitol Hill."
2. Lee, *Beyond Ideology*, 182.
3. As quoted in David Shribman, "Rep. Gephardt Is a Rising Star for Democrats, But Some Question Whether He Can Be a Leader," January 30, 1985, *Wall Street Journal*, 5.
4. See, for example, Alan Wiseman and Craig Volden, *Legislative Effectiveness in the United States Congress: The Lawmakers* (New York: Cambridge University Press, 2014); Alison W. Craig, *The Collaborative Congress: Reaching Common Ground in a Polarized House* (New York: Cambridge University Press, 2023); James M. Curry and Jason M. Roberts, "Interpersonal Relationships and Legislative Collaboration in Congress," *Legislative Studies Quarterly* 48, no. 2 (May 2023): 333–69.
5. Christopher H. Achen, "Measuring Representation," *American Journal of Political Science* 22, no. 3 (August 1978): 477.

6. Hanna F. Pitkin, *The Concept of Representation* (Berkeley: University of California Press, 1972), 166.

7. John R. Hibbing and Christopher W. Larimer, "What the American Public Wants Congress to Be," in *Congress Reconsidered*, 8th ed., ed. Lawrence C. Dodd and Bruce I. Oppenheimer (Washington DC: CQ Press, 2005), 55.

8. "Program on International Policy Attitudes, University of Maryland Poll: May 2010," Archive No. 31112214, Roper Center for Public Opinion Research, https://ropercenter.cornell.edu/ipoll/study/31112214/.

9. Skowronek, *Politics Presidents Make*, 6, 9.

10. Skowronek, *Politics Presidents Make*, 15.

11. Thomas E. Mann and Norm Ornstein, *It's Even Worse Than It Looks: How the American Constitutional System Collided with the New Politics of Extremism* (New York: Basic Books, 2012), xiv, 112.

12. Interview with staffer, October 2022.

13. Derek Kilmer, as quoted in Mark Warren, "Help, We're in a Living Hell and We Don't Know How to Get Out," *Esquire*, October 15, 2014.

14. As quoted in Siobhan Hughes, "Retirements Surge in Congress in Wake of GOP House Speaker Drama," *Wall Street Journal*, November 23, 2023.

15. Aaron Shock, as quoted in Warren, "Help, We're in a Living Hell."

16. Regardless, proposals to increase electoral competition would do little to entice more moderate candidates to run for Senate seats or to stay there for multiple terms, as their constituencies are not subject to gerrymandering. See Thomsen, *Opting Out of Congress*, 2–3.

17. See, for example, Seth J. Hill, "Institution of Nomination and the Policy Ideology of Primary Electorates," *Quarterly Journal of Political Science* 10, no. 4 (2015): 461–87.

18. Jon C. Rogowski and Stephanie Langella, "Primary Systems and Candidate Ideology: Evidence from Federal and State Legislative Elections," *American Politics Research* 43, no. 5 (2015): 846–71.

19. Lee Drutman, "Wanted: A Few Reasonable People to Run for Congress," *Undercurrent Events*, Substack, December 11, 2023, https://leedrutman.substack.com/p/wanted-a-few-reasonable-people-to.

20. See Thomsen, *Opting Out of Congress*, for a theory of "party fit" and moderate decline.

21. As quoted in Ashley Parker, "G.O.P. Moderate in the Middle . . . of a Jam," *New York Times*, October 8, 2013, A1.

22. Interview with member of Congress, November 2011.

23. Alexi McCammond, Andrew Solender, and Lachlan Markay, "New Label for Moderate Democrats: 'Normal,'" Axios, November 9, 2021, https://www.axios.com/2021/11/10/moderate-democrats-normal.

24. Russell Berman, "We Used to Be Called Moderate: We Are Not Moderate," *Atlantic*, January 27, 2023.

25. As quoted in Zwick, "Tuesday Mourning."

26. As quoted in Susan Page, "Inside Nancy Pelosi's War with AOC and the Squad," *Politico Magazine*, April 15, 2021, https://www.politico.com/news/magazine/2021/04/15/nancy-pelosi-alexandria-ocasio-cortez-481704.

27. See, for example, Manu Raju and Melanie Zanona, "Kevin McCarthy Leans on 'Five Families' as House GOP Plots Debt-Limit Tactics," CNN, February 13, 2023, https://www.cnn.com/2023/02/13/politics/kevin-mccarthy-debt-ceiling-strategy/index.html.

28. Mike Johnson, as quoted in Jordain Carney and Olivia Beavers, "Johnson Flails as Republicans Demand Consequences for Conservative Hijacking," *Politico*, January 11, 2024, https://www.politico.com/live-updates/2024/01/11/congress/conservatives-push-johnson-00135080.

Select Bibliography

Achen, Christopher H. "Measuring Representation." *American Journal of Political Science* 22, no. 3 (August 1978): 475–510.
Albert, Carl, and Danney Goble. *Little Giant: The Life and Times of Speaker Carl Albert*. Norman: University of Oklahoma Press, 1999.
Alberta, Tim. *American Carnage: On the Front Lines of the Republican Civil War and the Rise of President Trump*. New York: Harper, 2019.
Alphonso, Gwendoline. "One People, Under One God, Saluting One American Flag: Trump, the Republican Party, and the Construction of American Nationalism." In *American Political Development and the Trump Presidency*, edited by Zachary Callen and Phillip Rocco, 55–67. Philadelphia: University of Pennsylvania Press, 2020.
Ansolabehere, Stephen, James M. Snyder, and Charles Stewart. "The Effects of Party and Preferences on Congressional Roll-Call Voting." *Legislative Studies Quarterly* 26, no. 4 (November 2001): 533–72.
Badger, Anthony. "Republican Rule in the 80th Congress." In *Republican Takeover of Congress*, edited by Dean McSweeney and John E. Owens, 165–184. New York: St. Martin's Press, 1998.
Ball, Molly. *Pelosi*. New York: Picador, 2020.
Bartho, Jonathan. "Reagan's Southern Comfort: The 'Boll Weevil' Democrats in the 'Reagan Revolution' of 1981," *Journal of Policy History* 32 (2020): 214–38.
Bendiner, Robert. *Obstacle Course on Capitol Hill*. New York: McGraw-Hill, 1964.
Berinsky, Adam, and Gabriel Lenz. "Red Scare? Revisiting Joe McCarthy's Influence on 1950s Elections." *Public Opinion Quarterly* 78, no. 2 (2014): 369–91.
Binder, Sarah, and Frances Lee. "Making Deals in Congress." In *Political Negotiation: A Handbook*, edited by Jane Mansbridge and Cathie Jo Martin, 91–120. Washington, DC: Brookings Institution Press, 2016.
Bloch Rubin, Ruth. *Building the Bloc: Intraparty Organization in the U.S. Congress*. Cambridge: Cambridge University Press, 2017.
Bloch Rubin, Ruth. "Organizing at the Extreme: Hardline Strategy and Institutional Design." *Congress & the Presidency* 49, no. 1 (2022): 1–30.

Bloch Rubin, Ruth. "Organizing for Insurgency: Intraparty Organization and the Development of the House Insurgency, 1908–1910." *Studies in American Political Development* 27, no. 2 (October 2013): 86–110.

Boehner, John. *On the House: A Washington Memoir.* New York: St. Martin's Press, 2021.

Bolling, Richard. *House Out of Order.* New York: E. F. Dutton, 1966.

Bolling, Richard. *Power in the House: A History of the Leadership of the House of Representatives.* Boston: Dutton Press, 1968.

Bowen, Michael. *The Roots of Modern Conservatism: Dewey, Taft, and the Battle for the Soul of the Republican Party.* Chapel Hill: University of North Carolina Press, 2011.

Brandt, Karl Gerard. "Deficit Politics and Democratic Unity: The Saga of Tip O'Neill, Jim Wright, and the Conservative Democrats in the House of Representatives During the Reagan Era." PhD diss., Louisiana State University, 2003.

Brandt, Karl Gerard. *Ronald Reagan and the House Democrats: Gridlock, Partisanship and the Fiscal Crisis.* Columbia: University of Missouri Press, 2009.

Cameron, Charles, David Epstein, and Sharyn O'Halloran. "Do Majority-Minority Districts Maximize Substantive Black Representation in Congress?" *American Political Science Review* 90, no. 4 (December 1996): 794–812.

Caro, Robert A. *Master of the Senate: The Years of Lyndon Johnson.* New York: Alfred A. Knopf, 2002.

Champagne, Anthony. *Congressman Sam Rayburn.* New Brunswick, NJ: Rutgers University Press, 1984.

Chase Smith, Margaret. *Declaration of Conscience.* New York: Doubleday, 1972.

Chen, Anthony. *The Fifth Freedom: Jobs, Politics, and Civil Rights in the United States, 1941–1972.* Princeton, NJ: Princeton University Press, 2009.

Clapp, Charles. *The Congressman: His Work as He Sees It.* Washington, DC: Brookings Institution Press, 1963.

Clarke, Andrew J. "Party Sub-Brands and American Party Factions," *American Journal of Political Science* 64, no. 3 (July 2020): 452–70.

Cooper, Joseph, and David W. Brady. "Institutional Context and Leadership Style: The House from Cannon to Rayburn," *American Political Science Review* 75, no. 2 (June 1981): 411–25.

Cox, Gary W., and Mathew D. McCubbins. "Agenda Power in the U.S. House of Representatives, 1877–1986." In *Party, Process, and Political Change in Congress: New Perspectives on the History of Congress*, edited by David W. Brady and Mathew D. McCubbins, 107–45. Stanford, CA: Stanford University Press, 2002.

Cox, Gary W., and Mathew D. McCubbins. *Legislative Leviathan: Party Government in the House.* Berkeley: University of California Press, 1993.

Cox, Gary W., and Mathew D. McCubbins. *Setting the Agenda: Responsible Party Government in the U.S House of Representatives.* New York: Cambridge University Press, 2005.

CQ Almanac 1950. 6th ed. Washington, DC: Congressional Quarterly, 1951.

Craig, Alison W. *The Collaborative Congress: Reaching Common Ground in a Polarized House*. New York: Cambridge University Press, 2023.

Crandell, William F. "A Party Divided against Itself: Anticommunism and the Transformation of the Republican Right, 1945–1956." PhD diss., Ohio State University, 1983.

Critchlow, Donald. *The Conservative Ascendancy: How the GOP Right Made Political History*. Cambridge, MA: Harvard University Press, 2007.

Curry, James M. *Legislating in the Dark: Information and Power in the House of Representatives*. Chicago: University of Chicago Press, 2015.

Curry, James M., and Frances E. Lee. *The Limits of Party: Congress and Lawmaking in a Polarized Era*. Chicago: University of Chicago Press, 2020.

Curry, James M., and Jason M. Roberts. "Interpersonal Relationships and Legislative Collaboration in Congress." *Legislative Studies Quarterly* 48, no. 2 (May 2023): 333–69.

Dahl, Robert. "The Concept of Power." *Behavioral Science* 2 (1957): 201–15.

Dahl, Robert. *Who Governs? Democracy and Power in an American City*. New Haven, CT: Yale University Press, 1974.

Davidson, Roger H. "The New Centralization on Capitol Hill," *Review of Politics* 50, no. 3 (Summer 1988): 354–64.

Deering, Christopher J., and Steven S. Smith. "Majority Party Leadership and the New House Subcommittee System." In *Understanding Congressional Leadership*, edited by Frank H. Mackaman, 261–92. Washington, DC: CQ Press, 1981.

DiSalvo, Daniel. *Engines of Change: Party Factions in American Politics, 1868–2010*. New York: Oxford University Press, 2012.

Dixit, Avinash, Gene M. Grossman, and Faruk Gul. "The Dynamics of Political Compromise." *Journal of Political Economy* 108, no. 3 (2000): 441–662.

Dodd, Lawrence C., and Bruce I. Oppenheimer. "Consolidating Power in the House: The Rise of a New Oligarchy." In *Congress Reconsidered*, 4th ed., edited by Lawrence C. Dodd and Bruce I. Oppenheimer, 39–64. Washington, DC: CQ Press, 1989.

Dodd, Lawrence C., and Bruce I. Oppenheimer "The House in Transition." In *Congress Reconsidered*, 2nd ed., edited by Lawrence C. Dodd and Bruce I Oppenheimer, 31–61. New York: Praeger, 1981.

Eisenhower, Dwight D. *Waging Peace, 1956–1961*. Garden City, NY: Doubleday, 1965.

Evans, C. Lawrence. *The Whips: Building Party Coalitions in Congress*. Ann Arbor: University of Michigan Press, 2018.

Evans, C. Lawrence, and Walter J. Oleszek. *Congress under Fire: Reform Politics and the Republican Majority*. Boston: Houghton Mifflin, 1997.

Evans, C. Lawrence, and Walter J. Oleszek. "The Strategic Context of Congressional Party Leadership." *Congress & the Presidency* 26, no. 1 (1999): 1–20.

Evans, Diana. *Greasing the Wheels: Using Pork Barrel Projects to Build Majority Coalitions in Congress.* New York: Cambridge University Press, 2004.

Evans, Rowland, and Robert Novak. *Lyndon B. Johnson: The Exercise of Power.* New York: New American Library, 1966.

Ewald, William Bragg. *Who Killed Joe McCarthy?* New York: Simon & Schuster, 1984.

Farrell, John A. *Tip O'Neill and the Democratic Century.* Boston: Little, Brown, 2001.

Ferber, Mark F. "The Democratic Study Group: A Study of Intra-Party Organization in the House of Representatives." PhD diss., University of California, 1964.

Ferrell, Robert H. *The Diary of James C. Hagerty: Eisenhower in Mid-Course, 1954–1955.* Bloomington: Indiana University Press, 1983.

Feulner, Edwin Jr. *Conservatives Stalk the House: The Republican Study Committee, 1970–1982.* Ottawa, IL: Green Hill Publishers, 1983.

Follett, Mary Parker. *The Speaker of the House of Representatives* (New York: Longmans, Green, 1896).

Friend, Richard M. *Men against McCarthy.* New York: Columbia University Press, 1976.

Fuller, Helen. *Year of Trial: Kennedy's Crucial Decisions.* New York: Harcourt, Brace & World, 1962.

Gailmard, Sean. "Multiple Principals and Oversight of Bureaucratic Policy-Making." *Journal of Theoretical Politics* 21, no. 2 (2009): 161–86.

Gailmard, Sean, and Jeffery A. Jenkins. "Negative Agenda Control in the Senate and House: Fingerprints of Majority Party Power." *Journal of Politics* 69, no. 3 (August 2007): 689–700.

Galloway, George B. *History of the United States House of Representatives.* New York: Crowell, 1976.

Gerring, John. *Party Ideologies in America, 1828–1996.* New York: Cambridge University Press, 1998.

Gest, Justin, Tyler Reny, and Jeremy Mayer. "Roots of the Radical Right: Nostalgic Deprivation in the United States and Britain." *Comparative Political Studies* 51, no. 13 (2017): 1694–1719.

Goldwater, Barry. *Conscience of a Conservative.* Shepherdsville, KY: Victor Publishing, 1960.

Green, Matthew N. "Institutional Change, Party Discipline, and the House Democratic Caucus, 1911–19." *Legislative Studies Quarterly* 27, no. 4 (November 2002): 601–33.

Green, Matthew N. *Legislative Hardball: The House Freedom Caucus and the Power of Threat-Making in Congress.* New York: Cambridge University Press, 2019.

Green, Matthew N. *The Speaker of the House: A Study of Leadership.* New Haven, CT: Yale University Press, 2010.

Green, Matthew N., and Douglas B. Harris. *Choosing the Leader: Leadership Elections in the U.S. House of Representatives.* New Haven, CT: Yale University Press, 2019.

Griffith, Robert K. "About Face? The U.S. Army and the Draft." *Armed Forces & Society* 12, no. 1 (Fall 1985): 108–33.

Griffith, Robert K. *The Politics of Fear: Joseph R. McCarthy and the Senate.* Lexington: University Press of Kentucky, 1970.

Hacker, Jacob. *The Divided Welfare State: The Battle over Public and Private Social Benefits in the United States.* New York: Cambridge University Press, 2002.

Hacker, Jacob, and Paul Pierson. *Off Center: The Republican Revolution and the Erosion of American Democracy.* New Haven, CT: Yale University Press, 2006.

Haldeman, H. R. *The Haldeman Diaries: Inside the Nixon White House.* New York: G. P. Putnam's, 1994.

Hall, Richard, and Alan V. Deardorff. "Lobbying as Legislative Subsidy." *American Political Science Review* 100, no. 1 (February 2006): 69–84.

Hall, Richard, and Frank W. Wayman. "Buying Time: Moneyed Interests and the Mobilization of Bias in Congressional Committees." *American Political Science Review* 84, no. 3 (September 1990): 797–820.

Hardeman, D. B., and Donald C. Bacon. *Rayburn: A Biography.* Chicago: Madison Books, 1987.

Herman, Arthur. *Joseph McCarthy: Reexamining the Life and Legacy of America's Most Hated Senator.* New York: Free Press, 1999.

Hibbing, John R., and Christopher W. Larimer. "What the American Public Wants Congress to Be." In *Congress Reconsidered*, 8th ed., edited by Lawrence C. Dodd and Bruce I. Oppenheimer, 55–75. Washington, DC: CQ Press, 2005.

Hill, Seth J. "Institution of Nomination and the Policy Ideology of Primary Electorates." *Quarterly Journal of Political Science* 10, no. 4 (2015): 461–87.

Howell, William G. *Thinking about the Presidency: The Primacy of Power.* Princeton, NJ: Princeton University Press, 2015.

Jacobs, John. *A Rage for Justice: The Passion and Politics of Phillip Burton.* Berkeley: University of California Press, 1995.

Jardina, Ashley. *White Identity Politics.* New York: Cambridge University Press, 2019.

Jenkins, Jeffery A., and Nathan W. Monroe. "Negative Agenda Control and the Conservative Coalition in the U.S. House." *Journal of Politics* 76, no. 4 (October 2014): 1116–27.

Jones, Charles O. "Joseph G. Cannon and Howard W. Smith: An Essay on the Limits of Leadership in the House of Representatives." *Journal of Politics* 30, no. 3 (August 1968): 617–46.

Kabaservice, Geoffrey. *Rule and Ruin: The Downfall of Moderation and Destruction of the Republican Party, from Eisenhower to the Tea Party.* New York: Oxford University Press, 2012.

Katznelson, Ira. *Fear Itself: The New Deal and the Origins of Our Time*. New York: Liveright, 2013.

Katznelson, Ira, Kim Geiger, and Daniel Kryder. "Limiting Liberalism: The Southern Veto in Congress, 1933–1950." *Political Science Quarterly* 108, no. 2 (Summer 1993): 283–306.

Kernell, Samuel. *Going Public: New Strategies of Presidential Leadership*. Washington, DC: CQ Press, 1997.

Kiewiet, D. Roderick, and Mathew D. McCubbins. *The Logic of Delegation*. Chicago: University of Chicago Press, 1991.

King, David C., and Richard J. Zeckhouser. "Congressional Vote Options." *Legislative Studies Quarterly* 28, no. 3 (August 2003): 387–411.

Kofmehl, Kenneth. "The Institutionalization of a Voting Bloc." *Western Political Quarterly* 17, no. 2 (June 1964): 256–72.

Krehbiel, Keith. *Pivotal Politics: A Theory of U.S. Lawmaking*. Chicago: University of Chicago Press, 1998.

Krehbiel, Keith. "Where's the Party?" *British Journal of Political Science* 23, no. 2 (April 1993): 235–66.

Krehbiel, Keith, Adam Meirowitz, and Alan E. Wiseman. "A Theory of Competitive Partisan Lawmaking." *Political Science Research and Methods* 3, no. 3 (2015): 423–48.

Lasswell, Harold D. "Faction." In *Encyclopedia of the Social Sciences*, 49. New York: Macmillan, 1931.

Lawrence, John A. *Arc of Power: Inside Nancy Pelosi's Speakership, 2005–2010*. Lawrence: University Press of Kansas, 2023.

Lawrence, John A. *The Class of '74: Congress after Watergate and the Roots of Partisanship*. Baltimore: Johns Hopkins University Press, 2018.

Lee, Frances E. *Beyond Ideology: Politics, Principles, and Partisanship in the U.S. Senate*. Chicago: University of Chicago Press, 2009.

Lee, Frances E. *Insecure Majorities: Congress and the Perpetual Campaign*. Chicago: University of Chicago Press, 2016.

Levi, Margaret. "A Model, a Method and a Map: Rational Choice in Comparative and Historical Analysis." In *Comparative Politics: Rationality, Culture, and Society*, edited by Mark Irving Lichbach and Alan S. Zuckerman, 19–41. New York: Cambridge University Press, 2009.

Loomis, Burdett A. "Congressional Careers and Party Leadership in the Contemporary House of Representatives." *American Journal of Political Science* 28, no. 1 (February 1984): 180–202.

Mackaman, Frank H. *Understanding Congressional Leadership*. Washington, DC: CQ Press, 1981.

MacKaye, William R. *A New Coalition Takes Control: The House Rules Committee Fight of 1961*. New York: McGraw Hill, 1963.

Mackenzie, G. Calvin, and Robert Weisbrot. *The Liberal Hour: Washington and the Politics of Change in the 1960s* New York: Penguin, 2008.

MacNeil, Neil. *Forge of Democracy: The House of Representatives*. New York: David McKay, 1963.

Mann, Thomas E., and Norm Ornstein. *It's Even Worse Than It Looks: How the American Constitutional System Collided with the New Politics of Extremism*. New York: Basic Books, 2012.

Marshall, Bryan. "Explaining the Role of Restrictive Rules in the Postreform House." *Legislative Studies Quarterly* 27, no. 1 (February 2002): 61–85.

Martin, Cathie J. *Shifting the Burden: The Struggle over Growth and Corporate Taxation*. Chicago: University of Chicago Press, 1991.

Mason, Lilliana, Julie Wronski, and John V. Kane. "Activating Animus: The Uniquely Social Roots of Trump Support." *American Political Science Review* 115, no. 4 (November 2021): 1508–16.

Matthews, Chris. *Tip and the Gipper: When Politics Worked*. New York: Simon & Schuster, 2013.

Mayhew, David R. *Congress: The Electoral Connection*. New Haven, CT: Yale University Press, 1974.

Mayhew, David R. *Partisan Balance: Why Political Parties Don't Kill the U.S. Constitutional System*. Princeton, NJ: Princeton University Press, 2011.

Mayhew, David R. *Placing Parties in American Politics*. Princeton, NJ: Princeton University Press, 1986.

McCarty, Nolan. "In Defense of DW-NOMINATE." *Studies in American Political Development* 30 (October 2016): 172–84.

McGee, Zachary A. "Keeping Your Friends Close: How the House Freedom Caucus Organized for Survival." PhD diss., University of Texas–Austin, 2017.

McGirr, Lisa. *Suburban Warriors: The Origins of the New American Right*. Princeton, NJ: Princeton University Press, 2001.

Meinke, Scott R. *Leadership Organizations in the House of Representatives: Party Participation and Partisan Politics*. Ann Arbor: University of Michigan Press, 2016.

Miller, Edward H. *A Conspiratorial Life: Robert Welch, the John Birch Society, and the Revolution of American Conservatism*. Chicago: University of Chicago Press, 2022.

Moe, Terry M. "The New Economics of Organization." *American Journal of Political Science* 28, no. 4 (November 1984): 739–77.

Montgomery, Gayle B., and James W. Johnson. *One Step from the White House: The Rise and Fall of Senator William F. Knowland*. Berkeley: University of California Press, 1998.

Morse, Wayne. "Will We Have Industrial War or Peace with the Taft-Hartley Law?" *Cornell Law Review* 33 (1948): 524–57.

Moser, Charles. *The Speaker and the House: Coalitions and Power in the United States House of Representatives.* Washington, DC: Free Congress Research and Education Foundation, 1979.

Nelson, Garrison. *John William McCormack: A Political Biography.* New York: Bloomsbury Academic, 2017.

Neustadt, Richard E. *Presidential Power and the Modern Presidents: The Politics of Leadership from Roosevelt to Reagan.* New York: Free Press, 1990.

Noel, Hans. "Ideological Factions in the Republican and Democratic Parties." *The Annals of the American Academy of Political and Social Science* 667 (2016): 166–88.

Oleszek, Walter J. *Congressional Procedures and the Policy Process.* 4th ed. Washington, DC: CQ Press, 1996.

Olson, Mancur. *The Logic of Collective Action: Public Goods and Theory.* Cambridge, MA: Harvard University Press, 1965.

O'Neill, Thomas P. *Man of the House.* New York: St. Martin's, 1987.

Orren, Karen, and Stephen Skowronek. *The Search for American Political Development.* Cambridge: Cambridge University Press, 2004.

Page, Susan. *Madam Speaker: Nancy Pelosi and the Lessons of Power.* New York: Hachette, 2021.

Parker, Christopher S., and Matt A. Barreto. *Change They Can't Believe In: The Tea Party and Reactionary Politics in America.* Princeton, NJ: Princeton University Press, 2015.

Patterson, James T. *Mr. Republican: A Biography of Robert A. Taft.* Boston: Houghton Mifflin, 1972.

Patty, John W. "Equilibrium Party Government." *American Journal of Political Science* 52, no. 3 (July 2008): 636–55.

Pearson, Kathryn. *Party Discipline in the U.S. House of Representatives.* Ann Arbor: University of Michigan Press, 2015.

Pelosi, Nancy. *The Art of Power.* New York: Simon & Schuster, 2024.

Perlstein, Rick. *Before the Storm: Barry Goldwater and the Unmaking of the American Consensus.* New York: Bold Type Books, 2001.

Persily, Nathaniel. "Stronger Parties as a Solution to Polarization." In *Solutions to Political Polarization in America*, edited by Nathaniel Persily, 121–35. New York: Cambridge University Press, 2015.

Peters, Ronald M., Jr. *The American Speakership: The Office in Historical Perspective.* Baltimore: Johns Hopkins University Press, 1997.

Peters, Ronald M., Jr., and Cindy Simon Rosenthal. *Speaker Nancy Pelosi and the New American Politics.* New York: Oxford University Press, 2010.

Phillips-Fein, Kim. "Conservatism: A State of the Field." *Journal of American History* 98, no. 3 (November 2011): 723–43.

Phillips-Fein, Kim. *Invisible Hands: The Businessmen's Crusade Against the New Deal.* New York: W. W. Norton, 2010.

Pierson, Paul. "Increasing Returns, Path Dependence, and the Study of Politics." *American Political Science Review* 94, no. 2 (June 2000): 251–67.

Pierson, Paul. "Not Just What, but *When*: Timing and Sequence in Political Processes." *Studies in American Political Development* 14, no. 1 (April 2000): 72–92.

Pierson, Paul. *Politics in Time: History, Institutions and Social Analysis*. Princeton, NJ: Princeton University Press, 2004.

Pildes, Richard H. "Romanticizing Democracy, Political Fragmentation and the Decline of American Government." *Yale Law Journal* 124 (2014): 804–52.

Pitkin, Hanna F. *The Concept of Representation*. Berkeley: University of California Press, 1972.

Polsby, Nelson W. *How Congress Evolves: Social Bases of Institutional Change*. New York: Oxford University Press, 2004.

Remini, Robert V. *The House: The History of the House of Representatives*. Washington, DC: Smithsonian Books, 2006.

Ringe, Nils, Jennifer Nicoll Victor, and Christopher J. Carman. *Bridging the Information Gap: Legislative Member Organizations as Social Networks in the United States and European Union*. Ann Arbor: University of Michigan Press, 2013.

Ripley, Randall B. *Party Leaders in the House of Representatives*. Washington, DC: Brookings Institution Press, 1967.

Roberts, Cokie. "Leadership and the Media in the 101st Congress." In *Leading Congress: New Styles, New Strategies*, edited by John J. Kornacki, 85–96. Washington, DC: CQ Press, 1990.

Robinson, James A. *The House Rules Committee*. Indianapolis: Bobbs-Merrill, 1963.

Rogowski, Jon C., and Stephanie Langella. "Primary Systems and Candidate Ideology: Evidence from Federal and State Legislative Elections." *American Politics Research* 43, no. 5 (2015): 846–71.

Rohde, David W. *Parties and Leaders in the Postreform House*. Chicago: University of Chicago Press, 1991.

Rohde, David W. "Reflections on the Practice of Theorizing: Conditional Party Government in the Twenty-First Century." *Journal of Politics* 75, no. 4 (August 2013): 849–64.

Rohde, David W., and Kenneth A. Shepsle. "Leaders and Followers in the House of Representatives: Reflections on Woodrow Wilson's *Congressional Government*." *Congress and the Presidency* 14 (1987): 111–33.

Rosen, Elliot A. *The Republican Party in the Age of Roosevelt: Sources of Anti-Government Conservatism in the United States*. Charlottesville: University of Virginia Press, 2014.

Sandbrook, Dominic. *Mad as Hell: The Crisis of the 1970s and the Rise of the Populist Right*. New York: Knopf, 2011.

Scates, Shelby. *Maurice Rosenblatt and the Fall of Joseph McCarthy*. Seattle: University of Washington Press, 2006.

Schaffner, Brian F., Matthew MacWilliams, and Tatishe Nteta. "Understanding White Polarization in the 2016 Vote for President: The Sobering Role of Racism and Sexism." *Political Science Quarterly* 133, no. 1 (Spring 2018): 9–34.

Schattschneider, E. E. *The Semisovereign People: A Realist's View of Democracy in America*. New York: Cengage Learning, 1975.

Scheele, Henry Z. "Prelude to the Presidency: An Examination of the Gerald R. Ford–Charles A. Halleck House Minority Leadership Contest." *Presidential Studies Quarterly* 25, no. 4 (1995): 767–85.

Schickler, Eric. *Disjointed Pluralism: Institutional Innovation in the U.S. Congress*. Princeton, NJ: Princeton University Press, 2001.

Schickler, Eric. *Racial Realignment: The Transformation of American Liberalism, 1932–1965*. Princeton, NJ: Princeton University Press, 2016.

Schickler, Eric, and Kathryn Pearson. "Agenda Control, Majority Party Power, and the House Committee on Rules, 1937–52." *Legislative Studies Quarterly* 34, no. 4 (November 2009): 455–91.

Schickler, Eric, Kathryn Pearson, and Brian Feinstein. "Congressional Parties and Civil Rights Politics from 1933 to 1972." *Journal of Politics* 72, no. 3 (July 2010): 672–89.

Schickler, Eric, and Andrew Rich. "Controlling the Floor: Parties as Procedural Coalitions in the House." *American Journal of Political Science* 41, no. 4 (October 1997): 1340–75.

Schiller, Wendy J. "Senators as Political Entrepreneurs: Using Bill Sponsorship to Shape Legislative Agendas." *American Journal of Political Science* 39, no. 1 (February 1995): 186–203.

Schubert, Glendon. "The Politics of Legislative Procedure: The Twenty-One Day Rule." *Political Science* 5 (1953): 16–29.

Shales, John B., and Eric M. Licht. *Movers and Shakers: Congressional Leaders in the 1980s*. Washington, DC: Free Congress Research and Education Foundation, 1985.

Sheingate, Adam. "Political Entrepreneurship, Institutional Change, and American Political Development." *Studies in American Political Development* 17, no. 2 (October 2003): 185–203.

Sheingate, Adam. "Rethinking Rules: Creativity and Constraint in the House of Representatives." In *Explaining Institutional Change: Ambiguity, Agency, and Power* edited by James Mahoney and Kathleen Thelen, 168–203. New York: Cambridge University Press, 2010.

Sheingate, Adam. "Structure and Opportunity: Committee Jurisdiction and Issue Attention in Congress." *American Journal of Political Science* 50, no. 4 (October 2006): 844–59.

Shepsle, Kenneth. "The Changing Textbook Congress." In *Can the Government Govern?* edited by John H. Chubb and Paul Peterson, 238–66. Washington, DC: Brookings Institution Press, 1989.

Sides, John, Michael Tesler, and Lynn Vavreck. *Identity Crisis: The 2016 Presidential Campaign and the Battle for the Meaning of America*. Princeton, NJ: Princeton University Press, 2018.

Sin, Gisela. *Separation of Powers and Legislative Organization: The President, the Senate, and Political Parties in the Making of House Rules*. New York: Cambridge University Press, 2014.

Sinclair, Barbara. "House Special Rules and the Institutional Design Controversy." *Legislative Studies Quarterly* 19, no. 4 (November 1994): 477–94.

Sinclair, Barbara. "Leading the Revolution: Innovation and Continuity in Congressional Party Leadership." In *Republican Takeover of Congress*, edited by Dean McSweeney and John E. Owens, 71–95.

Sinclair, Barbara. *Legislators, Leaders, and Lawmaking*. Baltimore: Johns Hopkins University Press, 1998.

Sinclair, Barbara. *Majority Leadership in the U.S. House*. Baltimore: Johns Hopkins University Press, 1983.

Sinclair, Barbara. "Transformational Leader or Faithful Agent? Principal-Agent Theory and House Majority Party Leadership." *Legislative Studies Quarterly* 24, no. 3 (August 1999): 421–49.

Skocpol, Theda, and Caroline Tervo. *Upending American Politics: Polarizing Parties, Ideological Elites, and Citizen Activists from the Tea Party to the Anti-Trump Resistance*. New York: Oxford University Press, 2020.

Skocpol, Theda, and Vanessa Williamson. *The Tea Party and the Remaking of American Conservatism*. New York: Oxford University Press, 2016.

Skowronek, Stephen. *The Politics Presidents Make: Leadership from John Adams to Bill Clinton*. Cambridge, MA: Harvard University Press, 1997.

Smith, Richard N. *Thomas Dewey and His Times*. New York: Simon & Schuster, 1982.

Smith, Rogers, and Desmond King. "White Protectionism in America." *Perspectives on Politics* 19, no. 2 (2021): 460–78.

Smith, Steven S. *Call to Order: Floor Politics in the House and Senate*. Washington, DC: Brookings Institution Press, 1989.

Smith, Steven S. "O'Neill's Legacy for the House," *Brookings Review* 5, no. 1 (Winter 1987): 28–36.

Smith, Steven S. *Party Influence in Congress*. New York: Cambridge University Press, 2007.

Sparrow, James T. *Warfare State: World War II Americans and the Age of Big Government*. New York: Oxford University Press, 2011.

Steinberg, Alfred. *Sam Rayburn: A Biography*. New York: Hawthorn Books, 1975.

Strahan, Randall. *Leading Representatives: The Agency of Leaders in the Politics of the U.S. House*. Baltimore: Johns Hopkins University Press, 2007.

Sundquist, James L. *The Decline and Resurgence of Congress*. Washington, DC: Brookings Institution Press, 1981.

Thelen, Kathleen. "Historical Institutionalism in Comparative Politics." *Annual Review of Political Science* 2 (1999): 369–404.

Thelen, Kathleen. *How Institutions Evolve: The Political Economy of Skills in Germany, Britain, the United States, and Japan.* New York: Cambridge University Press, 2004.

Thomsen, Danielle M. *Opting Out of Congress: Partisan Polarization and the Decline of Moderate Candidates.* New York: Cambridge University Press, 2017.

Torcum, Jean E. "Leadership: The Role and Style of Senator Everett Dirksen." In *To Be A Congressman: The Promise and the Power*, edited by Sven Groennings and Jonathan P. Hawley, 191–92. Washington, DC: Acropolis Books, 1973.

Truman, David B. *The Congressional Party: A Case Study.* New York: John Wiley & Sons, 1959.

Tye, Larry. *Demagogue: The Life and Long Shadow of Senator Joe McCarthy.* New York: Houghton Mifflin Harcourt, 2020.

Wallace, Patricia Ward. *The Politics of Conscience: A Biography of Margaret Chase Smith.* Westport, CT: Praeger, 1995.

Waterhouse, Benjamin. *Lobbying America: The Politics of Business from Nixon to NAFTA.* Princeton, NJ: Princeton University Press, 2014.

Watkins, Arthur V. *Enough Rope: The Inside Story of the Censure of Joe McCarthy by His Colleagues.* Englewood Cliffs, NJ: Prentice Hall; Salt Lake City: University of Utah Press, 1969.

Wawro, Gregory. *Legislative Entrepreneurship in the U.S. House of Representatives.* Ann Arbor: University of Michigan Press, 2000.

White, William S. *The Taft Story.* New York: Harper & Brothers, 1954.

Wiseman, Alan. "Filters and Pegs in Holes: How Selection Mechanisms and Institutional Positions Shape (Perceptions of) Political Leadership." In *Leadership in American Politics*, edited by Jeffery A. Jenkins and Craig Volden, 267–88. Lawrence: University of Kansas Press, 2017.

Wiseman, Alan, and Craig Volden. *Legislative Effectiveness in the United States Congress:* New York: Cambridge University Press, 2014.

Zelizer, Julian E. *The American Congress: The Building of Democracy.* Boston: Houghton Mifflin, 2004.

Zelizer, Julian E. *Burning Down the House: Newt Gingrich, The Fall of a Speaker, and the Rise of the New Republican Party.* New York: Penguin Press, 2020.

Zelizer, Julian E. *On Capitol Hill: The Struggle to Reform Congress and Its Consequences, 1948–2000.* Cambridge University Press, 2004.

Zelizer, Julian E. "Rethinking the History of American Conservatism." *Reviews in American History* 38, no. 2 (2010): 367–92.

Zipp, Samuel. *The Idealist: Wendell Willkie's Wartime Quest to Build One World.* Cambridge, MA: Belknap Press of Harvard University Press, 2020.

Index

Page numbers in *italics* refer to tables.

Affordable Care Act (ACA), 43, 45–46, 48, 52–56, 66–67, 70, 85–86, 88–89
Aid to Families with Dependent Children program, 51
Albert, Carl, 97, 125, 128, 130
Aldrich, John, 7
American political development, 26–28, 188n97, 188–89n98, 189n101
Armey, Dick, 76
Army-McCarthy hearings, 149

Biden, Joe, 48, 59, 64, 91
Bipartisan Campaign Reform Act (McCain-Feingold Act), 51
Blue Dog Coalition, 44, 51–56, 59–63. *See also* Democratic Party; Pelosi, Nancy
Boehner, John: factional asymmetry and, 66–70, 156–57; federal budget and, 80–82, 197n18, 201n76, 202n79; government shutdown and, 67–68, 70–71, 84–88, 198n22; on leadership, 12, 201n72; leaving Speaker of the House post, 88–89; on Pelosi, 1; Republican Study Committee (RSC) and, 79–80; Tuesday Group and, 82–84, 202n93, 203n95, 203–4n113. *See also* Republican Party
Bolling, Richard, 117, 126–27
Boll Weevils. *See* Conservative Democratic Forum (CDF)
Brady, David, 97
Brown, Edmund G. "Pat," 154
Brown v. Board of Education, 102

Budget Control Act, 82
Bush, George W, 77–78, 107

Cannon Revolt (1910), 11–12, 132, 183n42
Cantor, Eric, 80, 86–87
Carlson, Frank, 151
Caro, Robert, 137, 223n18
Carter, Jimmy, 94
Case, Francis, 151, 232n112
case selection (for book), 40–42, *41*
Chase Smith, Margaret, 146, 227n79
civil rights: Democratic Party and, 27, 49, 95, 103, 105, 109, 115; Rayburn and, 119, 122, 124, 215n31, 216n49, 216–17n50, 218n66, 219n74; Republican Party and, 71, 102, 126
Civil Rights Act (1964), 95, 102
Clinton, Bill, 4
Cohn, Roy, 149
collaboration: comparing leaders by, 164–66; continuity and, 170–71; financial incentives and, 164; legislative politics and, 157–62; reform and, 166–70; representation and, 163–64. *See also* factions; leader power
collective action (within Congress), 14–19. *See also* factions
Colmer, William, 120–22, 125–28
conditional party government theory (CPG), 7, 180–81n22
Congressional Black Caucus, 105

INDEX

Congressional Progressive Caucus (CPC), 44–45, 50–51, 53, 55–59. *See also* Democratic Party
Conscience of a Conservative (Goldwater), 153
Conservative Action Team (CAT), 75–77. *See also* Republican Party; Republican Study Committee (RSC)
Conservative Democratic Forum (CDF), 50, 95–96, 99, 105–9, 209n71, 210n80, 211n94. *See also* Democratic Party
Conservative Opportunity Society (COS), 75. *See also* Republican Party
Contract with America, 75
Cooper, Jere, 121
Cooper, Joseph, 97
Cox, Gary, 8, 186n73
Cruz, Ted, 85
Curry, James, 12, 33
"Cut, Cap, and Balance." *See* Boehner, John

Dahl, Robert, 1, 32
Deering, Christopher, 13
Democratic Caucus, 104–5, 110, 125, 127
Democratic Leadership Council, 50
Democratic Party: civil rights and, 27, 49, 95, 103, 105, 109, 115; conservative collaboration during the 1970s in, 101–3, 207nn46–47, 207n49; contemporary reform and, 169–71; decline of progressives in, 49–52; factional asymmetry during O'Neill term within, 94–96, 98–99, 106–10, 112–14, 209n78; factional collaboration during Pelosi's term within, 43–45, 47, 59, 63; progressive collaboration during Pelosi's era of, 57–59; Rules Committee of, 115–16. *See also* Blue Dog Coalition; Congressional Progressive Caucus (CPC); Conservative Democratic Forum (CDF); O'Neill, Tip; Pelosi, Nancy; Rayburn, Samuel; United Democrats of Congress (UDC)
Democratic Study Group (DSG), 49–50, 103–5, 117–18, 123–30, 208nn59–61, 208n65, 217n54
Dent, Charlie, 86
Department of Education, 76
Devine, Sam, 73
Dewey, Thomas, 134, 136, 140
Dirksen, Everett, 13, 138, 147, 154

DiSalvo, Daniel, 36
Dodd, Lawrence, 100, 206n21, 208n59
Drutman, Lee, 168

Eisenhower, Dwight, 135, 138, 147–49, 152, 228nn84–85, 229n89
Elliot, Carl, 131
Ellison, Keith, 57
Encyclopedia of Social Sciences, 36
Equal Rights Amendment, 71, 137
Evans, C. Lawrence, 7–8

factions: American political development of, 27–28; asymmetric, 3, 20–24, 156, 160; collaboration within, 4–5, 14–21, 38–40, 39, 114, 157–71, 186–87n77, 188n91, 214n20; collective action within, 15–18; definition of, 3, 36; group dynamics and, 15–16; identification of, 36–37; symmetric, 3, 20–22, 156, 159–60, 187nn88–89; tracking activity of, 37. *See also* collaboration; Democratic Party; Republican Party
Fair Labor Standards Act, 131
Feingold, Russ, 51
Flanders, Ralph, 149–50
Foley, Tom, 112
Ford, Gerald, 72–73
Freedom Caucus, 20, 69, 88–91, 169, 196–97n7. *See also* Republican Party

Gingrich, Newt, 1, 13, 66, 75–77, 112, 200n53
Goldwater, Barry, 139, 153, 233n130
Gramm, Phil, 107–9, 112
Gramm-Latta, 108–9, 211n92
Green, Matthew, 12
Green New Deal, 61
Grijalva, Raul, 55
Gunderson, Steve, 73
Gypsy Moths, 100–101, 199n32. *See also* Republican Party

Halleck, Charles, 72, 123, 126, 128–29
Hance, Kent, 109
Harris, Douglas, 12
Hart, Gary, 104
Hastert, Dennis, 1, 77, 179n5
Hensarling, Jeb, 79, 84
Hibbing, John, 163
Hyde, Henry, 75

INDEX

Ibsen, Henrik, 153
Inflation Reduction Act of 2022 (IRA), 45–46, 48, 59–65

Jayapal, Pramila, 58
Jenner, William, 149
John Birch Society, 153
Johnson, Lyndon, 97, 125, 127, 131, 137, 147–48
Johnson, Mike, 2
Johnson, Nancy, 73
Jordan, Jim, 80–84, 88

Kennedy, John F., 97, 116, 119, 125, 127, 131
King, Peter, 86
Knowland, William: background of, 143–45, 222n9, 226n59, 226n66, 226n69, 228–29n86, 229nn87–88; factional symmetry and, 150–52, 155, 157; populist conservatism and, 135–37; rise to majority leader, 147–48; role in McCarthy's censure and, 137–39, 149–52, 154, 227n75, 230–31n101, 231nn107–8, 232n109, 232n124. *See also* Republican Party

Landon, Alf, 140
Larimer, Christopher, 163
Lasswell, Harold, 36
Lattimore, Owen, 145, 226n69
leader power: ambition and, 12–14, 185n63; authority and, 9–12; bipartisanship and, 5; definition of, 32–33; factional asymmetry, 160; factional collaboration and, 3–4, 14–19, 114, 157–71; factional symmetry and, 21–24, 156, 159–60; faction size and, 25; faction spatial position and, 25–26; institutionalism and, 9–12; measurement of, 33–36, 190n10; party divisions and, 2, 6–9, 21–24, 114, 156; size of the majority and, 24–25. *See also* collaboration
Lee, Frances, 8–9, 12, 186nn71–72
Lee, Mike, 85
legislative politics, 161–63
Legislative Reorganization Act (1970), 108–9
Lodge, Henry Cabot, Jr, 144
Long, Gillis, 104–5
Longworth, Nicholas, 12

Mahon, George, 101
Manchin, Joe, 64–65
Mann, Thomas, 167

Marshall, George C., 147
Martin, Joe, 123, 126, 129, 216n49
Matthews, Chris, 111
Mayhew, David, 35–36
McCain, John, 51
McCarthy, Joseph: background of, 143, 225n52; censureship of, 137–39, 149–52, 231nn107–8, 232n109, 232n124; communism and, 142–43, 152, 226–27n72, 227n76, 227n80, 230n95; party divide about, 148; political rise of, 145–47, 227–28n82, 228n85, 230n97, 230n100; populist conservatism and, 134–35, 233n129; various committee seats and, 148
McCarthy, Kevin, 1–2, 80, 90–91, 188n92
McCormack, John, 97, 121, 125, 128
McCubbins, Mathew, 8, 186n73
Meadows, Mark, 85, 88–89
Medicaid Act, 56
Medicare, 56, 61, 136
Michel, Bob, 72–73, 170
Miller, George, 53
Milliken, Eugene, 147
Mills, Wilber, 120
Moe, Terry, 11–12, 183n45, 187n90
Montgomery, Gillespie "Sonny," 106
Morse, Wayne, 141–42

National Endowment for Arts, 76
New Deal, 115, 119, 139–42
New Federalists, 75
New Frontier program, 119, 131
New York Times, 94, 110, 120, 122
Nixon, Richard, 73, 138, 154

Oakland Tribune, 143
Obama, Barack, 2, 43, 52–53, 57–58, 66, 79
Obamacare. *See* Affordable Care Act (ACA)
Ocasio-Cortez, Alexandria, 60
Olson, Mancur, 16
O'Neill, Tip: alternate explanations for Speaker term developments of, 99–101, 206n29; factional asymmetry of Democrats and, 94–96, 98–99, 106–10, 112–14, 157, 210n85, 210n87; Pelosi and, 97, 107; political biography of, 96–99, 205n9, 206n21; Rayburn and, 113, 117; Reagan and, 96, 107–12, 205n10, 210n90, 211n95; television and, 109–12, 211n103, 212nn105–6, 212n108, 212n114–15. *See also* Democratic Party

Oppenheimer, Bruce, 100, 206n21, 208n59
Ornstein, Norm, 167

partisan polarization, 7
party cartel theory, 8, 181n28, 181n30
party divisions: authority and, 11–12, 182–83n41, 183–84n47; collaborative dimension within, 14–19, 186–87n77; factions within, 3–4, 180n11; leader power and, 2, 6–9, 21–24, 114, 156; leadership constraints of, 6–9, 182n31; primitive preferences of, 15, 186n69
Patriot Act, 80
PAYGO provision, 60–61
Pelosi, Nancy: Affordable Care Act (ACA) and, 43, 45, 48, 52–56; alternate explanations for success of, 47–49, 191n15, 192n16; Blue Dogs and, 51–56, 59–63; climate change and, 48, 52, 59–65, 196n109; factional configurations and, 156; Inflation Reduction Act of 2022 (IRA) and, 43, 45, 48; leadership and, 156; legacy of, 1–2, 4, 45–47, 65, 170, 191n13; O'Neill and, 97, 107; Rayburn and, 47, 117, 133, 165–66. *See also* Democratic Party
Peters, Ronald M., Jr, 113
Pierson, Paul, 9
Pitkin, Hannah, 163
populist conservatism, 134–37, 142
Price, Tom, 84
principal-agent framework, 11–12, 183nn44–45

Rangel, Charles, 52
Rayburn, Samuel: alternate explanations for Rules Committee decision and, 118–19; civil rights and, 119, 122, 124, 215n31, 216–17n50, 216n49, 218n66, 219n74; Colmer's seat on Rules Committee and, 120–22, 125–28, 218nn63–64, 218n66; Democratic Study Group (DSG) and, 123–30, 217n54, 217n58; expansion of Rules Committee and, 125–33, 218n69, 218–19n72, 219nn73–75, 219n79, 220n80, 220n83, 220nn87–88, 220n90, 221n99, 221nn103–4, 221n107; factional symmetry and, 132–33, 157; leader power of, 116–18, 214n12, 215n30; O'Neill and, 113, 117; Pelosi and, 47, 117, 133, 165–66; policy gains from Rules Committee and,
131–32, 221n108; political biography of, 116–18, 221n110; Southern Delegations and, 119–20, 215n31; twenty-one day rule for Rules Committee and, 122–24, 216n46–47. *See also* Republican Party
Reagan, Ronald, 49–50, 72, 74, 94, 96, 100, 105, 107–12, 153
Reed, Thomas, 13
Reid, Harry, 56
reproductive rights, 56
Republican Governance Group, 20, 37, 169. *See also* Republican Party; Tuesday Group
Republican Party: civil rights and, 71, 102, 126; conservative decline within, 73–75; conservative power within, 68–70, 82–84, 92–93; contemporary reform and, 169–71; effects of the New Deal on, 139–42; factional asymmetry within, 66–68, 80, 88–91; factional symmetry within, 150–52; during George W. Bush presidency, 77–79; Gingrich as speaker for, 75–77; populist conservatism and, 134–37, 152–54; reduction of the federal budget by, 81–82. *See also* Boehner, John; Conservative Action Team (CAT); Conservative Opportunity Society (COS); Freedom Caucus; Gypsy Moths; Knowland, William; Republican Governance Group; Republican Study Committee (RSC); Tea Party; Tuesday Group; Wednesday Group
Republican Study Committee (RSC), 74–75, 78–82, 84–88, 169. *See also* Conservative Action Team (CAT); Republican Party
Rohde, David, 7, 98, 104, 186n70
Roosevelt, Franklin D., 119, 140
Rosenblatt, Maurice, 148
Ross, Mike, 54
Ryan, Paul, 1, 68, 84, 89–91

Sabath, A. J., 121–22, 125
Sanders, Bernie, 44, 50
Scalise, Steve, 84
Schattschneider, E. E., 2–3
Schickler, Eric, 10, 27
Sinclair, Barbara, 8, 25, 101
Sinema, Kyrsten, 64–65
Sisk, B. F., 131
Smith, "Judge" Howard, 123–24, 127–29, 216–17n50

INDEX

Smith, Steven, 13, 98, 184n49
Social Security program, 136, 140
Southern Delegations, 118–20, 123
Stenholm, Charlie, 105–6, 109
Strahan, Randall, 15, 21, 34, 184n52

Taft, Robert, 134–35, 138, 140–42, 145, 147, 154, 225n47, 226n65, 226nn61–62, 227n74, 228–29n86
Taft-Hartley Act, 141–42
Tea Party, 66–68, 79–80, 136. *See also* Republican Party
Thompson, Frank, 126–27, 130
Truman, Harry, 119, 122, 142, 146
Trump, Donald, 90, 136
Tuesday Group, 73, 75–78, 80–81, 83–84, 90, 199n34, 200–201n59. *See also* Republican Governance Group
Tydings, Millard, 145

United Democrats of Congress (UDC), 104–5. *See also* Democratic Party

Vietnam War, 97
Vinson, Carl, 126
Voice of America, 148, 229n91
vote-based metrics, 33–34, 36–37, 190nn6–7
Voting Rights Act (1965), 95, 100, 102

Warren, Earl, 143
Watergate scandal, 95, 104
Watkins, Albert, 150–51
Waxman, Henry, 53–54
Wednesday Group, 71–73, 198n25, 198nn27–28, 199n31, 199n33. *See also* Republican Party
Willkie, Wendell, 140, 224n36
Women's Republican Club of Wheeling, 143
Woolsey, Lynn, 55
World War II, 140
Wright, Jim, 107

Zelizer, Julian, 49, 105, 188–89n98, 208n59

CHICAGO STUDIES IN AMERICAN POLITICS

A series edited by Susan Herbst, Lawrence R. Jacobs, Adam J. Berinsky, and Frances Lee; Benjamin I. Page, editor emeritus

Series titles, continued from front matter:

THE OBLIGATION MOSAIC: RACE AND SOCIAL NORMS IN US POLITICAL PARTICIPATION *by Allison P. Anoll*

A TROUBLED BIRTH: THE 1930S AND AMERICAN PUBLIC OPINION *by Susan Herbst*

POWER SHIFTS: CONGRESS AND PRESIDENTIAL REPRESENTATION *by John A. Dearborn*

PRISMS OF THE PEOPLE: POWER AND ORGANIZING IN TWENTY-FIRST-CENTURY AMERICA *by Hahrie Han, Elizabeth McKenna, and Michelle Oyakawa*

DEMOCRACY DECLINED: THE FAILED POLITICS OF CONSUMER FINANCIAL PROTECTION *by Mallory E. SoRelle*

RACE TO THE BOTTOM: HOW RACIAL APPEALS WORK IN AMERICAN POLITICS *by LaFleur Stephens-Dougan*

THE LIMITS OF PARTY: CONGRESS AND LAWMAKING IN A POLARIZED ERA *by James M. Curry and Frances E. Lee*

AMERICA'S INEQUALITY TRAP *by Nathan J. Kelly*

GOOD ENOUGH FOR GOVERNMENT WORK: THE PUBLIC REPUTATION CRISIS IN AMERICA (AND WHAT WE CAN DO TO FIX IT) *by Amy E. Lerman*

WHO WANTS TO RUN? HOW THE DEVALUING OF POLITICAL OFFICE DRIVES POLARIZATION *by Andrew B. Hall*

FROM POLITICS TO THE PEWS: HOW PARTISANSHIP AND THE POLITICAL ENVIRONMENT SHAPE RELIGIOUS IDENTITY *by Michele F. Margolis*

THE INCREASINGLY UNITED STATES: HOW AND WHY AMERICAN POLITICAL BEHAVIOR NATIONALIZED *by Daniel J. Hopkins*

LEGACIES OF LOSING IN AMERICAN POLITICS *by Jeffrey K. Tulis and Nicole Mellow*

LEGISLATIVE STYLE *by William Bernhard and Tracy Sulkin*

WHY PARTIES MATTER: POLITICAL COMPETITION AND DEMOCRACY IN THE AMERICAN SOUTH *by John H. Aldrich and John D. Griffin*

NEITHER LIBERAL NOR CONSERVATIVE: IDEOLOGICAL INNOCENCE IN THE AMERICAN PUBLIC *by Donald R. Kinder and Nathan P. Kalmoe*

STRATEGIC PARTY GOVERNMENT: WHY WINNING TRUMPS IDEOLOGY *by Gregory Koger and Matthew J. Lebo*

POST-RACIAL OR MOST-RACIAL? RACE AND POLITICS IN THE OBAMA ERA *by Michael Tesler*

THE POLITICS OF RESENTMENT: RURAL CONSCIOUSNESS IN WISCONSIN AND THE RISE OF SCOTT WALKER *by Katherine J. Cramer*

LEGISLATING IN THE DARK: INFORMATION AND POWER IN THE HOUSE OF REPRESENTATIVES *by James M. Curry*

WHY WASHINGTON WON'T WORK: POLARIZATION, POLITICAL TRUST, AND THE GOVERNING CRISIS by Marc J. Hetherington and Thomas J. Rudolph

WHO GOVERNS? PRESIDENTS, PUBLIC OPINION, AND MANIPULATION by James N. Druckman and Lawrence R. Jacobs

TRAPPED IN AMERICA'S SAFETY NET: ONE FAMILY'S STRUGGLE by Andrea Louise Campbell

ARRESTING CITIZENSHIP: THE DEMOCRATIC CONSEQUENCES OF AMERICAN CRIME CONTROL by Amy E. Lerman and Vesla M. Weaver

HOW THE STATES SHAPED THE NATION: AMERICAN ELECTORAL INSTITUTIONS AND VOTER TURNOUT, 1920–2000 by Melanie Jean Springer

WHITE-COLLAR GOVERNMENT: THE HIDDEN ROLE OF CLASS IN ECONOMIC POLICY MAKING by Nicholas Carnes

HOW PARTISAN MEDIA POLARIZE AMERICA by Matthew Levendusky

CHANGING MINDS OR CHANGING CHANNELS? PARTISAN NEWS IN AN AGE OF CHOICE by Kevin Arceneaux and Martin Johnson

THE POLITICS OF BELONGING: RACE, PUBLIC OPINION, AND IMMIGRATION by Natalie Masuoka and Jane Junn

TRADING DEMOCRACY FOR JUSTICE: CRIMINAL CONVICTIONS AND THE DECLINE OF NEIGHBORHOOD POLITICAL PARTICIPATION by Traci Burch

POLITICAL TONE: HOW LEADERS TALK AND WHY by Roderick P. Hart, Jay P. Childers, and Colene J. Lind

LEARNING WHILE GOVERNING: EXPERTISE AND ACCOUNTABILITY IN THE EXECUTIVE BRANCH by Sean Gailmard and John W. Patty

THE SOCIAL CITIZEN: PEER NETWORKS AND POLITICAL BEHAVIOR by Betsy Sinclair

FOLLOW THE LEADER? HOW VOTERS RESPOND TO POLITICIANS' POLICIES AND PERFORMANCE by Gabriel S. Lenz

THE TIMELINE OF PRESIDENTIAL ELECTIONS: HOW CAMPAIGNS DO (AND DO NOT) MATTER by Robert S. Erikson and Christopher Wlezien

ELECTING JUDGES: THE SURPRISING EFFECTS OF CAMPAIGNING ON JUDICIAL LEGITIMACY by James L. Gibson

DISCIPLINING THE POOR: NEOLIBERAL PATERNALISM AND THE PERSISTENT POWER OF RACE by Joe Soss, Richard C. Fording, and Sanford F. Schram

THE SUBMERGED STATE: HOW INVISIBLE GOVERNMENT POLICIES UNDERMINE AMERICAN DEMOCRACY by Suzanne Mettler

SELLING FEAR: COUNTERTERRORISM, THE MEDIA, AND PUBLIC OPINION by Brigitte L. Nacos, Yaeli Bloch-Elkon, and Robert Y. Shapiro

WHY PARTIES? A SECOND LOOK by John H. Aldrich

OBAMA'S RACE: THE 2008 ELECTION AND THE DREAM OF A POST-RACIAL AMERICA by Michael Tesler and David O. Sears

NEWS THAT MATTERS: TELEVISION AND AMERICAN OPINION, UPDATED EDITION by Shanto Iyengar and Donald R. Kinder

FILIBUSTERING: A POLITICAL HISTORY OF OBSTRUCTION IN THE HOUSE AND SENATE by Gregory Koger

US AGAINST THEM: ETHNOCENTRIC FOUNDATIONS OF AMERICAN OPINION by Donald R. Kinder and Cindy D. Kam

THE PARTISAN SORT: HOW LIBERALS BECAME DEMOCRATS AND CONSERVATIVES BECAME REPUBLICANS by Matthew Levendusky

DEMOCRACY AT RISK: HOW TERRORIST THREATS AFFECT THE PUBLIC by Jennifer L. Merolla and Elizabeth J. Zechmeister

IN TIME OF WAR: UNDERSTANDING AMERICAN PUBLIC OPINION FROM WORLD WAR II TO IRAQ by Adam J. Berinsky

AGENDAS AND INSTABILITY IN AMERICAN POLITICS, SECOND EDITION by Frank R. Baumgartner and Bryan D. Jones

THE PARTY DECIDES: PRESIDENTIAL NOMINATIONS BEFORE AND AFTER REFORM by Marty Cohen, David Karol, Hans Noel, and John Zaller

THE PRIVATE ABUSE OF THE PUBLIC INTEREST: MARKET MYTHS AND POLICY MUDDLES by Lawrence D. Brown and Lawrence R. Jacobs

SAME SEX, DIFFERENT POLITICS: SUCCESS AND FAILURE IN THE STRUGGLES OVER GAY RIGHTS by Gary Mucciaroni